Wolves, Courts, and Public Policy

Wolves, Courts, and Public Policy

The Children of the Night Return to the Northern Rocky Mountains

Edward A. Fitzgerald

LEXINGTON BOOKS
Lanham • Boulder • New York • London

Published by Lexington Books
An imprint of The Rowman & Littlefield Publishing Group, Inc.
4501 Forbes Boulevard, Suite 200, Lanham, Maryland 20706
www.rowman.com

Unit A, Whitacre Mews, 26-34 Stannary Street, London SE11 4AB

British Library Cataloguing in Publication Information Available

Library of Congress Cataloging-in-Publication Data Available

ISBN 978978-1-4985-0267-2 (cloth: alk. paper)

™ The paper used in this publication meets the minimum requirements of American National Standard for Information Sciences Permanence of Paper for Printed Library Materials, ANSI/NISO Z39.48-1992.

Printed in the United States of America

This book is dedicated to the government agencies, groups, individuals, judges, lawyers, and law firms who have helped to restore the wolf to the Northern Rocky Mountains.

Contents

Acknowledgments

I want to thank Dr. Mary Ava Chamberlain and Dr. Sean Wilson for their support.

Parts of this work have appeared in modified form in several journals. I want to thank the following journals for their permission to reprint portions of these articles:

"*Wyoming Farm Bureau Federation v. Babbitt*: The Children of the Night Return to the Northern Rocky Mountains," 16 *Journal of Natural Resources and Environmental Law* 79 (2001-2002).

"Seeing Red: *Gibbs v. Babbitt*," 13 *Villanova Environmental Law Journal* 1 (2002).

"*New Mexico Cattlegrowers Association v. U.S. Fish and Wildlife Service*: Lobo Returns from Limbo," 46 *Natural Resources Journal* 9 (2006).

"*Defenders of Wildlife v. Secretary of Interior*: Dysfunctional Downlisting Defeated," 34 *Boston College Environmental Affairs Law Review* 37 (2007).

"Delisting Wolves: Are the Western Great Lake States Ready?" 37 *Environmental Law Reporter* 10863 (2007).

"*Defenders of Wildlife v. Salazar*: Delisting the Children of the Night in the Northern Rocky Mountains, 31 *Public Land & Resources Law Review* 1 (2010).

"Delisting Wolves in the Northern Rocky Mountains: Congress Cries Wolf," 41 *Environmental Law Reporte*r 10840 (2011).

"*Alliance for the Wild Rockies v. Salazar*: Congress Behaving Badly," 25 *Villanova Environmental Law Journal* 351 (2014).

"Wolf Delisting: Old Wine in New Bottles," 44 *Environmental Law Reporter* 10413 (2014).

Introduction

The reintroduction of the gray wolf to the Northern Rocky Mountains (NRM) has been controversial. Environmental groups assert that the wolf is necessary to maintain ecosystem balance and preserve biodiversity. Environmental groups argue that the wolf will not have a significant impact on livestock or big game. Western state and local governments oppose federal wolf reintroduction and recovery, which is viewed as an intrusion on their traditional management prerogatives and a threat to important economic interests. The livestock industry is concerned that the wolf will prey on cattle and sheep and compensation will not be forthcoming. Hunting groups fear the wolf will harm big game and jeopardize hunting opportunities. All of these concerns are subsumed within the larger battle over public land management in the West. State and local governments and traditional resource industries are concerned that resource development, which dominated federal public land policy, is being supplanted by environmental concerns.[1]

The wolf was driven to extinction by deliberate public policy. The Endangered Species Act (ESA), which was enacted in 1973, provided the means for the federal government to restore the wolf to its historic range and restore ecosystem balance. The Carter, Reagan, Bush, Clinton, Bush, and Obama administrations adopted different positions regarding wolf reintroduction and recovery efforts in the NRM. This generated public law litigation. Environmental and industry interest groups brought suits, challenging the federal implementation of public policy. Federal courts were called on to resolve this complex public policy dispute.[2]

Public law litigation allows groups whose interests were not adequately considered or compromised in the political process to question government action and vindicate the public values in the relevant statutes.[3] Public law litigation does not manifest the same characteristics as traditional litigation.

Traditional litigation is bipolar and focuses on a past event. The remedy sought flows directly from the right violated. The judge is a neutral arbiter applying the law to facts in a one-time event. Public law litigation involves multiple parties. The rules regarding standing and intervention have been broadened to provide interest groups access to the courts. The litigation focuses on present and future government actions. Groups seek injunctions to halt federal action. The judge plays an active role, interpreting the statutes and overseeing federal agency compliance with the statutory mandates. The judge has to consider legislative facts, which are policy oriented, and adjudicative facts, which are party oriented. The litigation is not a one-time endeavor, but is part of an ongoing political controversy.[4]

Supporters of public law litigation, judicial proponents, argue that judicial involvement in public policy disputes is beneficial. Public law litigation allows groups whose interests were underrepresented to challenge administrative action. Public law litigation brings public attention and mobilizes support on both sides of the issue. The neutral judge, who is the legal expert, must decide the issue in the context of a well-reasoned decision. The judge utilizes the tools of statutory interpretation—text, intent, and purposes—to determine the meaning of the law and reviews agency action to assess statutory compliance. The court ensures that the public values manifested in the statutes are realized and executive action comports with congressional will. The court's decision does not necessarily end the process, but often serves as a catalyst for subsequent congressional and executive action.[5]

Public law litigation is not universally applauded. Opponents, judicial skeptics, argue that the courts should follow the traditional model of litigation and resolve disputes involving the impingement of individual rights, not conflicts over public policy. Public law litigation is the extension of interest group politics in the guise of litigation. Groups unsuccessful in the congressional and executive branches utilize litigation to achieve their political goals. Judicial involvement in public policy conflicts detracts from the court's essential function of resolving disputes between individuals, not majoritarian interests. Courts lack the capacity to resolve complex policy disputes. Judges, who are generalists, lack the skills and information to comprehend technical and scientific issues. Judges employ the tools of statutory interpretation to substitute their own policy views for those of administrators. The courts' episodic involvement interferes with the agency's functions, fragments the process, disrupts the agency's agenda, misallocates scarce agency resources, precludes the necessary political tradeoffs, generates costly defensive procedures, and produces bad decisions. Federal courts should defer to democratically accountable executive agencies, which possess the requisite policy expertise.[6]

This book examines the reintroduction and recovery of the gray wolf in the NRM to assess the efficiency and impact of public law litigation. The assessment criteria are whether the federal courts correctly interpreted and enforced the statutory mandates and whether the judicial decisions advanced the statutory goals. The study reinforces the position of judicial proponents and demonstrates that public law litigation was instrumental in the return and recovery of the wolf to the NRM. The federal courts properly interpreted the ESA and National Environmental Policy Act (NEPA) mandates, both supporting and checking relevant executive action. As a result, the return of the wolf has restored balance to the NRM ecosystem and helped to preserve biodiversity.

Chapter 1 presents a theoretical model of the role of the courts in public law litigation. The role of Congress, the president, executive agencies, and federal courts in the policy-making process is examined. The debates regarding statutory interpretation and judicial review of administrative and congressional decisions, which were the central issues in the NRM wolf litigation, are discussed. The ongoing institutional dialogue regarding public policy is delineated.

Chapter 2 provides a historical overview of the extermination and resurrection of the wolf through conscious public policy. The wolf was driven from the East by the end of the nineteenth century as a result of settlement, development, and the loss of habitat. Wolf eradication in the West began after the Civil War and was completed in the early twentieth century. Changing federal public land policies and pressure brought by the livestock industry, hunters, and state governments prompted the federal government to establish a predator control program that effectively drove the wolf to the brink of extinction.

Public attitudes toward public lands and wildlife changed after World War II. Public land management moved away from resource development to greater environmental protection. Statutes were enacted in the 1960s and 1970s, which required federal agencies to consider environmental factors in their decision-making process. Environmental interest groups emerged. Public interest law firms were established. Public law litigation became prominent. Federal courts became the forum for resolving environmental disputes. Continued criticism of federal predator control and growing concern with species extinction led to enactment of the ESA. The ESA requires "all Federal departments and agencies . . . to conserve endangered species and threatened species" and "provide[s] a means whereby the ecosystems upon which endangered and threatened species depend may be conserved."[7] The U.S. Fish and Wildlife Service (FWS) in the Department of Interior (Interior) was delegated implementing authority to provide for the return and recovery of the wolf. The NRM wolf was listed as an endangered species in 1973. The gray wolf was listed as an endangered species across the continental United States, except Minnesota, in 1978.

Chapter 3 examines the reintroduction of the wolf to the NRM from the Carter through Clinton administrations. Different administrations adopted different positions regarding NRM reintroduction and recovery. The wolf was reintroduced to the NRM during the Clinton administration. Industry groups, which also utilize public law litigation, brought suit challenging federal wolf reintroduction. The Tenth Circuit, in *Wyoming Farm Bureau Federation v. Babbitt*,[8] properly determined that wolf reintroduction complied with the ESA and NEPA. The reintroduced populations were geographically separate from and released outside the current range of existing wolf populations. The potential environmental impacts of the NRM wolf reintroduction were adequately discussed by the FWS in the Environmental Impact Statement. Wolf reintroduction was allowed to proceed. Wolf recovery was so successful that the Clinton administration proposed creating four distinct population segments for the gray wolf in the Northeast, Western Great Lakes, West, and Southwest and downlisting the gray wolf to a threatened species where warranted. The designation of a distinct population segment (DPS) allows unique treatment for the discrete significant population.

Chapter 4 reviews the Bush administration's effort to establish three DPSs in the East, West, and Southwest and downlist, then delist, the gray wolf in the East and West DPSs. Environmental groups brought suit challenging the federal action. The U.S. District Court for the District of Oregon, in *Defenders of Wildlife v. Secretary of Interior*,[9] appropriately held that Interior could not delist the wolf across much of the United States because the wolf was still absent from significant portions of its historic range. The court's decision was consistent with the text, legislative history, and the purposes of the ESA, as well as the case law. Furthermore, suitable habitat remained in the wolf's historic range. Interior's decision regarding the establishment of three DPSs was also inconsistent with the legislative history, case law, and its own policy, which allows the designation of a distinct population segment to be used to circumscribe small populations for unique treatment, not delist large geographical areas.

Environmental groups also brought suit, challenging Interior's abandonment of the Northeast DPS. The U.S. District Court for the District of Vermont, in *National Wildlife Federation v. Interior*,[10] accurately invalidated Interior's decision. The court found Interior's amalgamation of the Northeast and Western Great Lakes DPSs into the single Eastern DPS constituted such a fundamental change in the proposed federal action that it undermined public comments on the proposal. The amalgamation also violated the ESA and Interior's DPS policy.

Chapter 5 reviews the Bush administration's creation and delisting of the wolf in the NRM DPS, which consists of Montana, Idaho, and Wyoming, eastern Washington, eastern Oregon, and north-central Utah. Environmental groups brought suit, challenging the action. The U.S. District Court for the

District of Montana, in *Defenders of Wildlife v. Hall*,[11] granted an injunction halting the action. The court took a "hard look" at Interior's decision and properly found that there was not an effective functioning metapopulation in the NRM DPS, which Interior insisted was a necessary precondition for delisting. Furthermore, Interior should not have approved Wyoming's 2007 wolf management plan because it suffered from many of the same defects as the earlier Wyoming plan invalidated in 2004. Following the decision, Wyoming submitted a revised wolf management program that was rejected in 2009.

Chapter 6 examines the Obama administration's attempt to subdivide the NRM DPS. The Obama administration, following a Bush administration proposal, delisted wolves in most of the NRM DPS, except Wyoming. Environmental groups brought suit. The U.S. District Court for the District of Montana, in *Defenders of Wildlife v. Salazar*,[12] appropriately held that the NRM DPS constituted a single unit that could not subdivided. The decision was consistent with the text, earlier Interior policy, and the case law. Furthermore, Wyoming constituted a significant portion of the range of the NRM population. Since Wyoming's wolf management plan had not been approved, wolves in the NRM DPS could not be delisted. Several subsequent events questioned the Montana federal district court's decisions. The U.S. District Court for the District of Wyoming held that Interior's rejection of Wyoming's wolf management plan in 2009 was not justified.[13] In addition, a new study demonstrated that there was genetic connectivity among the three wolf populations in the NRM DPS. The lack of genetic connectivity had been one of the reasons cited by the Montana federal district court for rejecting Interior's 2007 delisting proposal. Following the Montana and Wyoming district court decisions, wolf hysteria broke out in the NRM region, which generated congressional action.

Chapter 7 examines the congressional delisting of the NRM wolf. Congress in 2012 resurrected the Obama administration proposal and attached it to Interior's appropriation bill, delisting the wolf in the entire NRM DPS, except Wyoming. Congress went even further and precluded judicial review of the NRM wolf delisting. Environmental groups brought suit. The Ninth Circuit, in *Alliance for the Wild Rockies v. Salazar*,[14] correctly upheld the congressional delisting. Congress can alter a statute to affect the outcome of litigation and remove the federal courts' jurisdiction over statutory questions. There were, however, alternative novel legal theories that could have been pursued. The court could have engaged in structural review, enforced the congressional rule that prohibits the attachment of substantive legislation to an appropriation bill, and remanded the issue to Congress. The court could have found the delisting of the wolf in the NRM DPS through an appropriation rider that violated congressional rules, undermined federal public trust obligations, and compromised procedural due process. The court could have subjected the congressional action singling out the NRM wolf for unique treatment to more rigorous scrutiny because of the wolf's importance to the maintenance of biodiversity and ecosystem balance. Finally, Congress could not have removed federal court jurisdiction over the constitutional questions.

The conclusion summarizes the findings and examines several remaining issues that will affect the future of the NRM wolves. First, Interior approved Wyoming's wolf management plan. Environmental groups brought suit, challenging the action. The U.S. District Court for the District of Columbia found Interior's approval to be arbitrary and capricious.[15] Second, the Obama administration has proposed a complete reconceptualization of the wolf's taxonomy in North America and a delisting of the gray wolf across much of its current range. The proposal, which rests on questionable science, fails to recognize that the wolf is still missing from significant portions of its historic range. Finally, there are efforts under way in Congress to amend and weaken the ESA.

NOTES

1. Brian N. Beisher, "Comments: Are Ranchers Legitimately Trying to Save Their Hides or Are They Just Crying Wolf," 29 *Land and Water Law Review* 417, 430–42 (1994); Robert Keiter and Patrick Holshea, "Wolf Recovery Under the ESA: A Study in Contemporary Federalism," 11 *Public Land Law Review* 19, 30–35 (1990); Robert Moore, "The Pack is Back," 12 *Thomas M. Cooley Law Review* 647 (1995).
2. David Trubeck, "Environmental Defense I: Introduction to Interest Group Advocacy in Complex Disputes," in Burton A. Weisbrod, Joel F. Handler, and Neil K. Komesar, *Public Interest Law* (University of California, 1978), 153–54.
3. Robert A. Baum, *Public Interest Law: Where Law Meets Social Action* (Oceana, 1987), 1–4.
4. Abram Chayes, "The Role of the Judge in Public Law Litigation," 89 *Harvard Law Review* 1281 (1976).
5. Owen Fiss, "The Forms of Justice," 93 *Harvard Law Review* 1 (1979); John Denvir, "Towards a Political Theory of Public Interest Litigation," 54 *North Carolina Law Review* 1133 (1976).
6. Donald Horowitz, *The Courts and Social Policy* (Brookings Institution, 1977); Michael S. Greve, *The Demise of Environmentalism in American Law* (American Enterprise Institute, 1996); Gerald N. Rosenberg, *The Hollow Hope: Can Courts Bring About Social Change?* (University of Chicago, 1991).
7. 16 U.S.C. 1531.
8. 199 F.3d 1224 (10th Cir. 2000).
9. 354 F. Supp.2d 1156 (D. Or. 2005).
10. 386 F. Supp.2d 553 (D. Vt. 2005).
11. 565 F. Supp.2d 1160 (D. Mt. 2008).
12. 729 F. Supp.2d 1207 (D. Mt. 2010).
13. *Wyoming v. Interior,* Case No. 99-CV-118J (D. Wy. 2010).
14. 672 F.3d 1170 (9th Cir. 2012).
15. *Defenders of Wildlife v. Jewell,* Civil Action No. 12-1853 (September 23, 2014).

Chapter One

Theoretical Framework

Wolf reintroduction and recovery involved the interaction of the three branches of the federal government. Congress established the statutory framework in the Endangered Species Act (ESA) and National Environmental Policy Act (NEPA), which was the focus of the litigation. The debate between public choice theory, which views the goal of the legislative process as satisfying private interest, and civic republicanism, which envisions the legislative process as realizing the public interest, is discussed. Different presidents adopted different positions regarding the reintroduction and recovery of the NRM wolf. The U.S. Fish and Wildlife Service (FWS) in the Department of Interior (Interior) is the federal executive agency with the statutory authority to implement the ESA regarding land-based animals. Some of the constraints on executive agency decision making are explained. Federal courts were called upon to review the FWS statutory compliance. The public law litigation raised several questions: What tools should be used to define the statutory mandates? Whether the courts or administrative agencies should be principally responsible for defining the legal mandates? What is the role of the federal courts in overseeing administrative and congressional decisions? The answer to these questions depends to a degree on the court's assessment of congressional and executive action. The debates between judicial skeptics and proponents on these matters are discussed. Finally, the impact of public law litigation on the ongoing institutional dialogue regarding public policy is examined. This chapter discusses the underlying theoretical issues in the NRM wolf litigation.

CONSTITUTIONAL SETTING

Policymaking can be defined as "a course of action or inaction rather than specific decisions," which proceeds through a series of interrelated processes: agenda setting, policy formulation, implementation, and assessment. Policy making occurs within the constitutional framework, which separates power between the legislative, executive, and judicial branches; establishes a system of checks and balances; and divides power between the federal and state governments. Congress makes the law; the executive implements the law; and the courts adjudicate disputes. The vertical separation of powers between the three branches promotes efficiency and prevents the arbitrary exercise of power by any branch. The horizontal separation of power between the federal and state government prevents tyranny and preserves liberty.[1]

The constitutional structure requires governmental institutions to cooperate and collaborate with each other. Governmental institutions also compete with each other, attempting to read the signals sent by other institutions to maximize their opportunity for success. The policymaking process is "a spiral of institutional competition and cooperation," which provides numerous access points for competing interest groups to attempt to influence policy.[2]

Judicial skeptics argue that the Constitution provides for stability and continuity in governance. The separation of power restrains the federal government from interfering with authority left to other spheres. The people are represented by elected officials, not unelected judges. Elected officials are accountable for their decisions at the ballot box, not in federal courts.[3]

Judicial proponents counter that there are defects in the legislative and administrative process that exclude the consideration and implementation of important public values. There are differences between the law in action and the law on the books. Public law litigation addresses these problems and gives meaning to important public values inherent in the constitutional structure.[4]

CONGRESS

Congress enacted the statutes, the ESA and NEPA, which were the focus of the NRM wolf litigation. Congress also played a central role overseeing the FWS decisions and controlling the FWS budget. Congress registered its approval and disapproval of FWS action regarding wolf reintroduction and recovery through budget allocations. Ultimately, Congress delisted the NRM wolves through a rider on an Interior appropriation bill.

Congress is a bicameral institution, whose members are elected by distinct geographical constituencies. Congress helps to set the agenda by calling attention to problems through hearings, the introduction of bills, and speeches. Congress formulates policies and enacts them into law. The legislative process is decentralized and very fragmented. The majority party in each house, which controls the leadership positions and every committee, plays the crucial role. Legislation is drafted and altered in the committees, on the floor of each house, and revised by a conference committee. Legislation must be approved by both houses and signed by the president, who is often actively involved in the process. There is logrolling, political posturing, manipulation of procedures, and strategic voting throughout the process. Legislative decisions are the result of competing political pressures and driven by two- and four-year election cycles.[5]

There are contending views of the legislative process. Public choice theory considers the legislature to be a marketplace in which public goods are distributed to private interests. Legislation is economic transaction. Legislators, who are seeking reelection, enact policies that benefit private interests in return for votes, campaign contributions, and political influence. Interest groups compete for legislation, which will distribute public benefits to their members. The greater the benefits or costs, the more time and money will be spent by groups to achieve their goal. There is little demand or incentive to enact public interest legislation with dispersed benefits or costs. Such legislation is plagued by "free riders," who will not participate or invest in its enactment. Legislation does not further "some general social goal," but embodies deals that reflect private preferences. There is no deliberative process striving toward the achievement of the public interest.[6]

Civic republicanism posits that Congress is a deliberative body in pursuit of the "social good." Interest groups respond to problems and bring diverse perspectives to the deliberative legislative process, which is characterized by dialogue and discussion. Congress is the "forum for identifying or defining [objectives], and acting towards those ends." The legislative process is "one of mutual search through joint deliberation. . . . Moral insight, sociological understanding, and goodwill are legislative virtues." The end product is legislation that realizes the public interest.[7]

The deliberative process is reinforced by proper procedures. Henry Hart and Albert Sacks point out that "the substance of a decision cannot be planned in advance in the form of rules and standards," but "the procedure of decision commonly can be." Proper procedures ensure that all views are heard; factual information is subject to critical scrutiny; and the benefits and costs are adequately evaluated. Hart and Sacks assert that "the best criterion for sound legislation is the test of whether it is the product of a sound process of enactment."[8]

Neither model totally describes the legislative process. Legislators are not motivated by vague notions of the public interest, nor do they always behave as rational economic actors. Numerous factors influence their behavior, including reelection, policy objectives, ideology, and institutional power. Furthermore, the legislative process requires compromises at every level. Individuals and groups must bargain and compromise to achieve their ends in a complex institutional process. Legislation often reflects the harmonization of diverse self-interests to accomplish a common goal.[9] The fragmented legislative process also provides opponents with numerous opportunities to prevent the enactment of legislation.

PRESIDENT

Wolf reintroduction and recovery began during the Carter administration and continues through the Obama administration. Presidents Carter and Clinton were strong supporters of wolf reintroduction. Presidents Reagan, Bush Sr., Bush Jr., and Obama were more tempered in their support of wolf reintroduction and recovery.

The president, unlike Congress, serves a national constituency, so must service numerous interests. The president plays a crucial role as chief executive, commander in chief, diplomat, legislator, and public opinion and party leader. The president influences the political agenda by raising issues, structuring the public debate, and endorsing or discouraging policies. The president shapes the formulation of policy by generating proposals, mobilizing support for their enactment, and signing or vetoing legislation. The president's success is often determined by the partisan alignment in Congress, his standing in the polls, his administrative skills, and his leadership ability.[10] A first-term President must also be concerned about reelection, so must be aware of how his administration's policies will affect his chance of electoral success on a state-by-state basis.

EXECUTIVE AGENCIES

The Department of Interior is the executive department that is delegated the authority to implement the ESA. The FWS is the agency within Interior that is responsible for the reintroduction and recovery of the NRM wolf.[11] The FWS decisions were the focus of the public law litigation brought by industry and environmental groups.

Executive agencies, which are established by Congress, play a role in agenda setting and policy formulation by providing information that serves as the basis for executive and legislative actions. Executive agencies implement statutory policies. Congress generally delegates broad administrative authority to the agency because of election concerns, the need to achieve legislative compromises, the complexity of the problems, and unknown future contingencies. The agency implements statutory policies through rules and regulations enacted pursuant to the enabling statute or the Administrative Procedures Act (APA). Agency action proceeds through both formal and informal rulemaking. Formal rulemaking involves an adjudicatory hearing, followed by a decision based on substantial evidence. Informal rulemaking, also known as "notice and comment," involves the publication of the proposed agency action in the Federal Register. Public comment is taken on the proposal. The final agency decision, which addresses the public comments, is published in the Federal Register. Policymaking through informal rule-making has been described as "one of the greatest inventions of modern government."[12]

Executive agencies are supplementary lawmakers under conflicting pressures. Who controls agency action is at the center of the debate regarding public law litigation.[13] The agency responds to the President, who nominates agency officials and sets the direction of national policy. The Office of Management and Budget (OMB) reviews proposals for legislation, controls the agency's initial budget proposal, monitors proposed rules for compliance with executive orders, and communicates the White House position on important matters.[14]

Judicial skeptics argue that the president, who is democratically accountable, should police agency actions. The president represents a national constituency, so is not constrained by geographical interests. The president can enforce priorities and provide cohesion.[15] Judicial proponents counter that presidential oversight of administrative action is limited. The president has many responsibilities, so is not involved in most administrative decisions. Presidential appointments are usually done to service interest groups and/or congresspersons. Once appointed, administrators are constrained by statutory mandates and their constituencies. The president primarily influences agency action by providing a sense of direction.[16]

Executive agencies are subject to continued congressional influence. Congress defines the agency's jurisdiction and procedures, confirms its leadership, and approves its budget. Specialized committees oversee the agency's statutory implementation and review the agency's budget. Budgetary politics is a common means for formulating and influencing the implementation of policy. Congressional action continues, changes, or ends the policy.[17]

Judicial skeptics and proponents agree that congressional oversight is limited. Numerous committees and subcommittees with jurisdiction over agency action can be played off against one another. Committees usually do not have a national focus or a great deal of political accountability. Committees often reflect the view of the powerful chairperson and are composed of members interested in servicing their constituencies by providing public benefits to private interests. Committees are often sympathetic to the agency or regulated industry, so there is little public interest scrutiny.

Congressional oversight attracts little public attention, particularly when the same party occupies the White House and Congress. Stalemate occurs when the different parties control the different branches. Most importantly, congressional oversight ensures that the agency complies with the views of the current Congress, not the enacting Congress. Congresspersons gain no advantage from requiring the agency to adhere to the original legislative deal, but derive benefits from satisfying current interest group demands.[18]

Executive agencies are driven by their own internal dynamics. The agency serves the groups affected by its decisions. Interest groups provide information and generate political support for the agency with legislators. A symbiotic relationship develops between the agency and its clientele, which, unlike the public, are well organized and maintain constant contact with the agency.

Executive agencies are motivated by the bureaucratic desire to maximize their institutional importance and budget and minimize any threat to their functions. Organizational theory points out that various internal and external constraints explain agency behavior. Internal constraints consist of mission, goals, tasks, power structure, and autonomy. External constraints consist of political action regarding jurisdiction, funding, and cooperation from nongovernmental actors. The agency is led by a political appointee, who oversees career bureaucrats. The agency often seeks a "negotiated environment—a set of highly predictable interrelationships which serve to reduce in number and buffer unexpected threats to organizational well-being." The agency has to "discover, identify, or manufacture suitable combinations of means and ends to yield effective incentives for the constituents they desire." The agency is aware that "adaptation, innovation, and creation all involve risks of failure, with attendant discredit or disgrace as well as possible threat to job security."[19] Programs must be guarded from interference by other agencies with different missions. These internal bureaucratic needs cause the agency to focus on its own goals and adopt a narrow view of the public interest being served.

FEDERAL COURTS

This study focuses on the litigation regarding wolf reintroduction and recovery to the NRM. Environmental and industry groups unsuccessful in pursuing their policy demands in the legislative and executive arenas continued their struggle in the federal courts through public law litigation. The courts were called upon to evaluate Interior's implementation of policy.[20] The federal courts played an important role, interpreting the statutory mandates in the ESA and NEPA and reviewing Interior's decisions to ensure they conformed to the statutory mandates and were not arbitrary and capricious. The federal courts played an important role "articulate[ing] and enforce[ing] the public values and policies . . . in the governing constitutional or statutory provisions."[21]

Federal courts interact with the executive and legislative branches. The president nominates federal judges and attempts to influence the direction of policy through judicial appointments. The Senate Judiciary Committee reviews and the full Senate confirms federal judicial appointments. Congress also defines the federal court's jurisdiction and controls the federal court's budget and judicial pay.[22]

Federal courts are hierarchically organized. There are ninety-four federal district courts, thirteen appellate courts, and the Supreme Court. Federal district courts serve primarily as dispute resolvers. Federal appellate courts supervise the lower courts' decisions and promote uniformity within the circuit. Appellate courts are more concerned with the development and enunciation of broad rules and policies, rather than merely resolving the disputes between litigants. Appellate decisions are generally the final word on the issue because the Supreme Court only reviews a limited number of cases.[23]

STATUTORY INTERPRETATION

One of the court's major functions in public law litigation is to interpret statutes. Statutory interpretation is dependent on the court's view of the legislative process. There are different views regarding the relationship between the courts and Congress. Public choice adherents contend that courts are part of interest-group politics. Interest groups invest political capital and make legislative deals that favor their members. Groups are willing to invest time and capital for a long-term deal, which is essentially a contract between themselves and legislators. Groups are aware that future administrations and Congress' will not be committed to the past deal, so they need a way to ensure that deal will be enforced in the future. Judicial review by an independent court provides the means to ensure the longevity of the legislative deal. There is no place for public interest, which is anathema to interest group politics.[24]

Civic republicans take issue with this view. Civic republicans argue that the Constitution bars the naked transfer of public goods to interest groups through politics. The court's role is to discourage interest-group deals by raising their costs. The court must look past the deal and promote the public interest in the statute. Judicial review makes Congress accountable to the voters by making legislation transparent, exposing hidden deals, and enforcing only the provisions consistent with statutory purposes and policies.[25]

There are different theories of statutory interpretation, which are the subject of an ongoing debate regarding democratic legitimacy.[26] This study adopts the tradition position, originalism, which recognizes a statute as the command of the sovereign that must be interpreted by other agencies of government. Originalism presumes that the democratically elected legislature has the constitutional responsibility for making policy and the legislative command is supreme. The court, acting as the agent of the legislature, determines the legislative mandate by examining the text, intent, and purpose of the statute. The court, which is not accountable to the electorate, has some discretion, but is constrained to act within the parameters of the statute to carry out its purposes. Originalism is a positivist approach, which is consistent with the constitutional principles of popular sovereignty, majoritarianism, separation of powers, checks and balances, and federalism.[27]

An originalist interpretation begins by examining the text of the statute, which has been enacted into law through the constitutionally prescribed process. The text, which is known to the litigants and public, is the best evidence of legislative intent. Reliance on the text confines the court's inquiry; increases the probability of obtaining judicial agreement in particular cases; and provides certainty and predictability in the law.[28]

There are different textual positions. Strict textualism views the text as the only legitimate interpretive source. Weak textualism considers the statutory language to be the best guide regarding legislative intent or purpose. The latest variation on strict textualism, new textualism, attributes meaning to words solely within their statutory terrain by examining dictionary definitions, grammatical constructions, and the canons of statutory construction. The structure of the statute is analyzed to see how the words are utilized and how the definition fits in with the statute as a whole. The relationship of the statute with other statutes and the use of the words in other statutes are also relevant.[29]

New textualism rejects legislative intent and purposes that only serve as vehicles for judges to read their policy preferences into the statute. Justice Scalia noted that "judges interpret laws rather than reconstruct legislators' intentions. Where the language of those laws is clear, we are not free to replace it with an unenacted legislative intent."[30] New textualism incorporates the skepticism of public choice theory and mandates that statutes be strictly interpreted to decrease the public benefits dispensed to private groups by legislators seeking reelection.[31]

New textualism poses too many interpretative problems. First, the text alone is generally insufficient to determine statutory meaning because it is often ambiguous, vague, or incomplete. Since the words don't have clear meaning outside of the context in which they are used, external sources must be utilized to determine the meaning of the statutory language.[32]

Second, new textualism does not foster a sensible reading of the statute that is designed to carry out the legislative purpose. Instead, particular language is isolated from the legislative enterprise of which it is a part. Congress is unable to send messages to the court regarding agency behavior. This deprives the court of valuable information necessary to interpret the statute and frustrates the court's ability to carry out the design of the enacting legislative coalition. New textualism increases agency discretion and favors the executive branch in its competitive struggle with the Congress over the formulation and implementation of public policy. New textualism is a political strategy for disciplining legislatures and judges.[33]

Third, new textualism is built on the "benign fiction" that rational legislators know the canons of statutory construction, prior judicial precedents, and the existing statutory terrain, and that they write clear text. There is no support for these assumptions. Congressional staff and interest groups draft the text as well as the legislative history. Judges can manipulate the statutory text as easily as the legislative history.[34] Ignoring legislative history allows the court to assert sole dominance in the interpretative arena.

Since the text generally does not answer the interpretative problem, originalism requires the court to search through the "ash cans of the legislative process" to discover how the enacting legislature would have resolved the question. This inquiry can be either archeological or hypothetical. An archeological search entails a review of the text and the legislative history to determine the specific legislative position regarding the issue. A hypothetical inquiry is a reasonable projection about what the original legislature would have said if it possessed the foresight to anticipate what has happened since enactment.[35]

The court must be careful to distinguish between legitimate and manufactured legislative history. Legitimate history comprises statements that are designed to explain the meaning of the statute and build support for its enactment. These statements "illuminate the consensus view of the legislature where that view is left in doubt by the enacted language." Manufactured history consists of statements that are not designed to generate support for the statute, but appeal to particular constituencies and influence the judicial interpretation of the statute. These statements do not reflect the consensus of the legislature.[36]

Judicial skeptics are particularly wary of the use of legislative history, which enhances the power of lobbyists, committees and subcommittees, and staff. Legislative history elevates the views of committees and individuals over those of the Congress as a whole and enhances the power of committees over executive agencies. This is particularly true when the Congress and executive are controlled by different political parties. Justice Scalia contends that the use of legislative history is like looking over a crowd and picking out your friends.[37]

Judicial proponents counter that legislative history reflects the way Congress does business. Congress performs its responsibilities through committees, whose staff writes reports explaining what has been done. There is little danger that information is slipped past the full Congress. Judge Wald stated, "legislative history is the authoritative product of the institutional work of the Congress. It records the manner in which Congress enacts its legislation, and it represents the way Congress communicates with the country at large." Failing to acknowledge legislative history "is to second guess Congress's chosen form of organization and delegation of authority, and to doubt the ability to oversee its own constitutional functions effectively." Ignoring legislative history criticizes "the way a coordinate branch conducts its operations and, in that sense, runs the risk of violating the spirit if not the letter of the separation of powers."[38] Justice Breyer declared that "using legislative history to help interpret unclear statutory language seems natural. Legislative history helps a court understand the context and purposes of a statute."[39]

William Eskridge provides a hierarchy of legislative sources that is based on their comparative reliability. First, the most reliable sources are the committee reports, which represent the "collective understanding of those Congressmen involved in drafting and studying proposed legislation." Congress acts through committees, and "committee reports should be looked to for the most coherent, thorough, and authoritative explanation of a bill's purpose and intended meaning." The reports show areas of agreement between the House and Senate and issues of disagreement that are resolved by the conference committee.

Second, the "statements by sponsors and/or floor managers," who know the language, intent, and purpose of the statute, are important because other congresspersons defer to their judgment. Third, rejected proposals are relevant as "direct evidence that Congress considered an issue and agreed not to adopt a specified policy." Fourth, the statements of legislators in committee hearings and on the floor, while not as authoritative as the sponsors, show "the general assumptions made at the time a law was enacted." Fifth, statements by non-legislative drafters and sponsors are generally not important, unless "the statute was a careful compromise" or "there is virtually no other evidence." Finally, legislative silence and subsequent history are accorded little weight, unless "the precise intent of the enacting Congress is obscure."[40]

Critics assert that there can be no legislative intent because there is no lawmaker. The preferences of individual legislators cannot be aggregated into any collective intent because their psychological and political motivations cannot be known. Giving effect to legislative intent violates the constitutional requirements of bicameralism and the Presentment Clause that are necessary for the enactment of law. Even if legislative intent exists, it does not bind the court because the legislature's function is to pass statutes, not to apply the law in a particular factual situation. Finally, legislative intent is irrelevant because the language of the statute limits the court.[41]

Reed Dickerson rebuts this criticism and points out that all statutes rest on legislative intent, even though it might be difficult to discern. The best approximation of legislative intent is the statute, read in its proper context, supplemented by other reliable extrinsic evidence. Respecting legislative intent places the court in the proper deferential framework regarding the legislature and establishes a criterion of reliability that helps the court select and weigh elements of the language and legislative context.[42]

Public choice advocates also find legislative intent important. The court's role is to carry out the deals negotiated by the legislative coalition. This encourages future negotiations and leads to "stable and predictable methods of interpretation."[43]

An originalist interpretation is also guided by the legislative purpose, which is the ultimate motive of the legislature. Hart and Sacks assert that "every statute must be conclusively presumed to be a purposive act." The legislative purpose is the best justification that can be attributed to the statute in terms of its relationship with the set of legal norms operating at the time of the court's decision. The legislative purpose helps the court to determine the legislative intent, directs the court when intent has not been manifested, and allows the court to keep the statute in harmony with contemporary values.[44]

Critics argue that reliance on the legislative purpose is indeterminate for several reasons. First, since the legislative purposes are stated in general terms, the court has too much discretion. Second, a statute reflects many different purposes because it must be acceptable to a wide range of interests to be enacted. The different purposes reflected in the political bargain can't be aggregated into any particular public purpose. Third, focusing on the legislative purpose ignores the statutory text, which is the most legitimate source of legislative intent and is relied upon by the citizens. Finally, the optimistic assumptions regarding the purposeful legislative process are naive.[45]

Hart and Sacks address their critics, asserting that the attribution of purpose does not grant the court unbridled discretion. The court is constrained by the words of the statute, which are enacted by the legislature. The court must be careful not to give the words "a meaning that they will not bear." Words are not empty vessels into which the court pours meaning, but have a dual role "as guides to the attribution of general purpose and as factors limiting the particular meanings that can properly be attributed." The words must not be given "a meaning which would violate any established policy of clear statement." The court must "try to put itself in imagination in the position of the legislature which enacted the measure" and assume that the "legislature was made up of reasonable persons pursing reasonable purposes reasonably." The court asks, "why would reasonable men, confronted with the law as it was, have enacted this new law to replace it?" The court looks for the "mischief" in the prior statute and "the true reason of the remedy" provided by the new statute. Legislative history must be examined "for the light it throws on the general purpose."[46]

Public choice advocates find merit in Hart and Sacks's approach. Private interest legislation is generally based on a public purpose. An interpretative strategy that relies on public purpose ensures this purpose is carried out. The court places "subtle pressures on Congress to act in ways that benefit the public" and forces the Congress "to spell out more clearly the terms of its bargains with special interest groups." This raises the cost of interest-group activity.[47] Scholars note that "Hart and Sacks were not so much Panglossian empiricists as savvy normativists—crafters of assumptions that provide useful judicial and administrative side-constraints upon the less attractive features of politics."[48]

JUDICIAL REVIEW OF ADMINISTRATIVE DECISIONS

Another important role for the courts in public law litigation is to oversee the agency's legal, factual, and policy decisions to ensure compliance with the statutory mandates. There is an ongoing debate regarding the interpretative authority of the courts and administrative agencies.

The different positions regarding judicial-agency relationships can be aggregated into the deferential and supervisory models of administrative law. Judicial skeptics champion the deferential model, asserting that courts should defer to agency decision making for several constitutional reasons. First, the executive is mandated to "take care that the laws be faithfully executed." Second, Congress delegates its legislative authority to executive agencies to implement the statute. Third, federal agencies when implementing the statute engage in a political balancing process that belongs to the democratically accountable executive branch.[49]

Judicial skeptics argue that the deferential model is based on institutional competence. Executive agencies are more competent than courts to interpret statutes. Agencies have superior knowledge about legislative intent; are familiar with the problems being addressed; participate in the legislative process; know the consequences of the legislative action; and have better interpretative tools, such as staff, analytical skills, and political sophistication. Agency decisions, which are based on technological and policy concerns, are superior to judicial decisions, which are constrained by principles. Agency decisions provide for geographic uniformity, continuity, harmony and integration of policies, and quicker and more efficient implementation of the law.[50]

Skeptics assert that adjudication is piecemeal. Courts are reactive and must respond to the issues presented by the parties. Courts are not competent to resolve complex policy disputes that go beyond the declaration of rights and involve the implementation of rights through the oversight of the government bureaucracy. Judges are generalists, whose recruitment, socialization, and role precludes the development of the specialized knowledge involved in complex policy disputes. Courts are well suited to deal with party-oriented adjudicatory facts, but not with policy-oriented legislative facts. The necessity to provide a remedy for the violation of the rights infringed limits the court's ability to design and implement remedies to resolve complex policy disputes. Furthermore, courts do not provide for an ongoing review of policy.[51]

Skeptics point out that judicial involvement in complex policy disputes is based on inadequate knowledge of public bureaucracies. Courts do not understand economic and political constraints on agencies, the implications of various policy options, and the necessity for tradeoffs. Policymaking is done under conditions of uncertainty. Scientific and technological decisions involve much speculation. Judicial involvement interferes with policy implementation and "ossifies" the federal bureaucracy. Judicial decisions deflect policy concerns into narrow areas, paralyze policy innovation, foster contradictory policies, misallocate scarce resources, and force agencies to adopt policies that are often inimical to the public interest.[52] Martin Shapiro argues that "policy making via litigation means that the judge enters highly complex ongoing situations just far enough and just long enough to pull out a crucial brick and then scampers away, leaving it to the rest of the political system to somehow make sure that the wall does not fall down."[53]

Judicial skeptics are critical of liberal standing rules, which allow interest groups to utilize the courts to challenge political decisions. The plaintiffs to establish standing must show they will suffer an injury in fact, that is caused by the defendant, and the court is capable of providing redress for the injury. The plaintiffs must also demonstrate that the injury falls within the zone of interests to be protected by the statute.[54] Skeptics complain that the expansion of standing has made courts into just another forum for interest-group politics.[55] Only a litigant, who suffers an injury to her common law interest, should have standing to challenge government action. Individual harm is axiomatic to litigation. Public law litigation is parasitic on the court's function as a dispute resolver and norm enforcer. Granting interest groups standing to challenge government policy interferes with the executive's implementation of the law. Statutory beneficiaries should not be allowed to bring their complaints regarding policy implementation to the courts. Instead, they should focus their efforts in the congressional and executive branches.[56]

Justice Scalia as a professor advanced this object-beneficiary distinction. Professor Scalia asserted that the object of government regulation represents a minority interest that is entitled to the counter-majoritarian protection of the court. Statutory beneficiaries represent majoritarian interests that are best protected by political institutions. Professor Scalia recognized that "as long as no minority interests are affected 'important legislative purposes, heralded in the halls of Congress, [may be] lost or misdirected in the vast hallways of the federal bureaucracy.' And of course it does—and a good thing too."[57]

Judicial proponents argue that the deferential model fails to recognize that the implementation of statutory mandates is a political process. Agencies make choices when interpreting and implementing statutes. Agencies are not disinterested bureaucrats serving the public interest, but political actors under conflicting pressures, which often preclude statutory compliance. Courts oversee agency decisions "to see that important legislative purposes, heralded in the halls of Congress, are not lost or misdirected in the vast hallways of the federal bureaucracy."[58]

Proponents support the supervisory model, which recognizes the important role of the court in overseeing administrative actions and advances the constitutional separation of powers and checks and balances. Judicial review ensures that the executive branch faithfully executes the law and acts within the parameters of the statute to carry out its purposes. Judicial review prevents agency capture and keeps the agency accountable to Congress and ultimately to the voters.[59]

Proponents point out that the supervisory model is supported by the Administrative Procedures Act (APA), which declares that "the reviewing court shall decide all relevant questions of law, interpret constitutional and statutory provisions, and determine the meaning or applicability of the terms of an agency action." The court is also required to review the agency's factual and policy decisions to ensure that the agency has not acted in a manner that is "arbitrary and capricious, an abuse of discretion, or otherwise not in accordance with law." Furthermore, the APA grants parties aggrieved by federal government action generic standing to challenge federal administrative action.[60]

Proponents contend that judicial review promotes the legitimacy of administrative actions, which is defined as the "ensurance of legality, protection against arbitrariness and selectivity, promotion of procedural regularity, and ensurance against the twin evils of factional tyranny and self-interested representation."[61] Courts maintain the integrity of the system. Louis Jaffe stated, "the availability of judicial review is the necessary condition, psychologically if not logically, of a system of administrative power which purports to be legitimate, or legally valid." Courts serve as "a constant reminder to the administration and a constant source of assurance and security to the citizen."[62]

Proponents argue that the supervisory model recognizes the court's institutional advantages. The court must respond to the complaint. The judge, who is insulated from narrow political pressures, operates under "a professional ideal of reflective and dispassionate analysis of the problem before her and is likely to have had some experience in putting ideal into practice." The judiciary, which is not bureaucratic, can tap energies and resources in and outside of the government to seek a solution that can be tailored to meet the needs of the particular situation. National policy can be applied in limited situations. Litigation permits a high degree of participation by concerned parties without providing them with a veto and generates sufficient information to ensure the proper critical review. Judicial review is an effective mechanism for registering and responding to grievances generated by the operation of public programs in the regulatory state.[63]

Judicial proponents applaud the expansion of standing rules, which allow interest-group access to courts. The citizen suit provision in the ESA allows any person to "commence a civil suit on his own behalf to enjoin any person, including the U.S. and any other governmental instrumentality or agency . . . , who is alleged to be in violation of any provision of this chapter or regulation issued under the authority thereof."[64] General citizen standing is provided in the Administrative Procedures Act (APA).[65] The Supreme Court has recognized harm to "scenery, natural and historic objects and wildlife . . . may amount to an 'injury in fact' sufficient to lay the basis for standing under the APA."[66] The Supreme Court also acknowledged that an attenuated line of causation between the alleged environmental harm and the federal action can also support interest-group standing.[67] These changes promoted the growth of public law litigation.

Judicial proponents argue that statutory beneficiaries can be harmed by the agency's implementation of the law. Standing can't be limited to those suffering injury to their traditional common law interests. Congress created new statutory benefits that are entitled to protection. The agency is sometimes reluctant to implement the congressional mandate. Congress granted statutory beneficiaries standing to ensure that the agency follows the law. The citizen suit is a corrective action. The court is not forcing the agency to carry out policies not enacted in the political process, but ensures that the executive branch complies with statutory mandates.[68] Even some judicial skeptics recognize that "standing to obtain judicial review is a critical determination of a party's ability to participate effectively in agency decision-making process." Citizen suits require administrators to "respond to arguments made by parties that can challenge policy decisions in court . . . , but they can ignore with relative impunity arguments made by parties that lack this power."[69]

Judicial Review of Questions of Law

The courts are sometimes asked to review the agency's interpretation of the law in public law litigation. The courts have the constitutional authority to say what the law means. Alexander Hamilton in Federalist No. 78 stated "the interpretation of the laws is the proper and peculiar province of the courts."

Judges determine "the meaning of any particular act proceeding from the legislative body."[70] Justice Marshall reiterated this view in *Marbury v. Madison*, commenting that "it is emphatically the province and duty of the judicial department to say what the law is."[71] In the past, the courts adopted a case-by-case approach regarding the deference accorded to an agency's legal determination, considering such variables as "an agency's statutory mandate, its familiarity with the regulated industries, its expertise concerning the subject matter, and the type of interpretative problem at issue."[72]

This ad hoc approach was questioned in *Chevron v. Natural Resources Defense Council* (Chevron).[73] The Supreme Court developed a two-step process regarding judicial review of an agency's legal interpretations. The court first examines the text and legislative history of the statute to determine "whether Congress has directly spoken to the precise question at issue." If Congress has not directly addressed the question, the court can "not simply impose its own construction on the statute." The court moves to the second step to determine "whether the agency's answer is based on a permissible construction of the statute." The court does not have to conclude that the agency's construction is "the only one it permissibly could have adopted to uphold the construction, or even the reading the court would have reached if the question had arisen in a judicial proceeding." Instead, the court must defer to "a reasonable interpretation made by the administrator of the agency."[74]

Judges are admonished not to read their policy preferences into the law because they lack expertise and are not accountable to the electorate. Congress delegated its power to the agency, which can "properly rely upon the incumbent administration's views of wise policy to inform its judgments." The president makes policy choices that "resolve the competing interest which Congress itself either inadvertently did not resolve, or intentionally left to be resolved by the agency charged with the administration of the statute in light of everyday realities."[75]

Judicial skeptics applaud Chevron because it prevents the federal courts from imposing their views on the agencies. Chevron grants the president more authority and discretion to address problems. Agencies have more flexibility to change their statutory interpretation "in light of new scientific, industrial, or other developments or even because a recently elected administration has a new regulatory program." The development of national policy is facilitated by precluding different circuit courts from rendering different decisions on the same issue, preventing the "balkanization of federal law."[76]

Skeptics argue that agencies will be "encouraged to take more responsibility for interpreting the statutes they implement." Litigants will "make their best arguments, clearly and aggressively, before the agency rather than waiting for the main event in the courthouse."[77] Congress will be encouraged to write clear statutes.

Judicial proponents are critical of Chevron, which violates the separation of power by granting the agency unbridled discretion to enact executive policy. There is no judicial check on administrative agencies unless a clear signal has been sent by Congress, which never acquiesced to this transfer of authority.

Proponents assert that agencies lack the institutional capabilities to determine legal questions. Chevron fails to distinguish between the delegation of interpretative powers and statutory ambiguities. Chevron is based on a misconception of statutory interpretation. The question is not whether Congress has precisely addressed the issue, but whether the statute requires or forbids administrative action. Chevron fails to recognize that interest groups will continue to dominate executive agencies. Judicial review is necessary to prevent self-interested decisions: "foxes should not guard henhouses."[78]

Proponents contend that Chevron is inconsistent with evolution of the non-delegation rule, which posits that Congress cannot delegate legislative authority to agencies without providing adequate standards for its execution. The non-delegation rule reinforces the separation of powers and prevents the concentration of power in the executive. The Supreme Court abandoned the rigid non-delegation rule with the assurance that federal courts would watch over executive power. Executive authority must be constrained by adequate administrative procedures and judicial review. Congress delegates power to executive agencies to make policy within statutory limits, but not to define those statutory limits.[79]

Proponents argue that Chevron is overbroad. Each case presents different circumstances with different degrees of complexity. Justice Breyer pointed out that Chevron asks judges to develop a psychologically troubling perspective. After examining the legal question in depth, it is difficult for the judge to believe both that the agency interpretation is legally wrong and its interpretation is reasonable.[80] Justice Breyer maintains that the "the statute's text, its context, the structure of the statutory scheme, and canons of textual construction" as well as "statutory purposes, including those revealed in part by legislative and regulatory history" are relevant in determining whether the statute is ambiguous.[81]

Chevron has not repudiated the supervisory model because the courts employ Chevron in a strong or weak manner. A strong reading requires the court to defer to the agency's legal interpretation unless Congress has specifically addressed the legal issue. A weak reading stresses the continued use of the traditional tools of statutory interpretation. Only when these tools fail to yield an answer to the legal question is the court required to defer to the agency's legal interpretation.[82] The Court in Chevron specifically declared that "the judiciary is the final authority on issues of statutory construction and must reject administrative constructions which are contrary to clear congressional intent. If a court, employing the traditional tools of statutory construction, ascertains that Congress had an intention on the precise question at issue, that intention is the law and must be given effect."[83] Justice Marshall in a contemporaneous dissent remarked that "Chevron's deference requirement . . . was explicitly limited to cases in which congressional intent cannot be discerned through the use of traditional techniques of statutory construction."[84]

Justice Stevens, the author of the Chevron decision, later stated that a "pure question of statutory construction [is] for the courts to decide" by "employing traditional tools of statutory construction."[85] Justice Scalia took issue with this position, asserting that when the statute is not clear, the court must defer to the agency's interpretation.[86] Justice Stevens responded that "your criticism is based on a misreading of the Court's opinion in Chevron. That opinion did not announce a simple black letter rule requiring absolute deference to agencies unless there is clear evidence of congressional intent, and no deference when intent is clear. . . . The more important inquiry is whether the issue is one that Congress intended itself to resolve or whether it is an interstitial area in which Congress intended to delegate lawmaking authority to the agency."[87]

Federal courts have vacillated between strong and weak readings of Chevron.[88] Recent empirical studies demonstrate the following: First, Chevron has increased the likelihood of affirmance of agency interpretations of law, with deference rates above 60 percent. Second, while Democratic and Republican judges are likely to uphold agency interpretations, judges are more likely to support the interpretation that is consistent with their perceived policy preferences. Third, voting outcomes are influenced by panel effect. (Homogeneous panels are more likely to overturn an agency's interpretation that is inconsistent with their policy preferences.)[89] The selective application of Chevron indicates that the courts still have an important role to play in statutory interpretation. Chevron should only be viewed as a judicially imposed prudential concern that is to be applied in a flexible manner.

Judicial Review of Fact and Policy Questions

Federal courts are sometimes asked to review the agency's factual and policy decisions in public law litigation. The APA requires the court to ensure that agency actions are not "arbitrary, capricious, an abuse of discretion, or otherwise not in accordance with law." This standard of review supports both the supervisory hard-look doctrine and the deferential soft-glance approach.[90]

The hard-look doctrine requires agencies to consider all relevant factors, justify departures from past practices, furnish detailed explanations of their decision, explain the rejection of alternatives, and show the connections between statutory purposes and regulatory policies. The court examines the agency's action "to satisfy itself that the agency has exercised a reasoned discretion with reasons that do not deviate from or ignore the ascertainable legislative intent."[91] The court "attempts to make sense out of vague delegations, enforce policy declarations discernible there, and . . . reconcile contradictory and contrived legislative histories." The hard-look doctrine "ensures that the agency's decision was a 'reasoned' exercise of discretion and not merely a response to political pressures."[92]

Judicial skeptics have raised objections to the hard-look doctrine. First, a detailed explanation has little substantive effect on the agency's decision. Second, the courts lack the expertise and the political accountability to play a constructive role in administrative process. Third, the hard-look doctrine ignores the important role of politics in agency decisions. Fourth, judges use the hard-look doctrine to substitute their own policy choices for those of elected officials.[93] Fifth, the hard-look doctrine undermines the legitimacy of agency decisions. Sixth, the hard-look doctrine is not needed because better political alternatives are available. Finally, aggressive judicial review misappropriates limited agency resources.[94]

Judicial proponents point out that skeptics fail to recognize the necessity and value of the hard-look doctrine. Aggressive judicial review "gives those concerned with well-reasoned decision making a lever with which to move those who do not." Only the courts "have the time, the influence, and the freedom from ceremonial and political considerations that are necessary to a thorough, dispassionate and effective review of extremely complex and controversial matters."[95]

The hard-look doctrine advances the separation of powers. Judicial involvement prevents agency capture. The court ensures that the agency's decisions are based on technocratic expertise and conform to the statutory goals. Politics can influence value choice, but only within the constraints of the statute. Judge Leventhal, the father of the doctrine, noted that the hard-look doctrine combines "judicial supervision with a salutary principle of judicial restraint." Agencies and courts together constitute a "partnership in furtherance of the public interest" and the "court is in a real sense part of the total administrative process, and not a hostile stranger to the office of first instance."[96] Judicial review advances the republican ideal of honest disinterested deliberation regarding the public interest.[97] Federal courts continue to endorse and utilize the hard-look doctrine.[98]

Judicial Review of Congressional Decisions

Federal courts also examined the congressional delisting of the NRM wolves and the removal of federal jurisdiction over the issue. This posed interesting structural and constitutional issues. The federal courts properly upheld congressional delisting under existing precedent, but the congressional delisting could have been evaluated under more novel evolving legal theories.

Statutory interpretation is an effort by the court to give meaning to the statute, which is the end product of the political process. This assumes the statute is the result of a rational process that is governed by the Constitution and congressional rules. The Supreme Court is concerned with circumstances that "curtail the operation of . . . political processes."[99] Scholars have argued for structural review, which requires the federal court to review legislative procedures. When laws are enacted that impinge on important public values, the federal court should examine the procedures Congress followed. If the process was defective, the federal court should remand the legislation back to Congress. The court would not be telling Congress its goals cannot be achieved, but that the process followed was defective.[100]

Supporters of structural review argue that Congress should be required to produce a record of evidence or "clear statement" that demonstrates that it acted reasonably in concluding that federal legislation is necessary and proper to exercise its enumerated powers. Courts should police "Congress's deliberative process and its reasons for regulating" to ensure that Congress seriously considered federal concerns and adequately justified federal government action. Federal courts should conduct a "hard look review" of congressional action. This will promote procedural regularity, provide equal protection, protect due process, generate institutional dialogue, encourage deliberation, and ensure that the political process is open and fair.[101]

Opponents raise various objections to structural review: First, courts can't treat Congress like an administrative agency. Second, judicial interference with congressional procedures violates the separation of powers. Judicial review of congressional procedures presents a non-justiciable political question, which lacks judicially manageable standards. Third, judicial review will interfere with the unique way that Congress does business. Requiring Congress to follow its own rules, engage in an open deliberative process, and justify its positions undermines the efficacy of the institutional process. Fourth, imposing new procedural requirements is a post-hoc rationalization.[102]

DIALOGUE

Judicial decisions in the NRM wolf litigation did not end the conflict. Winners and losers in the litigation continued to pursue alternative strategies to advance their interests. The FWS and industry groups, whose arguments had not prevailed in the courts, were eventually successful in the legislative arena. Congress attached a rider to an appropriation bill that delisted the NRM wolves and precluded judicial review of the decision.

Judicial decisions in public law litigation do not end the ongoing institutional dialogue. Judicial decisions affirm or reject executive-legislative deals manifested in the statute; affect the competitive struggle between the legislative and executive branches over policy; impact executive implementation of policy; and structure federal-state relations. Judicial decisions are "political resources" that are "best viewed as the beginning of a political process."[103] Dissatisfied groups attempt to enlist the support of the executive and return to Congress, which is the "focal point for public reaction to judicial policies," to have the statutory decisions changed. Judicial decisions provide "strong ammunition for members of Congress who would defend the status quo,"[104] but also stimulate congressional action. Congress can incorporate the judicial decision into the statute; supplement, clarify, modify, or reverse the judicial decision; or establish exceptions to or limit the application of the statute. Statutory changes can reaffirm the original legislative bargains or establish new policy preferences.

Studies have examined congressional reversals of judicial statutory interpretations.[105] Recent studies demonstrate that Congress is very much aware of judicial interpretations, devotes significant time to analyzing their policy implications, and frequently overrides those interpretations. Congressional overrides are most likely "when a Supreme Court interpretation reveals an ideologically fragmented Court, relies on the text's plain meaning and ignores legislative signals, and/or rejects positions taken by federal, state, or local governments." The views of the current Congress are more important than those of the enacting Congress.[106]

Studies stress the importance of political factors in congressional reversals of judicial statutory decisions. Judicial decisions help to set the political agenda by demonstrating problems with the statute. Proposals for changes are presented. The political disposition of the executive and legislative branches is important if any change is to be forthcoming.[107] James Walker and Michael Solomine observed that "the last word in statutory interpretation belongs to no one institutional or individual, which is as it should be."[108]

NOTES

1. Walter A. Rosenbaum, *Environmental Policy and Politics,* 3d ed. (Congressional Quarterly, 1995), 82–87; *Misretta v. U.S.*, 488 U.S. 361, 380 (1989).

2. Daniel A. Farber and Philip P. Frickey, "Forward: Positive Political Theory in the Nineties," 80 *Georgetown Law Journal* 457, 462 (1992).

3. Edwin Meese III, "Foreword," in Lee Edwards (ed.), *Bringing Justice to the People: A Story of the Freedom Based Public Law Movement* (Heritage, 2004).

4. Burton A. Weisbrod, "Problems of Enhancing the Public Interest: Toward a Model of Government Failures," in Burton Weisbrod, Joel Handler, Neil Komesar, *Public Interest Law* (University of California, 1978).

5. William N. Eskridge Jr., "Dynamic Statutory Interpretation," 135 *University of Pennsylvania Law Review* 1479, 1530–31 (1987).

6. Eskridge, 1511–21. Mancur Olsen, *The Logic of Collective Action* (Harvard University, 1965).

7. Frank I. Michelman, "Political Markets and Community Self-Determination: Competing Models of Judicial Legitimacy," 53 *Indiana Law Journal* 145 (1977–78).

8. Henry M. Hart and Albert M. Sacks, *The Legal Process: Basic Problems in the Making and Application of Law* (Foundation, 1994), 694–95.

9. Daniel A. Farber and Philip P. Frickey, *Law and Public Choice: A Critical Introduction* (University of Chicago, 1991), 21–33.

10. Dennis L. Soden, *The Environmental Presidency* (SUNY Press, 1999). Norman J. Vig, "Presidential Leadership and the Environment: From Reagan to Clinton," in Norman J. Vig and Michael E. Kraft (eds.), *Environmental Policy in the 1990s* (Congressional Quarterly, 1997), 96. Michael E. Kraft, "Environmental Policy in Congress: Revolution, Reform, or Gridlock?" in Vig and Kraft, *Environmental Policy*, 120–23.

11. 50 *C.F.R.* 402.01(b) (2003).

12. Kenneth Culp Davis, *Administrative Law Treatise*, section 6.15 (1978).

13. Kathleen W. Marcel, "The Role of the Courts in a Legislative and Administrative Legal System: The Use of Hard Look Review in Federal Environmental Litigation," 62 *Oregon Law Review* 403, 408–9(1983). Cass R. Sunstein, "Factions, Self-Interest, and the APA: Four Lessons since 1946," 72 *Virginia Law Review* 271, 291–92 (1986). Richard Pierce, "Issues Raised by Laidlaw: Access to the Courts," 11 *Duke Environmental Law & Policy Forum* 207, 220–22 (2001).

14. Cynthia R. Farina, "Statutory Interpretation and the Balance of Power in the Administrative State," 89 *Columbia Law Review* 452, 504–6 (1989). Daniel B. Rodriquez, "The Substance of the New Legal Process," 77 *California Law Review* 919, 927 (1989). Alfred Aman, "Administrative Law in a Global Era," 73 *Cornell Law Review* 1101, 1236–42 (1988).

15. Richard J. Pierce, "*Lujan v. Defenders of Wildlife*: Standing as a Judicially Imposed Limit on Legislative Power," 42 *Duke Law Journal* 1170, 1171–88 (1993).

16. Harold H. Bruff, "Legislative Formality, Administrative Rationality," 63 *Texas Law Review* 207, 233–36 (1984).

17. Neil E. Devins, "Appropriations Redux: A Critical Look at Fiscal Year 1988 Continuing Resolution," 1988 *Duke Law Journal* 389. Louis Fischer, "The Authorization-Appropriation Process in Congress: Formal Rules and Informal Practices," 29 *Catholic University Law Review* 51 (1979).

18. Bruff, 229–33.

19. Notes, "Judicial Intervention and Organizational Theory: Changing Bureaucratic Behavior and Policy," 89 *Yale Law Journal* 513 (1980). Richard Allen Liroff, "Administrative, Judicial, and Natural Systems: Agency Response to the NEPA of 1969," 3 *Loyola University of Chicago Law Journal* 19, 29–30 (1972). Steven B. Fishman, "A Preliminary Assessment of the NEPA of 1969," 1973 *Urban Law Annual* 209, 237–40.

20. Jeremy A. Rabkin, *Judicial Compulsions: How Public Law Distorts Public Policy* (Basic Books, 1989), 4. Bradley Canon and Charles Johnson, *Judicial Policies: Implementation and Impact,* 2d ed. (Congressional Quarterly, 1998), 131–38.

21. Abram Chayes, "The Role of the Judge in Public Law Litigation," 89 *Harvard Law Review* 1281 (1976). Abram Chayes, "The Supreme Court 1981 Term, Forward: Public Law Litigation and the Burger Court," 96 *Harvard Law Review* 4, 58 (1982).

22. William E. Kovacic, "The Reagan Judiciary and Environmental Policy," 18 *Boston College Environmental Affairs Law Review* 669, 673–80 (1994). Robert Carp and Ronald Stidham, *The Federal Courts*, 3d ed. (Congressional Quarterly, 1998), 41–62, 183–206.

23. Christopher Smith, *Courts, Politics, and the Judicial Process,* 2d ed. (Nelson Hall, 1997), 225, 287. Sue Davis and Donald R. Songer, "The Changing Role of the U.S. Court of Appeals: The Flow of Litigation Revisited," 13 *Justice System Journal* 323, 338–40 (1988–89).

24. William M. Landes and Richard A. Posner, "The Independent Judiciary in an Interest-Group Perspective," 18 *Journal of Law and Economics* 875 (1975).

25. Cass R. Sunstein, "Naked Preferences and the Constitution," 84 *Columbia Law Review* 1689 (1984). Jonathan R. Macey, "Promoting Public-Regarding Legislation Through Statutory Interpretation: An Interest-Group Model," 86 *Columbia Law Review* 223 (1986). Susan Rose-Ackerman, "Judicial Review and the Power of the Purse," 12 *International Review of Law and Economics* 191, 192, 197 (1992).

26. Karen M. Gebbia-Pinetti, "Statutory Interpretation: Democratic Legitimacy and Legal System Values," 21 *Seton Hall Legislation Journal* 233 (1997).

27. Cass R. Sunstein, "Interpreting Statutes in the Regulatory State," 103 *Harvard Law Review* 405, 467 (1989). Martin H. Redish and Theodore T. Chung, "Democratic Theory and the Legislative Process: Mourning the Death of Originalism in Statutory Interpretation," 68 *Tulane Law Review* 803, 805 (1994). William N. Eskridge Jr., "The New Textualism," 37 *UCLA Law Review* 621, 626 (1990).

28. T. Alexander Alienikoff, "Updating Statutory Interpretation," 87 *Michigan Law Review* 20, 23–24 (1988).

29. William N. Eskridge Jr. and Philip P. Frickey, "Statutory Interpretation as Practical Reasoning," 42 *Stanford Law Review* 321, 340–41 (1990). Richard C. Ausness, "Federal Preemption of State Products Liability Doctrines," 44 *South Carolina Law Review* 187, 234–35 (1993).

30. *INS v. Cardoza-Fonseca,* 480 U.S. 421, 453 (1987).

31. Nicholas S. Zeppos, "Legislative History and the Interpretation of Statutes: Toward a Fact-Finding Model of Statutory Interpretation," 72 *Virginia Law Review* 1295, 1299–1305 (1990).

32. J. A. Corry, "The Use of Legislative History in the Interpretation of Statutes," 32 *Canadian Bar Review* 624, 625–26 (1954). Sunstein, "Interpreting Statutes," 418–24.

33. McNollgast, "Positive Canons: The Role of Legislative Bargains in Statutory Interpretation," 80 *Georgetown Law Journa*l 705, 738 (1992). Patricia M. Wald, "The D.C. Circuit: Here and Now," 55 *George Washington Law Review* 718, 727–28 (1987).

34. Eskridge, "New Textualism," 679–80. Redish and Chung, 823–26.

35. Charles Curtis, *It's Your Law* (Harvard University, 1954), 52. Redish and Chung, 813–15. Aleinikoff, 22–23.

36. Robert Weisberg, "The Calabresian Judicial Artist: Statutes and the New Legal Process," 35 *Stanford Law Review* 213, 246–47 (1983).

37. Antonin Scalia, *A Matter of Interpretation, Federal Courts and the Law* (Princeton University, 1997), 29–37.

38. Patricia M. Wald, "The Sizzling Sleeper: The Use of Legislative History in Construing Statutes in the 1988–89 Term of the U.S. Supreme Court," 39 *American University Law Review* 277, 306–7 (1990).

39. Stephen Breyer, "On the Uses of Legislative History in Interpreting Statutes," 65 *Southern California Law Review* 845, 848 (1992).

40. Eskridge, "New Textualism," 630–40. Ausness, 242–43.

41. Max Radin, "Statutory Interpretation," 43 *Harvard Law Review* 863 (1929–30). Eskridge, "Textualism," 643–50.

42. Reed Dickerson, *The Interpretation and Application of Statutes* (Little Brown, 1975), 68–79, 85–86.

43. Richard A. Posner, "The Jurisprudence of Skepticism," 86 *Michigan Law Review* 827, 848–52 (1988). Richard A. Posner, "Statutory Interpretation—in the Classroom and in the Courtroom," 50 *University of Chicago Law Review* 800 (1983). Rodriquez, 934–35.

44. Hart and Sacks, 1124. Vincent Wellman, "Dworkin and the Legal Process Tradition," 29 *Arizona Law Review* 413, 463 (1987). Dickerson, 86–102.

45. Eskridge and Frickey, "Practical Reasoning," 334–38. William N. Eskridge Jr. and Philip P. Frickey, "Legislation Scholarship and Pedagogy in the Post-Legal Process Era," 48 *University of Pittsburgh Law Review* 691, 704–9 (1987).

46. Hart and Sacks, 1374–80.

47. Macey, 261–67.

48. Farber and Frickey, 475.

49. Stephen Breyer, "Judicial Review of Questions of Law and Policy," 38 *Administrative Law Review* 363, 365–68 (1986). Clark Byse, "Judicial Review of Administrative Interpretation of Statutes: An Analysis of Chevron's Two Step," 2 *Administrative Law Journa*l 255, 257 (1988).

50. Colin S. Diver, "Statutory Interpretation in the Administrative State," 133 *University of Pennsylvania Law Review* 549, 568–92 (1985).

51. Donald Horowitz, *The Courts and Social Policy* (Brookings Institution, 1977).

52. R. Shep Melnick, *Administrative Law and Bureaucratic Reality,* 44 *Administrative Law Review* 245 (1992). R. Shep Melnick, *Regulation Through the Courts* (Brookings Institution, 1983). Rosemary O'Leary, "The Impacts of Federal Court Decisions on the Policies and Administration of the U.S. EPA," 41 *Administrative Law Review* 549 (1989). Robert A. Kagan, "Adversarial Legalism and American Government," 10 *Journal of Policy Analysis and Management* 369 (1991). Jerry L. Mashaw and David L. Harst, "Regulation and Legal Culture: The Case of Motor Vehicle Safety," 4 *Yale Journal of Regulation* 257 (1987).

53. Martin Shapiro, "Judicial Activism," in Seymour Lipset, *The Third Century: America as a Post Industrial Society* (Hoover Institute, 1979), 110, 129.

54. *Associated Data Processing Service Organizations v. Camp*, 397 U.S. 150 (1970).

55. Michael S. Greve, *The Demise of Environmentalism in American Law* (American Enterprise Institute, 1996), 42–63. Jeremy Rabkin, *Judicial Compulsions: How Public Law Distorts Public Policy* (Basic Books, 1989), 19–31.

56. Victor Aubert, "Competition and Dissensus: Two Forms of Conflict Resolution," 7 *Journal of Conflict Resolution* 26 (1963). Lon Fuller, "The Forms and Limits of Adjudication," 92 *Harvard Law Review* 92 (1978).

57. Antonin Scalia, "The Doctrine of Standing as an Essential Element of the Separation of Powers," 17 *Suffolk Law Review* 881, 897 (1983).

58. Rodriquez, 927. *Calvert's Cliff Coordinating Committee v. AEC,* 449 F.2d 1109, 1115 (D.C. Cir. 1971).

59. Abner J. Mikva, "How the Courts Should Treat Administrative Agencies," 36 *American University Law Review* 1, 3 (1986). Cass R. Sunstein, "What's Standing After Lujan? Of Citizen Suits, Injuries, and Article III," 91 *Michigan Law Review* 163, 212 (1993).

60. 5 U.S.C. §701, §706 (1988). Cass R. Sunstein, "Law and Administration After Chevron," 90 *Columbia Law Review* 2071, 2080–81 (1990).

61. Cass R. Sunstein, "On the Costs and Benefits of Aggressive Judicial Review of Agency Action," 1989 *Duke Law Journal* 522, 525.

62. Louis Jaffe, *Judicial Control of Administrative Action* (Little Brown, 1965), 320, 325.

63. Chayes, "Role of the Judge," 1307–8. Richard A. L. Gambitta, Marlynn L. May, and James C. Foster, *Governing Through Courts* (Sage, 1981).

64. 16 U.S.C. 1540 (g).

65. 5 U.S.C. 702 (1988).

66. *Sierra Club v. Morton,* 405 U.S. 727 (1972).

67. *U.S. v. Students Challenging Regulatory Agency Procedures,* 412 U.S. 699 (1973). *Duke Power v. Carolina Study Group,* 438 U.S. 59 (1978).

68. Gene R. Nichol Jr., "Justice Scalia, Standing, and Public Law Litigation," 42 *Duke Law Journal* 1141 (1993). Jonathan Poisner, "Environmental Values and Judicial Review after Lujan: Two Critiques of Separation of Powers Theory of Standing," 18 *Ecology Law Quarterly* 335 (1991).

69. Richard Pierce, "The Role of the Judiciary in Implementing an Agency Theory of Government," 64 *New York University Law Review* 1239, 1283–84 (1989).

70. Henry P. Monaghan, "Marbury and the Administrative State," 83 *Columbia Law Review* 1, 12 (1983).

71. 5 U.S. (Cranch) 137, 177-78 (1803).

72. Maureen B. Callahan, "Must Federal Courts Defer to Agency Interpretations of Statutes?" 1991 *Wisconsin Law Review* 1275, 1278–79. Thomas W. Merrill, "Judicial Deference to Executive Precedent," 101 *Yale Law Journal* 969, 972–73 (1992). Diver, 562.

73. 467 U.S. 837 (1984).

74. 467 U.S. 842–845.

75. 467 U.S. 865–866.

76. Byse, 259. Frank B. Cross, "Shattering the Fragile Case for Judicial Review of Rulemaking," 85 *Virginia Law Review* 1243, 1249–50 (1999). Peter L. Strauss, "One Hundred and Fifty Cases per Year: Some Implications of the Supreme Court's Limited Resources for Judicial Review of Agency Action," 87 *Columbia Law Review* 1093, 1122 (1987).

77. Kenneth W. Starr, "Judicial Review in the Post-Chevron Era," 3 *Yale Journal on Regulation* 83, 310–11 (1986).
78. Cass R. Sunstein, "Constitutionalism After the New Deal," 101 *Harvard Law Review* 421, 466–69, 488–99 (1987).
79. Farina, 478–88.
80. Stephen Breyer, 38 *Administrative Law Review* 363, (1986) 379.
81. *Arlington Texas v. FCC,* 133 S. Ct. 1863, 1876–77 (2013).
82. Kenneth W. Starr, Cass R. Sunstein, Richard K. Willard, Alan B. Morrison, "Judicial Review of Administrative Action in a Conservative Era," 39 *Administrative Law Review* 353, 367 (1987). Stephen Breyer, 38 *Administrative Law Review* 363 (1986), 373, 377, 379.
83. 467 U.S. 843 n.9.
84. *Chemical Manufacturers Assoc. v. NRDC,* 470 U.S. 116 n.15 (1985).
85. *INS v. Cardozo-Fonseca,* 480 U.S. 421, 446 (1987). Callahan, 1295–99.
86. 480 U.S. 452–56.
87. Bernard Schwartz, "Shooting the Piano Player? Justice Scalia and Administrative Law," 47 *Administrative Law Review* 1, 47–48 (1995).
88. Richard C. Pierce, "Two Problems in Administrative Law," 1988 *Duke Law Journa*l 300, 312–13 n.82. Strauss, 1118–19. Peter H. Schuck and E. Donald Elliot, "To the Chevron Station," 1990 *Duke Law Journal* 984. Patricia Wald, "The Contribution of the D.C. Circuit to Administrative Law," 40 *Administrative Law Review* 507, 530 (1988).
89. Jason J. Czarnezi, "An Empirical Investigation of Judicial Decisionmaking, Statutory Interpretations, and the Chevron Doctrine in Environmental Law," 79 *University of Colorado Law Review* 767, 782–83 (2008).
90. William H. Rodgers, *Environmental Law,* 2d ed. (West, 1994), 90–111.
91. *Greater Boston Television Corp. v. FCC*, 444 F.2d 841, 850–51 (D.C. Cir. 1970).
92. William H. Rodgers, "Judicial Review of Risk Assessments," 11 *Environmental Law* 301, 317 (1981). Cass R. Sunstein, "Deregulation and the Hard-Look Doctrine," 1983 *Supreme Court Review* 177, 181–84. William H. Rodgers, "A Hard-Look at Vermont Yankee: Environmental Law Under Close Scrutiny," 67 *Georgetown Law Journal* 699, 704–6 (1979).
93. Joseph L. Sax, "The (Unhappy) Truth About NEPA," 26 *Oklahoma Law Review* 239, 247–48 (1973). Antonin Scalia, "The Judicialization of Standardless Rulemaking: Two Wrongs Make a Right," *Regulation* (July–Aug. 1977), 38, 40. Martin Shapiro, "APA: Past, Present, Future," 72 *Virginia Law Review* 447, 478–79 (1986).
94. David M. O'Brien, "Marbury, the APA, and Science-Policy Disputes: The Alluring and Elusive Judicial/Administrative Partnership," 7 *Harvard Journal of Legislation and Public Policy* 443, 473 (1984). Peter L. Strauss, "Considering Political Alternatives to 'Hard Look' Review," 1989 *Duke Law Journal* 538, 548. Martin Shapiro, *Who Guards the Guardians? Judicial Control of Administration* (University of Georgia, 1988), 151–56.
95. William F. Pedersen Jr., "Formal Records and Informal Rulemaking," 85 *Yale Law Journa*l 38, 60 (1975).
96. Harold Leventhal, "Environmental Decisionmaking and the Role of the Courts," 122 *University of Pennsylvania Law Review* 509, 511–12 (1974).
97. Cass R. Sunstein, "Interest Groups in American Public Law," 38 *Stanford Law Review* 29 (1985).
98. *Motor Vehicle Manufacturers' Assoc. v. State Farm Mutual,* 463 U.S. 29 (1983). Alfred C. Aman and William T. Mayton, *Administrative Law* (West, 1992), 504–15.
99. *U.S. v. Carolene Products*, 304 U.S. 144, 152–53n.4 (1938).
100. Hans A. Linde, "Due Process of Lawmaking," 55 *Nebraska Law Review* 197, 222–24 (1976). Laurence H. Tribe, "Structural Due Process," 10 *Harvard Civil Rights–Civil Liberties Law Review* 269 (1975). Laurence Sagar, "Insular Minorities," 91 *Harvard Law Review* 1373, 1412 (1978). Dan T. Coenen, "The Rehnquist Court, Structural Due Process, and Semisubstantive Constitutional Review," 75 *Southern California Law Review* 1281 (2002).
101. Stephen Gardbaum, "Rethinking Constitutional Federalism," 74 *Texas Law Review* 795, 799–800, 825–26 (1996). William W. Buzbee and Robert A. Shapiro, "Legislative Record Review," 54 *Stanford Law Review* 87, 119–131 (2001). Vicki L. Jackson, "Federalism and the Uses and Limits of Law: Printz and Principle," 111 *Harvard Law Review* 2180, 2240 (1998).

Philip P. Frickey, "The Fool on the Hill: Congressional Findings, Constitutional Adjudication, and *United States v. Lopez*," 46 *Case Western Reserve Law Review* 695 (1996). Harold J. Krent, "Turning Congress Into an Agency: The Propriety of Requiring Legislative Findings," 46 *Case Western Reserve Law Review* 731, 743–46 (1966).

102. Dan T. Coenen, "A Constitution of Collaboration: Protecting Fundamental Values with Second-Look Rules of Interbranch Dialogue," 42 *William & Mary Law Review* 1575, 1835 n.1037, 1844–51 (2001). A. Christopher Bryant and Timothy J. Simeone, "Remanding to Congress: The Supreme Court's New 'on the Record' Constitutional Review of Federal Statutes," 86 *Cornell Law Review* 328, 370–89 (2001). Philip P. Frickey and Steven S. Smith, "Judicial Review, the Congressional Process, and Federalism Cases: An Interdisciplinary Critique," 111 *Yale Law Journal* 1707, 1723 (2002).

103. Stuart Sheingold, *The Politics of Rights: Lawyers, Public Policy and Political Change* (Yale University, 1974), 85.

104. Beth Henshen, "Statutory Interpretations of the Supreme Court: Congressional Response," 11 *American Political Quarterly* 441, 444, 447–53 (1983).

105. Note, "Congressional Reversals of Supreme Court Decisions: 1945–1957," 71 *Harvard Law Review* 1324, 1336–37 (1958). John Schmidhauser, Larry Berg, Albert Melone, "The Impact of Judicial Decisions: New Dimensions in Supreme Court–Congressional Relations," 1971 *Washington University Law Quarterly* 209. Richard A. Paschal, "Continuing Colloquy," 8 *Journal of Law and Politics* 143, 196–204 (1991). Harry P. Stumpf, "Congressional Response to Supreme Court Rulings," 14 *Journal of Public Law* 377, 394–95 (1965).

106. Thomas R. Marshall, "Policymaking and the Modern Court: When Do Supreme Court Rulings Prevail?," 42 *Western Political Quarterly* 493, 501 (1989). William N. Eskridge Jr., "Overriding Supreme Court Statutory Interpretation Decisions," 101 *Yale Law Journal* 331, 334–38 (1991).

107. Beth M. Henschen and Edward I. Sidlow, "The Supreme Court and the Congressional Agenda Setting Process," 5 *Journal of Law and Politics* 685 (1989).

108. James L. Walker and Michael E. Solomine, "The Next Word: Congressional Response to Supreme Court Statutory Decisions," 65 *Temple Law Review* 425, 453 (1992).

Chapter Two

The Extermination and Resurrection of the Wolf

The wolf was eliminated in the East by settlement and development and in the West through federal predator control, which was part of the change in public land management. In the early twentieth century, scientists began to criticize federal predator control and stressed that the wolf was necessary to maintain ecosystem balance. Changes in federal land management after World War II were promoted by the environmental movement. Federal statutes were enacted that protected wildlife and required executive agencies to consider environmental factors in their decision-making process. New access points were opened in Congress and the executive branch, which allowed environmental groups to participate in policymaking process. Environmental groups utilized public law litigation to challenge federal government decisions in federal courts. Continued criticism of federal predator control, coupled with concern for species extinction, led to the enactment of the Endangered Species Act (ESA), which provided the means for the wolf's return. This chapter examines the government policy that led to the wolf's eradication and resurrection.

EAST

Wolf Eradication

During the Middle Ages the wolf was called the "devil's dog" and vilified as a symbol of evil in Europe. Settlers brought their ancestor's enmity of the wolf to the New World. The wolf became the symbol of evil in the untamed forest and wilderness, which had to be conquered. Puritan ministers, such as

Cotton Mather, preached that wolves and wilderness were "an insult to the Lord."[1]

The wolf caused problems for settlers in colonial America. The wolf was a competitor for both land and game. It was also viewed as a threat to man, so it had to be eradicated. The prevailing philosophy was "that the only good varmint is a dead varmint."[2]

Settlers employed guns, drives, traps, pits, and dogs to kill wolves. Bounties were instituted. Massachusetts Bay Colony established the first wolf bounty in 1630, one penny per wolf. Virginia established the second wolf bounty in 1632. Different amounts were paid in different counties. Massachusetts and Virginia served as the models for other bounty laws, which were instituted in every colony.[3]

Bounties were notoriously inefficient and encouraged fraud. In some localities bounty hunters only had to state that a wolf was killed. There were many false statements. Hunters were often required to submit wolf body parts to collect the bounty. Proof of the kill was easily circumvented. Scalps and ears of dogs and coyotes were substituted for wolves. Body parts were shipped to the jurisdiction offering the highest bounty. Bounty hunters even bred wolves to maintain their livelihood. Female wolves were spared to ensure future breeding. The mass killing of wolves in an area did not ensure the destruction of individual predators, which learned to avoid men. Instead, it increased their fertility, providing them with a genetic advantage. Government expenditures increased, while predators survived.[4]

Other colonies, such as Pennsylvania and Rhode Island, employed professional hunters to kill wolves. Professional hunters were more successful than private bounty hunters. These colonies paid for the amount of predator control sought.[5]

After independence, the states controlled wildlife. States' rights were derived from English law. Title to land from the thirteenth through the fifteenth century was held by the King, who passed it to the nobility. Hunting was considered a royal prerogative, which passed to the states upon independence. The Supreme Court stated that when the states "took possession of the reins of government, and took into their own hands the powers of sovereignty, the prerogatives and regalities, which before belonged either to the crown or the parliament, became immediately and rightfully invested in the state."[6]

States and territories continued to utilize bounties. Poison joined the arsenal to eradicate the wolf in the East, beginning with the development of strychnine in 1847. Hunters put strychnine in tallow and spread it throughout the wolf's range. Poison killed wolves and other wildlife, but was also lethal for domestic animals. Poison was not the dominant mode of wolf eradication in the East. By the beginning of the twentieth century, settlement, development, habitat change, and the demise of its prey, rather than direct human efforts, eliminated the wolf in the East.

Rise of State Game Regulation

The demise of the wolf in the East corresponded with a changing attitude toward wildlife. Wildlife was considered to be an inexhaustible resource. This led to widespread extinction, despite early game laws. In the middle of the nineteenth century sport hunters organized and encouraged states to enact conservation laws, which included hunting seasons, bag limits, residency, and other limitations. This drove market hunters, who killed wildlife for profit, out of business.[7]

State game commissions were established to increase the supply of game and protect hunters' rights. The enforcement of game laws and stocking programs were expensive. State commissions were underfunded. States sold hunting and fishing licenses, which provided the game commissions with a steady source of income. State commissions promoted the interests of hunters, who demanded government action to eradicate the wolf, which preyed on game.[8]

There was little understanding of the importance of the wolf. Conservationists believed that wolves "certainly needed killing, fewer of these there are, the better for the useful and beautiful game." Teddy Roosevelt felt that wolves were "the archetype of raven, the beast of waste and desolation." William Hornaday, a noted naturalist, stated "of all the wild animals in North America, none are more despicable than wolves." There was no room for the wolf in the conservation ark.[9]

WEST

History Repeats Itself

Poison played a major role in the eradication of the wolf in the West. Western trappers initially sought beaver pelts. After the call for beaver pelts decreased, the demand for wolf pelts increased, particularly for Russian soldiers. The price of wolf pelts increased from one dollar in the 1840s to two dollars by the mid-1860s and again to two dollars and fifty cents a decade later.[10] This provided an economic incentive for wolf killing. Wolfers shot and skinned buffalo, filled the carcasses with strychnine, and left the carcasses to be eaten by scavengers. Wolves feasted and died. Wolfers returned, skinned the wolf carcasses, and moved on. Between 1870 and 1877, approximately 55,000 wolves were killed annually.[11]

But the livestock industry, not trappers, was the major cause of wolf eradication. After the Civil War, the livestock industry expanded in the West. Transcontinental railroads linked the country. Cattlemen shipped their livestock to eastern and western cities. Short-horned cattle replaced long-horned cattle to facilitate transportation, removing the cattle's major defense mechanism against predators. The sheep industry, whose ranchers were termed "woolgrowers," expanded in the West at this time.

Bison competed with livestock for grass, so they had to be removed. Hunters decimated the buffalo population. By 1884, the buffalo was gone from the plains east of the Northern Rocky Mountains (NRM). At the same time, market hunters severely reduced the native ungulate population. This permitted the expansion of the livestock industry and the removal of the Indians from western lands. The wholesale killing of buffalo provided nourishment, which allowed the wolf population to expand. The destruction of the buffalo and other large ungulates, however, forced the wolf to turn to livestock as a food source.[12]

Severe winters in the late 1880s caused the livestock industry to collapse. Previously, livestock grazed on the open range and were rounded up several times per year. After the Depression, there were smaller herds and fences. All livestock had to be accounted for, and any loss to predators was evident. Ranchers pushed for bounties, which were established at the state, county, and local levels. By the mid-1890s, nearly all the western states had bounties that were supplemented by stockmen's associations. The western states experienced the same inherent problems with bounties, but wolf numbers were gradually being diminished. In 1899, the National Stockmen's Association suggested that a uniform western wolf bounty be established. It was never realized because there was no agreement regarding its amount or funding mechanism. The Bureau of Biological Survey (BBS) in the Department of Agriculture became the central clearinghouse for state bounty laws. The BBS worked with state and local officials to strengthen bounty systems, which were present in thirty-nine of the forty states and territories.[13]

Federal Involvement

The livestock industry, farmers, hunters, and western states exerted pressure on the federal government to eradicate the wolf, which became intertwined with the change in public land policy. Throughout the nineteenth century acquisition and disposal dominated federal public land policy. In the early twentieth century the federal government, which held title over much of the western land, began to set aside and manage public lands. The Supreme Court accepted this exercise of sovereign power pursuant to the Property Clause in the Constitution and the implied public trust doctrine.[14] The first major set-aside was the national forests in 1897. This caused a schism in the nascent conservation movement. Conservationists, including President Roosevelt and Gifford Pinochet, believed in the efficient scientific management of national forest resources to produce the "greatest good of the greatest number for the longest time." Preservationists, who were led by John Muir, the founder of the Sierra Club, believed that undeveloped public lands should be preserved, not developed for resource exploitation.[15]

The newly created National Forest Service (NFS) in the Department of Agriculture (Agriculture) began to regulate and charge fees for grazing in the national forests. The NFS, seeking the support of the livestock industry, asked the BBS for help in "ridding the forest reserves and cattle range of gray wolves," which were ostensibly killing 20 percent of the livestock.[16] In 1906, the BBS conducted "a study to determine methods for the extermination of wild animals which prey upon livestock in the forest reservations."[17] The BBS declared that wolf extermination was "a paramount objective of the government," which could only be achieved by "a concerted interstate campaign."[18] In 1907, forest rangers reported a record kill of 1,723 wolves and 18,000 coyotes in thirty-nine western national forests, which was estimated to be one-tenth of the total area inhabited by wolves. This resulted in an estimated savings of two million dollars.[19] Western states were generally suspicious of federal intervention into traditional areas of state control such as wildlife management, but they supported aggressive federal predator control. The federal government eventually co-opted state and local predator control programs.[20]

Wolves and Soldiers

Wolf hysteria plagued the West in the early twentieth century. The livestock industry claimed annual losses of fifteen million dollars per year to predators. States were paying one million dollars per year in bounties for nonexistent wolves. The imminent entry of the United States into World War I signaled the beginning of the end for the wolf. Allies and American soldiers needed to be fed. Livestock depredation by wolves was characterized as taking food from soldiers. Wolves and coyotes were also blamed for the outbreak of a rabies epidemic in the West in 1915, which resulted in the death of livestock. The livestock industry put pressure on western congressmen for greater federal predator control.[21]

In 1914, Congress instructed the BBS to spend money for "experiments and demonstrations in destroying wolves, prairie dogs, and other animals injurious to agriculture and animal husbandry." In 1915, Congress allocated $125 to the BBS to conduct an all-out war against the wolf on public lands and national forests. The BBS was transformed from an advisory to a service agency. Eight districts were established, each with its own supervisor. Professional hunters and trappers were hired to kill predators.[22] Bounties were not offered. Instead, predator fur was sold at auction and the funds deposited into the Treasury. There was constant friction between private trappers and salaried government hunters.[23]

The demand for federal predator control exceeded the available funding, so the costs were shifted to the livestock industry. In 1918, the BBS began cooperative programs with states, counties, and livestock associations. The BBS investigated complaints and provided hunters and equipment, while its clientele funded the effort through a head tax on livestock in the affected areas. The BBS budget increased in 1918–1919.

Ranchers and woolgrowers gained more influence because they paid the bills. Regional stockmen's associations sprang up to deal with predator control. The associations elected managers, levied assessments, and paid the salaries of hunters, who coordinated their activities with the BBS. By 1922, there were forty associations advising the BBS's new Division of Predatory and Animal and Rodent Control (PARC). By the mid-1920s, the BBS received one quarter of its funding from its clients.[24] In 1928, the secretary of agriculture was called on to investigate and report on "the feasibility of a five-year cooperative program . . . for the purposes of eradication, suppression, or bringing under control of predatory animals within the U.S., and estimated costs thereof." The secretary reported that such an effort would be possible over the next ten years and would save ten dollars for every one dollar spent. Complete eradication was not possible, but the wolf could be brought under control. The cost of federal predator control over the previous thirteen years averaged $432,042 per year. The annual price tag for the new ten-year program was $1,378,700, or 243 percent more than apportioned for fiscal year 1929. From 1915 through 1928, federal and cooperative hunters killed 133 wolves in Idaho, 596 wolves in Montana, 707 wolves in Wyoming, 31 wolves in Oregon, 188 wolves in Utah, and 2 wolves in Washington.[25]

Scientific Backlash

Scientists voiced their criticism of federal predator control at the American Society of Mammology meeting in 1924. The BBS responded that large predators "no longer have a place in our advancing civilization." Predators caused significant economic losses to ranchers, who were unable to control them. The BBS was simply assuming this responsibility.

The Society appointed a scientific committee to study federal predators. In 1928, the committee reported that predators should be restricted to national parks and wilderness areas. Many scientists disagreed with the report's findings. Critics accused the BBS of colluding with the western livestock industry and state governments to conduct a politically motivated extermination campaign that was based on false data and bad science. Ranchers and state officials exaggerated their livestock losses. Predators did not pose a serious threat to livestock. Critics suggested that predator control should be replaced by a "system of intelligent controls" adapted to the specific needs of different western regions.[26]

The Kaibab disaster in the 1920s demonstrated the adverse ecological consequences of federal predator control. In 1906, President Roosevelt designated the Kaibab portion of Grand Canyon Forest Reserve as a national game preserve, which also supported twenty thousand sheep and cattle. Hunting was outlawed to increase the deer population. Government hunters proceeded to kill all the predators in the area. By 1924, over six thousand wolves, coyotes, and mountain lions had been killed. With the absence of predators, the deer population exploded from four thousand to over one hundred thousand, denuding the vegetation and causing an ecological disaster. The Secretary of Agriculture ordered the killing of the deer to stop the overgrazing. Colorado brought suit alleging a violation of state gaming law, but the Supreme Court upheld the federal government's authority "to protect its land and property."[27]

The Society protested the killing of wildlife, particularly predators. In response, Congress delayed the BBS's appropriation in 1930. The BBS pleaded with the Society to withdraw its opposition and promised to target its killing. The Society sent a letter to Congress limiting its opposition solely to federal predator control. Congress then released the BBS's appropriation. PARC returned to its indiscriminate killing of predators. Ironically, the Society's letter was used to justify aggressive predator control.[28]

The war against predators continued. In 1931, Congress enacted the Animal Damage Control Act (ADCA), which provided statutory authority and a budget line for PARC. The secretary of agriculture was authorized to investigate "the best methods of eradication, suppression, or bringing under control on national forests and other areas of the public domain, as well as on state, territorial, or private owned lands, mountain lions, wolves, . . . other animals injurious to agriculture, horticulture, forestry, animal husbandry, wild game, fur, birds . . . ; and to conduct campaigns for the destruction or control of such animals."[29] The ADCA authorized expenditures of one million dollars per year from 1932–1941, but funding was limited because of the Depression and preparations for World War II.[30]

The federal government took over control of the remaining federal grazing lands in the Taylor Grazing Act of 1934.[31] The Grazing Service, now Interior's Bureau of Land Management (BLM), was granted regulatory authority over federal grazing lands. PARC's role expanded with this major federal set-aside of public lands. Livestock owners were charged a fee to graze on public lands. Part of the fee was dedicated to predator control. Critics continued to accuse PARC of "organized slaughter" in its effort to make the West safe for livestock, causing the nation's wildlife "the most serious crisis in its history."[32]

Changes in Wildlife Management

Scientific management of wildlife emerged in the 1930s.[33] State wildlife management focused on the creation of a surplus of game animals that could be harvested by hunters, who paid license fees that funded state wildlife agencies. Aldo Leopold's 1933 seminal work, "Game Management," introduced the concepts of ecosystem management and carrying capacity as wildlife management tools. The Wildlife Society, which was established in 1937, promoted these goals.[34]

The federal government, building on its earlier efforts to manage wildlife (i.e., the Lacey Act, which outlawed the interstate transport of wildlife taken in violation of state law, and the Migratory Bird Treaty Act, which granted the federal government jurisdiction over migratory birds), enacted the Federal Aid in Wildlife Restoration Act, which provided funds to states for "wildlife restoration projects."[35] Statutory objectives were defined in terms of habitat. States had to meet federal standards and were only eligible for funding if hunting license fees were used exclusively to support state fish and game commissions. This freed wildlife agencies from state legislatures, lowered political influence, and increased the role of science.[36]

Criticism of federal predator control continued. Aldo Leopold declared that "no predatory species should be exterminated over a large area" and "rare predatory species . . . should not be subject to control." Paul Errington's study demonstrated that predation was only one of several factors that determined prey species' success or failure. Sigurd Olsen's study of wolves and coyotes in Superior National Forest demonstrated the necessity of predators in the wilderness to maintain ecological balance. Olsen stated that the wolf "is an integral part of the wilderness community, the destruction of which would destroy the fine balance between related forms." He pointed out that "the politics of wolf preservation and the science of studying wolves are more vicious and complicated than any wolf pack I've had the pleasure of studying."[37]

In the 1930s, the National Park Service (NPS), which had been established in 1916,[38] changed its policy regarding predator control. The NPS declared that "no native predator shall be destroyed on account of its normal utilization of any other park animal, excepting if that animal is in immediate danger of extermination, and then only if the predator is not itself a vanishing form."[39] Agriculture and Interior did not follow this policy, but continued predator control on remaining public lands.

In 1939, the BBS moved to Interior, where the livestock industry exerted even greater control over the program. The BBS was combined with the Bureau of Sport Hunting and Fisheries to form the U.S. Fish and Wildlife Service (FWS) in 1940. Predator control expanded. Congress doubled PARC's budget from 1940 through 1950. As federal efforts increased, state efforts decreased. Many states and counties repealed bounty laws and enacted appropriations for cooperation with the federal government, which were supplemented by private efforts. By 1937, only twelve states and territories specifically mentioned wolves in their bounty laws.[40]

The development of the pesticide industry in the 1940s intensified chemical warfare against predators. Two new toxicants, thallium sulfate and compound 1080, were introduced. The coyote getter, which consisted of an exploding cyanide capsule hidden in material attractive to animals, was developed. Aerial hunting also became a popular form of predator control.[41] Federal efforts regarding wolf eradication were so successful that in 1944 Stanley Young concluded that "the wolf has been definitely brought under control and presents a very minor problem except in limited areas in the U.S."[42]

POST WORLD WAR II

Changing Attitudes

Public attitudes toward public lands, wildlife, and the wolf changed after World War II. With growing economic prosperity, citizens took advantage of recreational opportunities. Public lands and wildlife were no longer viewed exclusively as a source of commodities, but their scientific, recreational, commercial, and ecological values were recognized. Aldo Leopold, the forefather of conservation biology, proposed the "land ethic" for public land management, which preserves biodiversity and ecosystems. According to Leopold, "a thing is right when it tends to preserve the integrity, stability, and beauty of the biotic community. It is wrong when it tends otherwise."[43]

The view of the wolf was also changing. Adolph Murie's study of wolves at Mt. McKinley in 1944 demonstrated the importance of wolves for conservation. A. M. Stebler warned about the extinction of wolves in Michigan in 1944. New TV shows, including *Walt Disney*, *Wild Kingdom*, and *National Geographic*, made people more aware of wildlife, particularly the wolf. Farley Mowat's "Never Cry Wolf" in 1963 showed the wolf was not the evil demon vilified by man.[44]

There was a change in public land management, which stressed greater protection for wildlife. There was a growing recognition that "interest group liberalism" had failed.[45] Congress delegated broad administrative authority to public land agencies, including the NFS and BLM, which became captured by the regulated commodity industries, particularly timber and livestock. Public land policy was being made through sub-governments or "iron triangles of government," consisting of interest groups, congressional committees, and executive agencies. Public land policy did not serve the public interest, but private interests.[46]

In the early 1960s, there was a political effort to move away from dominant-use toward multiple-use public land management. New statutes (i.e., the Multiple Use and Sustained Yield Act and Classified Multiple Use and Sustained Yield Act) were enacted that expanded federal agency mandates and provided for greater interest group participation in the administrative process.[47] Congress created an "interest representation scheme," which was based on the premise that increased pluralism in the administrative process would create a more balanced approach to realize the public interest.[48]

The multiple-use statutes did not remedy agency capture. There was little change in the direction of policy because the statutes did not establish priorities in public land management. Administrators, working under the same political constraints, were only required to consider enumerated factors, but had discretion regarding their importance. George Cameron Coggins stated that "the Multiple Use and Sustained Use statutes are not very good laws. They represent congressional buck-passing, and they allow bureaucratic lawmaking. They give managers latitude that would be deemed undue in other more visible areas of the law. It is easy to see why courts assiduously avoid interpreting them and why the agencies persist in emphasizing the single resources that they can measure in dollars."[49]

Conservation groups did achieve some success regarding the protection of species habitat. The Wilderness Act of 1964 "secure[d] for the American people of present and future generations the benefits of an enduring resource of wilderness."[50] The National Wildlife Refuge System Act of 1966 consolidated the management of wildlife refuges and set aside public lands for the benefit of wildlife.[51] The Wild and Scenic Rivers Act of 1968 preserved selected rivers and their immediate environs for future generations.[52]

The emergence of the environmental movement in the 1960s united the preservation and conservation factions. Stuart Udall, Secretary of Interior under Presidents Kennedy and Johnson, wrote that "the resources humankind needs for the long haul can only be husbanded if we nurture an ever-widening concept of land stewardship."[53] President Johnson in 1965 noted that "our conservation must be not just the classic conservation of protection and development, but a creation conservation of restoration and innovation. Its concern is not with nature alone, but with the total relation between man and the world around him. Its object is not just man's welfare but the dignity of man's spirit."[54]

The modern environmental movement arose with the baby boomer generation, which was raised during economically affluent times and manifested post-industrial values. Faith in science and technology and unfettered economic growth were questioned. Right's consciousness emerged. There was recognition of the collective nature of social problems and demand by affected groups and citizens for government relief. Events in the 1960s, such as the Santa Barbara oil spill and the Cuyahoga River fire, provided the impetus for environmental movement.[55]

There was an explosion of congressional and administrative activity in the 1960s and 1970s. The nation experienced a "republican moment" that entailed an "outburst of democratic participation and ideological policies," which overcame the political barriers precluding the enactment of environmental legislation.[56] New statutes were enacted with bipartisan support that established broad environmental mandates and provided planning processes and public participation, which applied to all federal agencies, (i.e., NEPA, ESA). New congressional committees and subcommittees were established with jurisdiction over environmental statutes, which provided interest groups more points of access into the political process. New executive agencies were formed to provide advice and implement environmental statutes (i.e., Environmental Protection Agency [EPA] and Council on Environmental Quality [CEQ]). New environmental groups emerged who, along with established groups, promoted non-consumptive values in Congress and executive agencies.[57] Environmental groups were able to participate in the "iron triangles" of government to influence policy.

Federal courts became the forum for resolving policy conflicts. Public interest law firms, which were funded by foundations and member contributions, emerged (i.e., Natural Resources Defense Council, Sierra Club Legal Defense Fund [now Earthjustice], and Defenders of Wildlife). Citizen suit provisions in the environmental statutes and Administrative Procedures Act (APA) allowed environmental groups to act as private attorney generals and enforce statutory mandates. Federal courts were sympathetic to environmental concerns and recognized that broad-based environmental injuries supported environmental-group standing. Environmental groups, which learned from earlier NAACP and ACLU litigation efforts, brought suits, challenging federal government action. Federal courts scrutinized agency decision making to ensure compliance with the myriad environmental statutes. Public law litigation emerged.[58]

Federal Predator Control and Endangered Species Act

Species destruction and preservation were among the major concerns of the emerging environmental movement. There had been some earlier concern with species extinction. Aldo Leopold in 1936 wrote "Threatened Species," which argued that the preservation of threatened species "was a primary duty of the conservation movement." The NPS and FWS in 1942 published "Fading Trails: The Story of Endangered American Wildlife," which argued for the preservation of wildlife species, including predators, "to help maintain the elusive 'balance' between all living things."[59]

Rachael Carson's *Silent Spring* in 1962 pointed out the environmental dangers of pesticides. Federal predator control was criticized for using poisons, which killed wildlife and upset the ecological balance and biodiversity. The seeds of doubt sown in the 1930s regarding poison blossomed in the 1960s. Nevertheless, PARC was still eradicating wildlife.[60] The coyote replaced the wolf as the principal culprit to justify the program.

Facing congressional pressure, Secretary Udall created the Leopold Commission to examine federal predator control. The Leopold Report in 1964 concluded that federal predator control was not a balanced component of animal husbandry. PARC was killing more predators than necessary. PARC had become a semi-autonomous agency, whose role had expanded beyond any need. PARC was servicing the livestock and agriculture industry, which paid its bills. A reassessment of PARC goals and implementation was necessary to reflect the public interest. PARC and the livestock industry disagreed with the findings, but the level of predator killing subsided.[61]

The Leopold Report led to the transformation of PARC into the Division of Wildlife Services (DWS) in Interior in 1965. The DWS was responsible for pesticide appraisal and monitoring, as well as wildlife enhancement. The DWS recognized that all wildlife was valuable, so "government policy should be one of husbandry of all forms of wildlife." Furthermore, predator control should be limited to "troublesome species, preferably troublesome individuals, and only to localities where substantial damage or danger exists." Nevertheless, most of DWS's attention continued to focus on control, which satisfied its principal constituent, the livestock industry. There were unsuccessful efforts in Congress to prevent the use of poisons and limit federal predator control. Secretary Udall, along with the livestock industry, vigorously opposed the bills because internal changes were under way, and efforts to protect endangered species had begun.[62]

Federal predator control became intertwined with species extinction. Interior in 1964 created the Committee on Rare and Endangered Wildlife Species. The Committee in 1966 published the Redbook, a preliminary list of rare and endangered species. The Redbook was not legally enforceable, but turned attention to species extinction. Scientists who worked on the Redbook became advocates for species preservation legislation.[63] Congress recognized that habitat destruction was a significant factor in species extinction. The Land and Water Conservation Act of 1964 provided federal funds for the acquisition of land "for the preservation of species of fish or wildlife that are threatened with extinction."[64] The need to protect habitat and preserve all species, not just game animals, was acknowledged.

The Endangered Species Preservation Act (ESPA) was enacted in 1966. The Secretary of Interior was directed to carry out a program to conserve and encourage the growth and replacement for selective species of native fish and wildlife threatened with extinction. The ESPA did not engender the same degree of hostility as the predator control bills, so it did not generate opposition. The timber wolf was listed as an endangered subspecies in 1967.[65]

The ESPA was strengthened by the enactment of the Endangered Species Conservation Act (ESCA) in 1969, which protected species and subspecies of wildlife threatened with worldwide extinction, including the wolf. The ESCA expanded earlier legislation in several ways. First, it authorized the establishment of a list of fish and wildlife threatened with extinction and prohibited the importation of such species. Second, the buying or selling of any animal taken in violation of state or foreign country law was proscribed. Third, the authorization for implementation funds was increased.[66]

The Public Land Law Review Commission Report in 1970 fueled further opposition to federal predator control. The report concluded that federal "predator control programs should be eliminated or reduced on Federal public lands." Federal predator control programs "have substantially reduced and in some cases virtually eliminated certain species that are natural predators." While these programs may have been of some benefit to livestock operators, "they have upset important natural mechanisms for the population control of other species." This caused an increase in the ungulate populations "in some localities to levels far above the capacity of the natural habitat to support them . . . resulting in habitat destruction and starvation."[67]

Books and articles continued to focus public attention on the chemical warfare against wildlife.[68] The federal poisoning of predators became a national issue. The CEQ and Interior sponsored a joint study of federal predator control in 1971. The Cain Commission, echoing the Leopold Report, recognized that the federal predator control program "contains a high degree of built-in resistance to change." The public-private funding scheme "maintains a continuity of purpose in promoting the private interest of livestock growers, especially in the western rangeland states." The livestock industry's financial contribution "serves as a gyroscope to keep the bureaucratic machinery pointed toward the familiar goal of general reduction of predator populations, with little attention to the effects of this on the native wildlife fauna."

The Cain Commission found that predator control had little impact on predator populations. Livestock loss to predators was not constant and difficult to measure. Although the overall losses were slight, some ranchers suffered an inordinate burden. Heavy livestock losses were isolated and attributed to individual predators, which acquired a taste for livestock. Furthermore, the resulting ecological disruptions raised questions regarding the costs and benefits of federal predator control. The Commission called for an end to nonselective control methods and a focus on individual depredating animals.[69]

The Cain Commission prompted President Nixon in 1972 to issue Executive Order 11,643, which restricted the use of toxins for predator control on federal lands.[70] President Nixon stated, "Americans today set high value on the preservation of wildlife. The old notion that 'the only good predator is a dead one' is no longer acceptable." Predator control was not an end in itself, but must be more selective and ecologically friendly. The EPA halted interstate shipment of all pesticides registered for use against predators and suspended and canceled the registration for nineteen products containing thallium sulfate, sodium cyanide, strychnine, and compound 1080.[71]

President Nixon proposed a new Animal Damage Control Act, which would end federal predator control. Supporters of the bill argued that predators fill an important niche in the ecosystem and play an important role to keep prey in check. Prey populations that exceed their habitat's carrying capacity overgraze. Predators serve as natural regulators of prey populations in the ecosystem. Predators provide important aesthetic value for people and enhance the tourist industry. Predators are intimately linked to the idea of the West and wilderness. Hunters value predators as trophy game. Man has an ethical and moral obligation not to destroy species, but to share the land with species.[72]

The livestock and agriculture industries vigorously opposed the bill. They demanded more predator control and the transfer of the DWC back to the Department of Agriculture. The bill passed the House, but was defeated in the Senate. Other bills, which prohibited the poisoning of predators, provided for a study of predator control methods, established a national policy on predators, and prohibited the killing of endangered species, were also defeated.[73]

The Secretary of Interior's narrow interpretation of the ESCA precluded its proper implementation.[74] President Nixon in 1972 acknowledged that "even the most recent act to protect endangered species . . . simply does not provide the kind of management tools needed to act early enough to save a vanishing species."[75] Several events facilitated the enactment of ESA. The Golden Eagle Protection Act of 1972 expanded the scope of federal protection under the Bald Eagle Protection Act of 1940.[76] The Wild Free-Ranging Horses and Burros Act protected wild horses and burros on public lands.[77] The Marine Mammal Protection Act extended federal authority over marine mammals.[78] The United States signed and ratified the Convention on International Trade in Endangered Species (CITES), which required implementing legislation.[79] A wolf specialist group of the International Union for the Conservation of Nature provided a blueprint for global wolf conservation, which declared that wolves, like other wildlife, "have a right to exist in a wild state," one that "derives from the right of all living creatures to co-exist with man as part of natural ecosystems."[80]

The livestock industry fought hard to oppose President Nixon's Animal Damage Control Act, so had little political will to fight expanded species protection. The ESA was enacted in 1973, which protected endangered and threatened species and required federal government to restore endangered species. President Nixon's signing statement declared that "nothing is more priceless and more worthy of preservation than the rich array of animal life with which our country has been blessed. It is a many-faceted treasure, of value to scholars, scientists, and nature lovers alike, and it forms a vital part of the heritage we all share as Americans."[81]

The ESA prevents federal, state, and private action that poses a danger to endangered species. Citizens are granted standing to enforce the ESA. The Supreme Court declared the ESA was "the most comprehensive legislation for the preservation of endangered species ever enacted by any nation." Congress intended "to halt and reverse the trend towards species extinction, whatever the cost." The legislative history indicated that federal agencies must "afford first priority to the declared national policy of saving endangered species," which has "priority over [their] primary missions." Courts must "afford endangered species the highest priorities," and act with "institutionalized caution" when reviewing ESA cases.[82] The ESA established the means to restore and protect the wolf.

The ESA provides for the listing and delisting of endangered and threatened species based on the following five factors: "A) the present or threatened destruction, modification, or curtailment of its habitat or range; B) overutilization for commercial, recreational, scientific, or educational purposes; C) disease or predation; D) the inadequacy of existing regulatory mechanisms; or E) other natural or manmade factors affecting its continued existence."[83] Interior's FWS is granted regulatory authority over land-based animals. The National Marine Fisheries Service has regulatory authority over aquatic species. The NRM wolf was listed as an endangered subspecies in 1973.[84] The gray wolf population in the United States was listed as endangered in 1978, except in Minnesota where it was downlisted to a threatened species.[85]

The field of conservation biology pioneered by Aldo Leopold was also emerging at this time. Conservation biology supports rewilding, the restoration and protection of big wilderness and wide-ranging carnivores to maintain ecosystems. Rewilding is based on three Cs: carnivores, core, and corridors. Large carnivores, like the wolf, institute beneficial top-down trophic cascades. Large core areas must be protected to sustain the large carnivores. Corridors connecting the core areas are required because core areas will not be sufficient.[86] Conservation biology provides the scientific underpinning for wolf reintroduction and recovery.

CONCLUSION

The wolf was driven from the East because it posed a threat to man and livestock and was a competitor for big game. States, counties, localities, and professional associations employed bounties, professional hunters, and poison to eradicate the wolf, but the principal reason for the wolf's demise in the East was settlement, development, and loss of habitat and prey. The wolf was gone from the East by the beginning of the twentieth century.

The war against the wolf in the West began during the nineteenth century. The wolf was eliminated because it posed a threat to livestock industry, which expanded after the Civil War. The demise of the wolf in the West was linked to federal public land policy. At the beginning of the twentieth century the federal government began to set aside and manage federal public lands. Ranchers were charged a fee to graze on public land. Ranchers, in turn, demanded protection from wolf depredation. The BBS became the agent of the wolf's demise, which was accomplished by the early 1930s. There was, however, a great deal of criticism of federal predator control by scientists engaged in the emerging field of wildlife management.

After World War II the management of public lands and attitudes regarding wildlife in general and the wolf in particular began to change. Public land policy moved from dominant-use to multiple-use management. New federal statutes allowed federal agencies to consider wildlife protection in management of public lands, but federal land policy was still dominated by commodity interests. The rise of the environmental movement in the 1960s led to the enactment of new statutes that required federal agencies to consider environmental factors in their decision-making process. These statutes diminished the hold of commodity interests on public land policy and created an implied public trust responsibility on the federal government. These statutes were accompanied by the emergence of public law litigation, which provided judicial oversight of federal agency decisions. This ensured that the legislative goals did not get lost in the labyrinth of the administrative process. Federal predator control continued to be criticized. Unsuccessful efforts to curtail federal predator control, along with the growing concern for species extinction, led to the enactment of the ESA. The emergence of the field of conservation biology stressed that the wolf was important for the maintenance of ecosystem health and biodiversity. The change in public land policy was not welcomed by resource and development interests. This gave rise to the Sagebrush Rebellion in which western states representing commodity interests challenged federal ownership of public lands.

NOTES

1. Christopher J. Kirwan, "Wolves and Recovery Plans," 60 *University of Missouri Kansas City Law Review* 517, 519 n. 24.

2. Senate Appropriation Committee, *Dept. of Labor, and Health and Education and Welfare and Related Appropriations FY 1972* (June 3, 1971), Statement Russell Train, chair CEQ, 115.

3. Stanley P. Young and Edward A. Goldman, *Wolves of North America* (Dover, 1944), 340. Bruce Hampton, *The Great American Wolf* (H. Holt & Co., 1997), 72–76.

4. Young and Goldman, 367.

5. George Cameron Coggins and Evans, "Predators Rights and American Wildlife Law," 24 *Arizona Law Review* 821, 827–29 (1982).

6. *Martin v. Waddell*, 41 U.S. (16 Pet.) 367, 410 (1842).

7. Coggins and Evans, 829–31. Jenks Cameron, *The Bureau of Biological Survey: Its History, Activities and Organization* (John Hopkins University, 1929), 1–11.

8. David Todd, "Wolves—Predator Control and Endangered Species Protection," 33 *South Texas Law Review* 459, 469–70 (1992).

9. Coggins and Evans, 830–31. Hampton, 127–30.

10. Hampton, 107. Young and Goldman, 165–71.

11. Timothy Strauch, "Wolf Conservation," 27 *Land and Water Law Review* 33, 38–39 (1992).

12. Young and Goldman, 377–78. Hampton, 114.

13. Young and Goldman, 358–66.

14. Charles F. Wilkerson, "The Public Trust Doctrine in Public Land Law," 14 *University of California Davis Law Review* 269, 280–84 (1980).

15. Christopher McGrory Klyza, *Who Controls Public Lands?* (MIT, 1996), 15–26.

16. Hampton, 131. David E. Brown, *The Wolf in the Southwest* (University of Arizona, 1984), 48.

17. Michael J. Robinson, *Predatory Bureaucracy: The Extermination of Wolves and the Transformation of the West* (University of Colorado, 2005), 62.

18. Elizabeth Cowan Brown, "The 'Wholly Separate' Truth: Did Yellowstone Wolf Reintroduction Violate Section 10(J) of the ESA?" 27 *Boston College Environmental Affairs Law Review* 425, 426–27 (2000).

19. Hampton, 132. Young and Goldman, 383. Cameron, 46–47.

20. Coggins and Evans, 834–35.

21. Hampton, 133–35. James B. Trefethen, *An American Crusade for Wildlife* (Wincesters, 1975), 284.

22. Cameron, 5–14, 46–47. Young and Goldman, 383–84. Robinson, 78.

23. Robert K. Mortensen, *In the Cause of Progress: History of New Mexico Cattlegrowers Assoc.* (New Mexico Cattlegrowers Association, 1983), 71. Daniel Miles Gish, *A Historical Look at the Mexican Gray Wolf in Early Arizona Territory and Since Statehood* (U.S. FWS, 1978), 65 (nd).

24. Thomas R. Dunlap, "Values for Varmints: Predator Control and Environmental Ideas, 1920–1939," 53 *Pacific Historical Review* 141, 147–158 (1983). Coggins and Evans, 835–837. Thomas R. Dunlap, *Saving America's Wildlife* (Princeton University, 1988), 39.

25. Mortensen, 72–73. Cameron, 54, 315.

26. Dunlap, "Varmints," 147–53.

27. *Hunt v. U.S.*, 278 U.S. 96 (1928). Coggins and Evans, 837.

28. Dunlap, "Varmints," 154–55. Faith McNulty, *Must They Die?* (Doubleday, 1971), 14–16. Wick Corwin, "Predator Control and the Federal Government," 51 *North Dakota Law Review* 787, 802 (175).

29. 7 U.S.C. 426. Coggins and Evans, 835–37. June C. Edvenson, "Predator Control and Regulated Killing: A Biodiversity Analysis," 13 *Journal of Environmental Law* 31, 45 (1995).

30. Mortensen, 73. Hampton, 147.

31. 43 U.S.C. 315–315r.

32. Hampton, 148.

33. Dale D. Goble, "Evolution of At Risk Species Protection," in Frank W. Davis, J. Michael Scott, and Dale D. Goble (eds.), *The Endangered Species Act at Thirty* (Island Press, 2005), 12–13.

34. Dunlap, *Saving*, 65–83. Coggins and Evans, 838–39. George C. Coggins, "Federal Wildlife Management," 60 *Oregon Law Review* 59, 64–75 (1981).

35. 16 U.S.C 661–667e.

36. Goble, 13.

37. Adrian Weydeven and Timothy R. Van Deelen, *Recovery of the Gray Wolf in the Great Lakes Region of the U.S.: An Endangered Species Success Story* (University of Wisconsin, 2009), 4–7. Rick McIntyre, *War Against the Wolf* (Voyager Press, 1995), 318.
38. 16 U.S.C. 1–18f.
39. Paul Schullery (ed.), *The Yellowstone Wolf: A Guide and Source Book* (High Plains, 1996), 236. Durwood L. Allen, *Our Wildlife Legacy* (Funk and Wagnalls, 1962), 237.
40. Corwin, 802–3.Young and Goldman, 366.
41. Coggins and Evans , 839–40.
42. Young and Goldman, 385.
43. Aldo Leopold, *A Sand County Almanac* (New Press, 1968), 225.
44. Weydeven and Van Deelen, 9
45. T. Lowi, *The End of Liberalism*, 2d ed, (Norton, 1979).
46. Todd, 485. James P. Lester, and Joseph Stewart, *Public Policy: An Evolutionary Approach* (Wadsworth, 1996), 69–70. Martin Nie, *Beyond Wolves* (University of Minnesota Press, 2003), 48.
47. 16 U.S.C. 528–31.
48. Richard Stewart, "The Reformation of American Administrative Law," 88 *Harvard Law Review* 1667 (1975).
49. George Cameron Coggins, "Of Succotash Syndromes and Vacuous Platitudes: The Meaning of Multiple Use and Sustained Yield for Public Land Management," 53 *University of Colorado Law Review* 229, 279–80 (1982).
50. 16 U.S.C. 1131 et. seq.
51. 16 U.S.C. 668dd–668ee. Coggins and Evans, 843–44.
52. 16 U.S.C. 1271 et. seq.
53. Stewart L. Udall, *The Quiet Crisis and the Next Generation* (Gibbs-Smith, 1988), 270.
54. Goble, 15.
55. Stuart Sheingold, *The Politics of Rights: Lawyers, Public Policy and Political Change* (Yale University, 1974). James S. Bowman, "The Environmental Movement: An Assessment of Ecology Politics," 5 *Environmental Affairs* 649, (1976). Andrew S. McFarland, *Public Interest Lobbies: Decision Making on Energy* (AEI, 1976), 1–5.
56. Daniel Farber, "Politics and Procedure in Environmental Law," 8 *Journal Law Economics & Organization* 59, 66 (1992).
57. McFarland, 8–24.
58. Burton Weisbrod, Joel Handler, and Neil Komesar, *Public Interest Law* (University of California, 1978). Robert L. Rabin, "Lawyers for Social Change: Perspectives on Public Interest Law," 28 *Stanford Law Review* 207 (1976). Sandra Davis, "Fighting Over Public Lands: Interest Groups, States, and the Federal Government," in Charles Davis (ed.), *Western Public Lands and Environmental Politics*, 2d ed. (Westview, 2001), 14–30.
59. Goble, 5–6.
60. Todd, 484–87. J.J. McCoy, *Wild Enemies* 157-75 (Hawthorne Books 1974).
61. Leopold et al., "Predator and Rodent Control in the U.S." (1964), reprinted in House Committee on Merchant Marine and Fisheries, *Predatory Mammals and Endangered Species: Hearings on H.R. 689 and Related Bills* (1972), 495–506. Edvenson, 42–43. McCoy, 168–69.
62. McNulty, 34–40. Corwin, 804–6. Coggins and Evans, 845–50.
63. Goble, 6. Daniel J. Rohlf, *ESA: A Guide to Its Protections and Implementation* (Stanford Environmental Law Society, 1989), 20.
64. 16 U.S.C. 4601-9(a)(1).
65. 32 *Federal Register* 4001 (1967).
66. Robinson, 306–15.
67. Public Land Law Review Commission, *One Third of the Nation's Land* (1970), 168.
68. Ronald Rood, "Animals Nobody Loves," and Jack Olson, "Poisoning of the West," cited in McCoy, 168–71. Dunlap, *Saving*, 131–41.
69. Cain et al., *Predator Control—1971, Report to the CEQ and the Department of Interior* (1972), 2–14. Coggins and Evans, 851–52. Corwin, 804–6
70. 37 *Federal Register* 2875 (1972).
71. 37 *Federal Register* 5718–20 (1972). Coggins and Evans, 852–56.

72. Train, 274–75.
73. Nancy E. Marion, *Making Environmental Law: The Politics of Protecting the Earth*, (Praeger, 2011), 233.
74. Steven Yaffee, *Prohibitive Policy: Implementing the Federal ESA* (MIT, 1982), 49.
75. President Richard Nixon, *Special Message to Congress Outlining the 1972 Environmental Program* (February 8, 1972).
76. 16 U.S.C. 668–668(d)
77. 16 U.S.C. 1331–40.
78. 16 U.S.C. 1361–1421h.
79. Goble, 17. Rohlf, 22–23.
80. Hampton, 176.
81. "President Nixon Signing Statement," 374 Public Papers 1027, 1027–28 (Dec. 23, 1978), cited in *Alliance for the Wild Rockies v. Salazar*, 800 F. Supp. 2d 1123, 1126 (2011).
82. *TVA v. Hill*, 437 U.S. 151, 180–86, 195 (1973).
83. 16 U.S.C. 1533.
84. 38 *Federal Register* 14678 (1973).
85. 43 *Federal Register*. 9612 (1978).
86. Michael E. Soule and Reed F. Ross, "Rewilding and Biodiversity as Complementary Tools for Continental Conservation," 8 *Wild Earth* 18 (1998). Michael E. Soule and John Terborgh, "The Policy and Science of Regional Conservation," in Michael E. Soule and John Terborgh (eds.), *Continental Conservation, Scientific Foundations of Regional Reserve Networks* (Island Press, 1999), 1–18.

Chapter Three

The Return

Wyoming Farm Bureau Federation v. Babbitt

The wolf was eradicated from the Northern Rocky Mountains (NRM) as the result of federal predator control. Wolf reintroduction began in the Carter administration and was completed in the Clinton administration. Industry groups, utilizing public law litigation, brought suit, challenging the federal action. The Tenth Circuit in *Wyoming Farm Bureau Federation v. Babbitt*[1] upheld Interior's decision. The court found that Interior's decision was consistent with the text, intent, and purposes of the Endangered Species Act (ESA). Interior's consideration of environmental impacts did not violate the National Environmental Policy Act (NEPA). Wolf reintroduction into the NRM was allowed to proceed. Wolf recovery was so successful that Secretary of Interior Bruce Babbitt proposed downlisting the wolves across much of the United States. This chapter traces the history of wolf reintroduction into the NRM, analyzes the resulting litigation, and reviews subsequent developments in the Clinton administration.

WOLF REINTRODUCTION

Wolves were once abundant throughout the Rocky Mountains. After the Civil War the livestock industry expanded in the West. The buffalo was exterminated. The native game population was reduced by market hunters. By 1885, there were over two million head of cattle in Wyoming and six hundred thousand head of cattle in Montana. Experiencing the loss of their primary food source, wolves turned to livestock.[2]

The livestock industry and hunters lobbied for the establishment of state, county, and local bounties. The industry argued that livestock was a source of tax revenue that was lost through wolf predation. Hunters, who significantly contributed to the state economies through license fees, asserted that bounties increased the flow of revenue into public coffers and maintained an abundant supply of big game. Public bounties were supplemented by private funds provided by local stockmen.[3]

Wyoming established the first wolf bounty of fifty cents per wolf in 1873. The bounty was increased in 1893 to eight dollars per wolf, which was paid from general county funds. This was replaced by a three-dollar-per-wolf bounty in 1895, which was paid from the state treasury. From 1897 to 1907, Wyoming paid over sixty-five thousand dollars in wolf bounties. Wyoming in 1913 imposed a three-hundred-dollar fine for releasing a wolf from a trap. From 1895 to 1917, thirty thousand wolves were killed for the bounty in Wyoming. The wolf bounty was increased to fifteen dollars per wolf in 1917.[4]

Montana established a state bounty of one dollar per wolf in 1883, which was supplemented by county bounties. In the first year, 5,450 wolf hides were presented for payment. In 1905, Montana instructed veterinarians to infect captured wolves with mange and release them to infect other wolves. This program lasted for eleven years, but was suspended because of the fear that mange would be spread to livestock. From 1883 to 1918, 80,730 wolves were killed for the bounty in Montana. By the late 1920s, wolves were gone from Montana. Idaho established a predator control program in the early 1900s. From 1919 to 1928, 258 wolves were terminated under this program.[5]

Bounties were unsuccessful, so the livestock industry, hunters, and western states turned to the federal government. The Bureau of Biological Survey (BBS) began a concerted effort to eradicate the wolf in 1915. From 1915 to 1928, the BBS killed 174 wolves in Idaho, 596 wolves in Montana, and 707 wolves in Wyoming. Cooperative money spent on predator control through 1928 was \$116,356 in Idaho, \$228,602 in Montana, and \$215,271 in Wyoming.[6]

The federal and state eradication campaign was successful. The wolf was eliminated from the Great Plains by 1926. The BBS in 1927 reported that "large gray or lobo wolves have been almost cleared from livestock ranges . . . only a few scattered individuals remain." By 1942, government hunters had killed 24,132 wolves in the region. The last wolves in Washington were killed in 1940 and in Colorado and Wyoming in 1943.[7] The gray wolf was reduced to less than 1 percent of its original population and eliminated from 96 percent of its original habitat in the lower forty-eight states.

Yellowstone National Park

The federal government set aside 2.2 million acres in 1872 and created Yellowstone National Park "for the benefit and enjoyment of the people." The Secretary of Interior (Secretary) was authorized to stop "the wanton destruction of the fish and game found within the park."[8] President Grover Cleveland in 1886 assigned U.S. Army personnel to "guard Yellowstone and protect its features and wildlife." Congress limited hunting in the park in 1894. The U.S. Cavalry protected wolves in the park until Congress authorized predator control on public lands in 1915. Only fourteen wolves were killed in the Cavalry's thirty-two years of park management.[9]

The National Park Service (NPS) was authorized to conserve the scenery, natural and historic objects, and wildlife for the enjoyment of future generations. The Secretary of Interior was allowed to "provide in his discretion for the destruction of such animals . . . as may be detrimental to the use of said parks."[10] The NPS utilized the BBS predator control program to protect animals that people wanted to see; expand its budget; bolster support with game associations, which viewed the parks as game reserves; and build broad-based support with the livestock and agriculture industries. From 1914 to 1926, the BBS killed 136 Yellowstone wolves, including 80 pups. The wolf was virtually eliminated from Yellowstone by 1926.[11]

NPS policy toward the wolf began to change in 1931. The NPS announced that all animals "should be kept inviolate within the parks." There no longer would be "widespread campaigns of destruction" particularly against "disappearing species" that might be making their "last stand." The NPS in 1933 declared that "no native predator shall be destroyed on account of its normal utilization of any other park animal . . . [and] no management measure or other interference with biotic relationships shall be undertaken prior to a properly conducted investigation." Each park species was "a priceless creation." Large predators like the wolf and coyote were particularly important for the parks where they "find their only sure haven" and "are given opportunity to forget that man is the implacable enemy of their kind."[12] The change in policy was too late for the wolf, and the systematic extermination of predators continued on the park borders.

Wildlife management in national parks changed in the 1960s. Aldo Leopold in 1963 recommended that natural ecosystem management be implemented. The artificial feeding of wildlife and reductions in herd populations should stop. Nature should regulate activities in the parks. This became the official NPS policy in 1967. The 1973 Master Plan for Yellowstone promised to perpetuate the park's ecosystem by restoring the natural species exterminated by man. Between 1967 and 1986, the bison population in Yellowstone grew from between 400 and 600 to 2,100 head. The northern elk herd swelled from 5,000 to 18,000. Natural resources in the park were being depleted. Wolves were suggested as the answer, but ranchers said no.

Carter Administration

James E. Carter lost all of the western states except Texas in his 1976 presidential victory. Former Idaho governor, Cecil Andrus, became Secretary of Interior in the Carter administration. President Carter became embroiled in numerous public land conflicts with the western states, including the cancellation of dams, the development of coal shale, and the location of the MX missile system. Colorado governor Richard Lamm proclaimed that the federal government had declared war on the West.[13]

The new policy of environmental protection angered resource interests, which historically dominated western public land management. Traditional benefactors saw their access to western lands and water being threatened by a new set of policy actors with different agendas. The enactment of the Federal Land Policy and Management Act (FLPMA) in 1976, which ended the disposition of most public lands and established permanent federal retention, was the final straw.[14] Resource industries joined with disaffected western state governments to demand the federal government surrender control over public lands. This federal-state struggle became known as the Sagebrush Rebellion or "the Great Terrain Robbery."[15]

When western states were admitted into the Union, the federal government retained title to public lands. When the federal government set aside public lands for specific purposes, western states complained this violated state sovereignty. As long as public lands were being managed for resource development and offsetting federal compensation was provided, western state objections were only rhetorical.

The Sagebrush Rebellion began in 1978 when the Western Council of State Governments and Western Region of National Association of Counties decided to challenge federal ownership of public lands. Different strategies were pursued. Bills were introduced in Congress, which transferred federal lands to state governments, but none made it out of committee.[16] In 1979, Nevada passed a statute asserting state ownership of public lands controlled by the Bureau of Land Management (BLM). State legislatures in Arizona, New Mexico, Colorado, Hawaii, Idaho, Utah, Washington, and Wyoming did the same. Nevada brought suit challenging the FLPMA. The U.S. District Court for the District of Nevada rejected the claim and held that "the Property Clause in Article IV grants the federal government unlimited authority over public lands. Congress, not the courts, determines how the public trust is administered. The federal government can sell or retain ownership of public lands without state consent."[17]

The Sagebrush Rebellion failed because political, social, and economic changes were under way in the West. Proponents were poorly organized. There was a split between western ranchers, who wanted state ownership, and economic libertarians, who supported private ownership. All of the western states did not seek ownership of federal lands. Some realized that the benefits of federal ownership, including cheap grazing fees, reclamation projects, federal roads, and subsidized timber sales, far outweighed the costs of administering public lands.[18]

Despite the loss, strident opposition to federal environmental regulation on western lands had just begun. Business objected to the costs of federal regulation. Conservatives created their own foundations (i.e., the Heritage Foundation) and public interest law firms (i.e., the Mountain States Legal Foundation) to advance industry interests and oppose environmental initiatives. Appeals to federalism and harm to traditional economic interests become the central themes in the opposition to wolf reintroduction.

President Carter supported wolf reintroduction. In his 1977 environmental message to Congress, President Carter stated:

> The public's interest in wildlife specifically includes predators, which have in the past sometimes been regarded as competitors for livestock or game leading to their destruction. . . . Because we now realize the importance of the role that predators play in the various ecosystems, our goals should be not to destroy them but to reduce the occasion for their conflict with livestock . . . . If control is necessary, it should focus on the individual predators causing the problem—not the species as a whole.[19]

The ESA required the FWS to bring the wolf "back from the brink so that [it] may be removed from the protected class." The first step was to "develop and implement" a recovery plan, which contains site management actions; objective and measurable criteria to remove species from the list; and an estimate of the time required and costs to carry out the plan's goals. The plan is "a basic road map to recovery, i.e. the process that stops or reverses the decline of a species and neutralizes threats to its existence. It is supposed to provide a means for achieving the species' long-term survival in nature."[20]

The Carter administration in 1980 developed the first NRM wolf recovery plan, which proposed natural recovery in Montana and reintroduction into Yellowstone and central Idaho. The plan reclassified the wolf from an endangered to threatened species and established two populations within its historic range, which included all of Idaho and Oregon, most of Montana, the northern two-thirds of Wyoming, and the Black Hills of South Dakota. The plan was vague and only provided a list of prerequisites for reintroduction.

The plan was not implemented because amendments to ESA in 1978 required recovery plans to provide "a framework for actions directed at conserving or, at least insuring the survival" of listed species. New planning guidelines had to be established. The FWS promulgated a revised *Recovery Planning Guidelines Manual* in 1981 that imposed a standard system to improve efficiency in tracking recovery tasks and increase the utilization of recovery plans in the budget review process. The 1980 recovery plan had to be revised to meet the new format.[21]

Reagan Administration

Ronald W. Reagan won all the western states in the 1980 and 1984 presidential elections. Ronald Reagan, an avowed Sagebrush rebel, did not support the transfer of public lands to the states, but eased the pain of defeat by appointing leaders of the Sagebrush Rebellion to important positions. James Watt, the former head of the conservative Mountain States Legal Foundation, became the first Secretary of Interior in the Reagan administration. The executive bureaucracy was staffed by westerners sympathetic to the goals of the Rebellion, who managed federal lands as a good neighbor. This quelled western anger and decreased the influence of environmental groups over public land policy.[22]

President Reagan criticized environment laws and opposed government regulation, which represented federal intrusion into state authority and impeded economic growth. The Reagan administration followed the dictates of the ESA, but did not support wolf reintroduction. The Assistant Secretary of Interior in 1983 testified that "there was going to be no introduction of the wolf into Yellowstone at this time."[23] The wolf was not waiting for political action, but returned to the NRM on its own with full ESA protection. Canadian wolves migrated into Glacier National Park (GNP) and sired pups in 1982. Another pack established territory in GNP in 1984. The wolves split into various packs and produced pups. One of the packs on the Blackfeet Indian Reservation was destroyed for livestock depredation.[24] This prompted the Defenders of Wildlife (DOW) in 1987 to establish a fund that compensated livestock owners, who suffered losses due to wolf depredation.

The FWS submitted a revised recovery plan in 1987, which called for the reintroduction of ten breeding pairs for three consecutive years in three recovery areas that were chosen for their wilderness characteristics and remoteness from human activity. The Montana recovery area included GNP, Bob Marshall, Great Bear, and Lincoln-Scapegoat wilderness areas. The Idaho recovery area consisted of Selway-Bitterroot, Gospel Hump, Frank Church River of No Return, and Sawtooth wilderness areas. The Greater Yellowstone recovery area comprised Yellowstone National Park, Absaroka-Beartooth, North Absaroka, Washakie, and Teton wilderness areas. The objective of the plan was to establish three distinct populations in three areas, which would ensure that two would survive a catastrophic event.

Each recovery area was divided into three zones, with wolves receiving diminished protection outside the central zone. Zone One, the primary recovery area, contained the key habitat components necessary for wolf recovery, which was prioritized. Zone Two, the buffer area, contained some components of wolf habitat, but was not sufficient to support a viable population. Wolf recovery was important, but not paramount. Zone Three was unsuitable for wolves because of human activity and development. Wolf recovery was not encouraged, and depredation could be addressed by lethal control. The plan forecast natural recovery in Montana and Idaho from wolves migrating from Canada. If natural recovery did not occur in central Idaho, an experimental population would be introduced. A nonessential experimental population, which had less ESA protection, would be introduced into Yellowstone to decrease local opposition. Dispersal corridors would facilitate the wolf's southern migration and connect the three recovery areas and GNP with Canada.[25]

The 1987 plan was driven primarily by economic factors and was designed to placate the livestock industry. The criteria for the three recovery areas included 1) a large ungulate population, 2) three thousand square miles of wilderness, 3) a maximum of 10 percent privately owned land, 4) livestock grazing on less than 20 percent of the land, and 5) isolation from humans. No critical habitat was designated. There was no protection for the ecosystems on which the wolf depended. Livestock grazing was prioritized. Wolves moving outside Zone One could be killed to protect livestock. The plan subsidized the livestock industry by providing predator-free zones and shifting the cost of production to the public.[26]

The recovery plan faced local opposition. Prior to issuance of the plan, the NPS and NFS developed a vision document calling for joint management of the Greater Yellowstone Ecosystem (GYE), which contains private and public lands that are subject to twenty-eight different federal, state, and local jurisdictions. The federal government owns 58 percent of the land in GYE. Approximately 107 million acres of private ranchland are dependent to some extent on the 254 million acres of BLM and NFS lands in the GYE.[27] The vision document was vigorously opposed by economic interests, which viewed the plan as an effort to undermine local autonomy, increase federal authority, and promote environmental protection at the expense of the traditional western way of life. The wolf recovery plan was seen as a subtle effort to resurrect the vision document.[28]

Idaho, Montana, and Wyoming officials joined with the livestock industry, hunters, outfitters, and land developers to oppose the recovery plan. Opponents raised several arguments. The gray wolf was not an endangered or threatened species because there were numerous wolves in Canada and Alaska. The Canadian wolves proposed for reintroduction were not native to the NRM region. Wolves were hybrids that could not be considered endangered species. Wolves posed a threat to other endangered and threatened species in the region. The reintroduction of the wolves would take private property and livestock, and no compensation would be forthcoming. Wolves carried diseases that would adversely impact livestock. Wolves would harm wildlife, particularly elk, deer, and moose. This would have an adverse impact on hunting and recreational activities resulting in the loss of state revenues. Wolf reintroduction would intrude on traditional state authority over wildlife and impose costs on the states. Wolves were an endangered species, which would be difficult to manage and hamper predator control. Natural ecosystem management in Yellowstone was a failure. The overpopulation of elk and bison was due to poor management, not the absence of the wolf. Finally, wolf reintroduction was a land-use control that was designed to limit development and access to public lands.[29]

Wolf reintroduction generated interagency conflict. William Mott, the Director of the National Park Service (NPS), supported reintroduction, stating, "we do not have the right to eliminate these animals from the web of life. Future generations have a right to go to Yellowstone and hear those magnificent animals howl." Frank Dunkle, the Director of the FWS, opposed reintroduction, arguing that it was a misguided attempt to "undo the disastrous conditions" the NPS had created in the park by years of mismanagement of elk and bison herds.[30]

After the recovery plan was announced, Dunkle put the program on hold. At a Wyoming woolgrowers' meeting, Dunkle declared "that he would not allow the FWS to fund any wolf recovery work. The wolf stops at my desk." Dunkle stated that "the only wolves I will bring to Wyoming or that I will sponsor in Wyoming . . . are on this tie." He warned that any attempt to reintroduce the wolves would encounter "the full range of bureaucratic roadblocks. . . . If you've seen bureaucracy in action, you know the Glacier wolves are likely to reach Yellowstone before the paperwork is done." A reporter noted that "if Dunkle was a wolf, he would have licked the woolgrower's nose, rolled over on his back and peed on himself. Any wolf would recognize that as submissive behavior."[31]

The reintroduction plan faced regional opposition. Senator Alan Simpson (R. Wyo.) pointed out that wolf reintroduction posed "a very serious threat to the livestock industry." Representative Richard Cheney (R. Wyo.) stated, "I am strongly opposed to [wolf recovery]." Representative Ronald Marlenee (R. Mt.) declared, "Montana needs wolves like we need another drought." There was also an unsuccessful effort to delist the gray wolf. Facing congressional pressure, Director Mott retreated, and the Reagan administration backed off wolf reintroduction. Interior decided to delay implementation of the recovery plan until additional studies were completed.[32]

Wolf supporters pursued congressional action. Representative Wayne Owens (D. Ut.) introduced a bill that required Interior to conduct an Environmental Impact Statement (EIS) and reintroduce wolves to Yellowstone by 1991. He noted that, "Yellowstone Park has an almost perfectly operating ecosystem, lacking only one element. The predator, the wolf, is needed." He observed that "there is a theory among Wyoming and Montana congressional delegations that they own Yellowstone." Wolf reintroduction has been "completely side tracked by political interference" that is motivated by "hatred of wolves."[33]

Congress responded through the appropriations process. The House Appropriations Committee in 1988 approved funds for an EIS, but the funds were deleted in conference. Instead, two hundred thousand dollars was granted for studies on the wolf's impact on wildlife. The conference committee noted that "the return of the wolf to Yellowstone is desirable."[34]

The Wise-Use movement arose from the ashes of the Sagebrush Rebellion at the end of the Reagan administration. The Wise-Use movement advocates the termination of environmental controls on development, the exclusive use of federal lands by extractive industries, the protection and subsidization of commodity interests on public lands, and support for motorized recreation. The movement claims to be a grassroots campaign, but is subsidized and supported by major resource and commodity industries. The movement, which promotes the myth that resource development is the dominant interest of the West, supports property rights and county supremacy.[35] The movement opposed the reintroduction of the wolf, which was essentially "a conflict . . . over the management of public lands."[36]

Bush Administration

George H.W. Bush in his 1988 presidential victory won most of the western states, except Washington and Oregon. President Bush promised to be the environmental president. Manuel Lujan became Secretary of Interior in the Bush administration. The appointment was criticized by environmental groups, who questioned Representative Lujan's poor environmental record in Congress. The Bush administration acknowledged the importance of wolf reintroduction, but decided to wait for the report authorized in the 1988 appropriation bill.[37]

Action began in Congress. Representative Owens reintroduced legislation that compelled the Secretary to conduct an EIS on the 1987 plan by December 31, 1991, and implement its recommendations. Senator Simpson characterized the bill as "a misguided and zealous effort to accelerate wolf reintroduction without considering in any way how wolves will affect other animals in Yellowstone and the very real human beings that also live in Wyoming." Representative Marlenee called the bill "blatantly anti-sportsmen." Senator Larry Craig (R. Id.) asserted, "we do not need this legislation."[38]

The Bush administration did not support the bill. FWS director John Turner stated that the bill was "premature at this time." The NPS opposed the bill stating that "any legislative effort to short circuit our scientific investigations . . . is a very bad policy precedent." Environmental groups also opposed the legislation because it did not comply with the ESA requirements. Hearings were held, but the bill did not move forward.[39]

Senator James McClure (R. Id.) proposed a compromise in 1989, which called for the introduction of three mating pairs into the Yellowstone and central Idaho reintroduction areas. Wolves leaving the reintroduction areas would be subject to state control. The bill failed. Despite these efforts, no EIS for wolf reintroduction was authorized in 1989. Congress did, however, appropriate $175,000 to continue reintroduction studies in 1990.[40]

The FWS issued a report in 1990, *Wolves for Yellowstone*, which was based on the studies authorized in 1988.[41] The FWS decided to proceed with wolf reintroduction as proposed in the 1987 recovery plan. Environmental groups were pleased. The Defenders of Wildlife (DOW) declared that "politics has dictated the outcome of the Yellowstone wolf debate for far too long. Now it is time to listen to the facts. The government studies show we can meet the needs of ranchers and outfitters while meeting the desire of millions of Americans to see wolves restored to our best known national park."[42] After the report was released, Senator McClure reintroduced his earlier bill, but opposition from the FWS, NPS, and environmental groups proved fatal.[43]

Wolf recovery continued to be dealt with in the appropriation process. The House Appropriation Committee earmarked funds for an EIS regarding reintroduction. The conference committee deleted the provision, but directed the Secretary to appoint a ten-member Wolf Management Committee to develop gray wolf reintroduction and management plans for Yellowstone and central Idaho and issue its report by May 15, 1991. The conference committee authorized $375,000 for the study.[44]

The Wolf Management Committee report in 1991 recommended that Idaho, Montana, and Wyoming be designated as nonessential experimental area for the purposes of wolf recovery. Nonessential experimental populations receive less protection under the ESA. The FWS should manage wolves in the experimental population area according to the plan until the EIS, rulemaking, and state management plans are completed. The states should assume primary management authority for wolves outside national parks and national wildlife refuges and adopt wolf management plans agreed to by the Secretaries of Interior and Agriculture and their governors prior to any release in Yellowstone.[45]

The Wolf Management Committee report was "dead on arrival in Congress." Wolf advocates opposed the plan because the designated experimental area, the Greater Yellowstone Ecosystem, included the naturally repopulating wolves in northwestern Montana, which were protected as endangered species. Wolf advocates were also wary of state management.[46] The DOW stated the plan is "more of an extermination policy than a restoration plan." The National Audubon Society declared that the committee "capitulated to livestock industry and delivered a plan that flies in the face of ESA."[47]

Wolf opponents were divided. Representative Marlenee stated that "wolves are worse than cockroaches. There is no method of control we can establish that will ensure that the wolf will not devastate other wildlife populations and whole segments of industry in Montana, Wyoming, and Idaho." Wyoming governor Mike Sullivan supported the return of wolves to Yellowstone, but only if wolves outside the park were managed by the state; no additional land use restrictions were imposed outside the park; an efficient compensation program for depredation was created; sport hunting was not curtailed; and the wolf was delisted as soon as possible.[48]

The DOW filed suit in August 1991 to force the Secretary to implement the 1987 recovery plan. Congress then enacted a rider to the 1992 Appropriation Act, which prohibited the expenditure of funds for wolf reintroduction into Yellowstone National Park and central Idaho.[49] The D.C. federal district court ultimately rejected the DOW suit, declaring that "the Recovery plan itself has never been an action document." The court noted that it could not order the Secretary to perform a task, which Congress has specifically prohibited.[50] Nevertheless, Congress directed the FWS to prepare an EIS regarding wolf reintroduction into Yellowstone and central Idaho by January 1994.[51]

Clinton Administration

William J. Clinton carried some western states in the 1992 presidential election, including Montana, Colorado, Washington, and Oregon, but lost Montana and Colorado in the 1996 presidential election. Former Arizona governor, Bruce Babbitt, became Secretary of Interior in the Clinton administration. Secretary Babbitt was a strong supporter of wolf reintroduction. He stated that "the [Yellowstone] Park needs the wolf. . . . There are an awful lot of ungulents in that Park, some 30,000 elk, 4,000 bison, and one reason that these animals are moving up the population curve is precisely the absence of this predator."[52]

The Final EIS (FEIS), which was released in May 1994, supported wolf reintroduction.[53] The FWS planned to obtain forty-five to seventy-five wolves from southwest Canada and transfer them to Yellowstone and central Idaho. Fifteen wolves fitted with collars would be reintroduced into Yellowstone and central Idaho annually for three to five years and monitored. The goal was to establish a population of three hundred wolves, which would allow the species to be delisted by 2002. The reintroduced wolves would be classified as nonessential experimental populations to reduce local concerns about the regulation of private lands, livestock depredation, big-game predation, and the lack of state involvement.[54]

Environmental groups were pleased. The DOW declared that "historians will mark the restoration of wolves to our first national park and the rest of the Yellowstone ecosystem as a turning point in the annals of wildlife conservation. It will mark the beginning of a new era of predator protection and the end of an era of predator exploitation." Predator Friendly Wool pointed out that "this all has to do with basic changes taking place in the west. Bringing back the wolf is a turning point for this region. . . . Things are changing, and the wolf has become the most dramatic symbol of this struggle."[55]

Western congressmen were angry. Senator Craig Thomas (R. Wy.) declared, "Yellowstone Park has real priorities . . . like road repairs, adequate staffing levels and building upkeep . . . this proposal takes money away from those areas that really need it." Senator Simpson (R. Wy.) acknowledged that "[I]t could have been worse. At least an experimental population means we have the flexibility to control it." Five western senators, Conrad Burns (R. Mt.), Alan Simpson (R. Wy.), Craig Thomas (R. Wy.), Larry Craig (R. Id.), and Dirk Kempthorne (R. Id.) asked Secretary Babbitt to delay reintroduction.[56]

In November 1994, the Wyoming Farm Bureau Federation (WYFB) filed suit to enjoin the FWS from releasing the wolves, alleging NEPA, ESA, and Administrative Procedures Act (APA) violations. Industry groups had learned the lessons from environmental groups and were willing to use public law litigation to further their political goals.[57] The National Wildlife Federation and DOW intervened on behalf of the FWS.

In January 1995, the federal district court denied the injunction, but issued a temporary stay preventing the release of wolves pending appeal. The Tenth Circuit lifted the stay, which allowed reintroduction to proceed. FWS director Mollie Beattie stated, "Now we don't have to say to our kids that we used to have something called the wolf, and there used to be something called the Yellowstone ecosystem."[58]

The first four wolves were brought in from Canada and released into the Frank Church River of No Return Wilderness in central Idaho in January 1995. One week later eleven more wolves were released in Idaho. Beginning in March 1995, eighteen wolves were released into Yellowstone. Following the initial release, Secretary Babbitt testified that "our aim is to speed the recolonization of wolves so that they can be removed from the endangered species list and federal protection by the year 2002."[59]

Western congresspersons continued to criticize reintroduction, which had cost $6 million and was projected to cost another $6.8 million by 2002. Senator Craig stated that "this amounts to $65,000 for each wolf." Representative Helen Chenoweth (R. Id.) declared that the program "violates state rights, abuses the Constitution, drains millions of dollars" from more deserving programs and "was just jammed down the throats of Westerners." Representative Barbara Cubin (R. Wy.) noted that the "blatant disregard shown by the Interior Department toward the people of Wyoming is symptomatic of an uncaring bureaucracy." After the Republican takeover of Congress in 1995, the budget for wolf reintroduction was slashed by $200,000. This represented a sizeable cut in the $527,000 wolf budget for the next fiscal year.[60]

Western governors criticized federal wolf reintroduction. Montana governor Marc Racaciot complained that "Montana is caught in the awkward situation . . . no matter how many hundreds of wolves inhabit Montana, unless recovery goals are met in Wyoming and Idaho, we cannot delist wolves here." Wyoming governor that Jim Geringer declared federal reintroduction "has been by unilateral actions and blatant disregard" for its partnership with the state. Western state legislatures also responded. The Wyoming legislature enacted a one-thousand-dollar bounty on wolves that strayed out of Yellowstone Park, but Governor Geringer vetoed the bill. Idaho enacted a law that prevented state officials from cooperating with wolf reintroduction.[61]

Groups on both sides recognized the underlying problem with wolf reintroduction. The WYFB noted that "in reality, this thing is not so much about wolves." Rather it is about "limits on the land, the defining feature of the West." The Wolf Fund declared that "wolves aren't the cause of the changes occurring in the West . . . but they have become the means by which ranchers can voice their concern about what's happening around them."[62]

Wyoming Farm Bureau Federation (WYFB) v. Babbitt

The WYFB suit continued. Several environmental groups also filed suit opposing wolf reintroduction, but for totally different reasons. The National Audubon Society filed a second complaint, alleging that the demotion of the naturally occurring wolves in the experimental population area from an endangered to a threatened species violated the ESA. The Urbigkits, a couple who studied the Yellowstone wolves, filed a third complaint, asserting that the EIS failed to discuss the impacts of reintroduction on the naturally occurring subspecies of wolves in Yellowstone, *Canis lupus irremotus*.

In December 1997, the U.S. District Court for the District of Wyoming held the reintroduction of wolves into Yellowstone and central Idaho violated section 10(j) of the ESA, which grants the Secretary flexibility to establish and decrease the legal protection afforded to any reintroduced species. Section 10(j)(1) identifies an experimental population as "any population (including any offspring arising solely thereof) authorized by the Secretary for release under paragraph (2), but only when, and at such times as, the population is wholly separate geographically from non-experimental populations of the same species." Section 10(j)(2) authorizes the Secretary to release "any population (including eggs, propagules, or individuals) of an endangered species or threatened species outside of the current range of such species if the Secretary determines that such release will further the conservation of such species." Before authorizing such a release, "the Secretary shall by regulation identify the population and determine, on the basis of the best available information, whether or not such population is essential to the continued existence of an endangered species or a threatened species." All members of the experimental population "shall be treated as a threatened species." A nonessential population is only managed as a threatened species "within the National Wildlife Refuge System or the National Park System." Otherwise it is treated "as a species proposed to be listed." No critical habitat is designated for any nonessential population.[63]

The federal district court determined that individual dispersing wolves could enter the experimental population area. The potential overlap of the natural and experimental populations violated section 10(j) because the experimental population was not "wholly separate geographically" and had not been released outside "the current range" of the natural population. Furthermore, the reduction in the status of individual dispersers from endangered to threatened in the experimental population area violated the ESA. The district court found no violation of the NEPA.[64]

Wolf opponents were happy with the court's decision. The Mountain States Legal Foundation, which represented WYFB, declared that the "program was illegal from day one, and Babbitt knew it . . . but his obsequious obsession to do the bidding of environmental groups and his narcissistic need for a photo opportunity in the snows of Yellowstone made him think he could get away with it." Wolf supporters were disappointed. The DOW announced that "it is a real tragedy even to discuss dismantling the greatest wild restoration effort in our nation's history. The idea of removing wolves defies common sense." Secretary Babbitt vowed that "no wolves will be removed from Yellowstone on my watch."[65]

The Tenth Circuit reversed the district court on each of the three ESA issues. First, the Tenth Circuit accepted the FWS's definition of population and determined that individual dispersing wolves did not constitute a population. Second, the FWS's determination that the experimental population was "wholly separate geographically" from the natural population and released outside "the current range" of the natural population was upheld. Third, the Secretary could treat all wolves in the experimental population area as part of the experimental population. This would help to achieve the recovery goals and avoid enforcement problems. The Tenth Circuit concurred with the district court's determination that the EIS complied with the NEPA.[66]

Wolf supporters were happy. Secretary Babbitt stated the court's decision is "a ringing endorsement of our wolf reintroduction program in Yellowstone

National Park and central Idaho and . . . welcome vindication of our efforts to preserve this magnificent species." The DOW declared that "the Yellowstone wolves have been given a new lease on life and so has the principle that science—not politics—should guide wildlife restoration efforts in America."[67]

ANALYSIS

The Tenth Circuit adopted a weak version of Chevron, employing the traditional tools of statutory interpretation to evaluate the FWS decision. The Tenth Circuit correctly determined that the FWS decision was consistent with the text, intent, and purposes of section 10(j). Congressional inaction regarding the FWS's interpretation and implementation of section 10(j), the enactment of appropriations for the program, and the rejection of proposals jeopardizing wolf reintroduction indicated that the FWS's decision was consistent with the "presumed intent" of Congress. Furthermore, both federal courts properly determined that the EIS did not violate the NEPA.

Wholly Separate Geographically

Section 10(j)(1) requires the experimental population to be "wholly separate geographically from non-experimental populations of the same species." The FWS defined a wolf population to be "at least two breeding pairs of wild wolves successfully raising at least two young each (until December 31 of the year of their birth), for two consecutive years in an experimental area." The FWS drew the boundaries for all known wolf packs in the NRM. The FWS focused on breeding pairs within a defined territory, rather than individual dispersers, which move great distances. The boundary of the experimental population was based on distribution of the wolf population in Montana. After studying the experimental population area for two years, the FWS found that no portion of the area was used by the breeding wolves in Montana. The FWS also determined that any wolf population inside experimental boundaries would be the result of reintroduction or the natural dispersal of wolves from Montana or Canada.[68]

The Tenth Circuit upheld the FWS definition of population. The Tenth Circuit determined that "lone dispersers do not constitute a population or even part of a population, since they are not in 'common spatial arrangement' sufficient to interbreed with other members of a population." Moreover, it was highly unlikely that lone dispersers would meet another solitary wolf, breed, and produce two pups yearly for two consecutive years. The population left behind was unlikely to expand because the lone wolf would move on.[69]

The Tenth Circuit's decision, which upheld the FWS reliance on breeding pairs, was consistent with text of section 10(j), which refers exclusively to populations. Population is not defined in the text, but is used synonymously with species. The ESA defines a species as a "distinct population segment which interbreeds when mature."[70] The FWS generally defines population as "a group of fish or wildlife . . . in common spatial arrangement that interbreed when mature."[71] The FWS definition was also harmonious with the plain meaning rule, which dictates "where the language of an enactment is clear and construction according to its terms does not lead to absurd or impracticable consequences, the words employed are to be taken as the final expression of the meaning intended."[72] Population refers to a group, not to an individual.

The FWS definition of a population to be breeding pairs, which was based on reproduction and sustainability, was consistent with wolf biology. The gray wolf is a social animal that "lives in packs of related individuals that range in size from 2 to 25." The wolf pack, not individuals, is the crucial social unit. The wolf pack is central for breeding, hunting, feeding, teaching, rest, and play. The pack establishes and defends its territory, which can "range from 125 km to over 2,541 km; ranges of unmated individuals are larger and are not defended." Gray wolves maintain their territories through howling and scent markings. Lone wolves, who are unmated, scent mark infrequently, "whereas newly formed pairs scent-mark frequently until they become established." Most importantly, "because of the large distances that dispersing individuals may move and the abundance of potential dispersers, individual gray wolves occur outside the species range in the lower 48 states."[73]

The Tenth Circuit decision was consistent with legislative intent. The legislative history demonstrates congressional concern with populations, not individuals. The House Merchant Marine and Fisheries Committee referred to "population" or "populations" sixteen times, "individuals" one time, and "specimens" two times.[74] Two noted experts, Michael J. Bean and Melanie J. Rowland, declared that "the legislative history is clear that it is the population itself, and not its individual members, that is to be treated as threatened."[75]

This issue was addressed by the Ninth Circuit in *United States v. McKittrick.*[76] McKittrick was convicted of killing a wolf that was part of an experimental population. McKittrick claimed that the experimental population designation was invalid because the wolves were not "wholly separate geographically" from the naturally occurring wolves present in Yellowstone. The Ninth Circuit specifically rejected the district court's reasoning in the Wyoming Farm Bureau Federation case and upheld the FWS findings that the experimental population of gray wolves was wholly geographically separate and no natural populations were in the area. The Ninth Circuit concluded that "sporadic sightings of isolated indigenous wolves in the release area, lone wolves, or 'dispersers,' do not constitute a population."[77]

Judicial skeptics point out that public law litigation poses the danger of policy fragmentation and balkanization of the law. Different federal courts can make different decisions regarding the same legal issue. This causes confusion and paralysis on the part of the agency and makes it difficult to implement a coordinated national policy.[78] There was no policy fragmentation because both the Ninth and Tenth Circuits adopted the same interpretation of section 10(j).

Current Range

Section 10(j)(2)(a) states that the Secretary "may authorize the release . . . of any population . . . of any endangered species or a threatened species outside the current range of such species if the Secretary determines that such release will further the conservation of such species." The FWS utilized the sum total of pack territory to establish the current range of the species. Wolves had been sighted in Montana, Idaho, and Wyoming since the 1970s, but there was no documentation of any breeding pairs within the experimental population area. There was no geographical overlap between any Montana wolf population's home range and the experimental area. The northern boundary of the Idaho experimental area was moved further south when active breeding pairs from Montana located below the experimental boundary recommended in the proposed rule. If any natural wolf population was discovered in the experimental population area within ninety days, the experimental population would be removed.[79]

The Tenth Circuit determined that the territory occupied by a single wolf did not constitute the current range of the species. The definition of species must be consistent with conservation and recovery. The FWS properly focused on distinct, interbreeding population segments or subspecies, not individual animals. The Tenth Circuit declared that "an individual animal does not a species, population or population segment make."[80]

The Tenth Circuit's decision was consistent with the text of the statute. Range is not defined in statute. Webster's dictionary defines range as "the region to which a plant or animal is native."[81] Native assumes a regular ongoing presence that depends on the existence of a breeding pair. Prominent wolf experts recognize that "because of the large distance that dispersing individuals may move and the abundance of potential dispersers . . . individual gray wolves occur outside the species range in the lower 48 states."[82]

The text refers to "the current range of such species." Species is defined as a "distinct population segment, which interbreeds when mature."[83] This assumes a breeding pair. The current range of the species refers to areas where the populations, which are individuals belonging to packs, reside.

Furthermore, species have specific ranges, which depend on their biological characteristics. Ranges can vary depending on natural and man-made events. If the trade winds blow a single bird across the ocean or an animal becomes a stowaway on a far-ranging vessel, this individual does not expand the species' current range.[84]

The Status of Dispersers

The status of natural individual wolves that migrate into the experimental population area was a crucial issue in the litigation. The FWS acknowledged that wolves can migrate over five hundred miles, but there was no evidence of wolves in central Idaho or Yellowstone for the past ten years. The FWS admitted that from a management standpoint it would be difficult to determine if a wolf was a member of the experimental population or a natural disperser. The initial experimental population would be collared and differentiated. Once they reproduced, it would be hard to distinguish members of the experimental population from natural dispersers. This distinction could not be dealt with by regulation. Furthermore, an individual disperser might arrive in the experimental population area, stay, and mate. This would increase the population, but would not have a major impact because the majority of the breeding wolves would still be reintroduced animals. The FWS avoided any conflict by treating all wolves in the experimental population area as a threatened species.[85]

The Tenth Circuit held that the ESA granted broad discretion to the Secretary regarding experimental populations. The FWS determined that no wolf populations were present in the experimental population area. Wolves migrate, so the intermingling of the natural and experimental populations might occur. The best management strategy was to treat all wolves in the experimental population area as part of the experimental population.[86]

The Tenth Circuit's decision was consist with the text, intent, and purposes of section 10(j), which grants the Secretary broad discretionary authority regarding the experimental population. Section 10(j)(2) allows the Secretary to release the experimental population and determine if it is essential or nonessential. Section 10(j)(3) permits the Secretary to re-designate a population as experimental, which had previously been released.

The legislative history supports the delegation of broad authority to the Secretary regarding section 10(j). The conference committee stated that "the purpose of requiring the Secretary to proceed by regulation . . . is to provide a vehicle for the development of special regulations for each experimental population that will address the particular needs of the population." The experimental population is treated as a threatened species. The conference committee noted that "this provision obliges the Secretary to issue such regulations as he deems necessary and advisable to provide for the conservation of the experimental population." The Secretary is granted "broad flexibility in promulgating regulations to protect such species" and "to avoid potentially complicated problems of law enforcement."

Section 10(j) allows the Secretary to establish an experimental population according to its location, not its origin. The conference committee stated that the Secretary can identify the experimental population "on the basis of location, migration pattern, or any other criteria that would provide notice as to which populations of endangered or threatened species are experimental."[87]

Congress was well aware that the status of individual dispersers depends on their location. When a species is listed, the Secretary establishes its status as endangered or threatened depending on its location. The Secretary can treat different populations of the same species differently. The legislative history shows that a population can be a distinct portion of a species or subspecies. The House Merchant Marine and Fisheries Committee stated that "species" is defined "broadly enough to include any subspecies of fish or wildlife or plants, or any population of such species."[88]

The Secretary utilized this discretionary authority to extend different levels of protection to different populations of the same species depending on their location. For example, grizzly bears south of the Canadian border were listed as threatened, while those north of the border were unlisted.[89] Alligators were once listed as endangered everywhere, except in three Louisiana parishes.[90] Until 1978, bald eagles were listed as endangered south of forty degrees north latitude, while those to the north were unlisted.[91] In 1978, wolves were listed as an endangered species in the lower forty-eight states, except Minnesota where they were only a threatened species.[92]

The General Accounting Office (GAO) was critical of Interior's ability to attribute a different status to different populations of the same species. This allowed the FWS to list squirrels in one park as endangered, while the same species of squirrels was abundant in other parks in the same city. The GAO recommended an amendment that would prevent the FWS from listing geographically limited populations of vertebrates as threatened or endangered. The FWS and National Marine Fisheries Service (NMFS) opposed any change, which "would severely limit their ability to require the appropriate level of protection for a species based on its actual biological status." The agencies noted that one of the improvements in the 1973 ESA was the ability of the "FWS to adopt different management practices for healthy, threatened or endangered populations." Congress rejected the GAO suggestion. The Senate Interior Committee declared that "there may be instances in which the FWS should provide for different levels of protection for populations of the same species."[93]

Section 10(j) was enacted to increase the chances of successful recovery of endangered species. The Secretary was granted discretion to overcome local opposition and achieve cooperation regarding controversial reintroductions, like the wolf. Congress assumed that some individuals would lose their protection. The experimental population is usually taken from the native endangered species population in the wild or in captivity. The protection granted to the individual decreases when it becomes part of the experimental population. The Secretary is granted broad authority to retroactively designate any previously introduced population to be an experimental population, changing its status from endangered to threatened.

Treating the individual dispersers as part of the experimental population furthers the primary purpose of the ESA to conserve wildlife. Conservation is defined as "use of all methods and procedures which are necessary to bring any endangered species or threatened species to the point at which the measures provided . . . are no longer necessary."[94] The Ninth Circuit in McKittrick declared that "the statute's essential purpose . . . is the conservation of species."[95] The Supreme Court in *TVA v. Hill* announced that "the plain intent of Congress in enacting this statute was to halt and reverse the trend towards species extinction whatever the cost."[96] A narrow interpretation of section 10(j) would frustrate the Secretary's ability to carry out its purposes. The survival of the species is greater than the protection of any individual. The species cannot be sacrificed to protect an individual.

Legislative Inaction

Congress was well aware of the NRM wolf reintroduction, including the definitions of population and current range, the intermingling of individual dispersers with the experimental population, and the possible status change of the wolves. The failure of Congress to act, its continual support through appropriations, and its rejection of proposals that threatened wolf reintroduction demonstrated congressional acquiescence to the FWS statutory interpretation.[97] The Supreme Court held that congressional failure to disapprove an executive regulation, while "not dispositive, . . . strongly implies that the regulations accurately reflect congressional intent." Deference is appropriate when "an agency interpretation involves issues of considerable public controversy, and Congress has not acted to correct any misperception of its statutory objectives."[98]

The 1987 wolf recovery plan sought to achieve recovery in three areas: northwest Montana, central Idaho, and Yellowstone. The plan noted that if the wolves in any area increased sufficiently, they would be reclassified as threatened, while others would remain endangered. Barriers between populations were not contemplated. Instead, the plan sought to bring about such movement by maintaining suitable travel corridors among populations. As individual wolves moved, so did their status.[99]

The FWS's quarterly reports to Congress before the Final EIS (FEIS) indicated the possible intermingling of individual dispersers with members of the experimental population. The FEIS addressed the possible intermingling of the natural and experimental populations. The Final Regulation specifically addressed the intermingling of dispersers with the experimental population.[100]

Congress not only acquiesced, but also supported the FWS decisions by continually appropriating funds for the reintroduction. The appropriations process is one of the principal ways to enact and influence policy.[101] Efforts to curtain funding for wolf reintroduction were rejected. In 1995, Senator Burns (R. Mt.), a wolf opponent, attempted to add language to the Interior appropriation bill that would bar bringing any additional wolves into Yellowstone. This effort failed, but the FWS's annual six-hundred-thousand-dollar budget for wolf reintroduction was reduced by one third.[102] In 1998, Representative Chenowith (R. Id.) sponsored an amendment to the National Fish and Wildlife Foundation reauthorization bill, which prohibited the use the funds "for any activity related to the introduction of wolves or grizzly bears in Idaho, Montana, Utah, or Wyoming." The amendment was not enacted.[103] Congress continued to appropriate funds for the monitoring of wolves in Yellowstone and central Idaho.[104]

Other reliable indicators of congressional acquiescence are the proposals rejected by Congress. Rejected proposals indicate that Congress specifically considered the administrative action and refused to act.[105] The Supreme Court stated that "one must assume that a deliberate policy decision informed Congress' rejection of these alternatives in favor of the language presently contained in the [statute]."[106] Republicans gained control of Congress in 1995, promising to decrease federal regulatory activities, increase state control, protect private property rights, and decrease environmental controls. There were several efforts in 1995 to reauthorize and amend the ESA that would have changed the focus of section 10(j).

Senator Slade Gorton (R. Wash.) introduced legislation that required the Secretary to identify the "precise boundaries of the geographic area for the release," which should only occur in national parks and wildlife refuges. No member of the experimental population found outside of the release area would "be treated as a threatened species if the member poses a threat to the welfare of the public." This bill ceased to receive serious consideration after Senator Gorton admitted that significant sections of the bill were written by lawyers for the mining, timber, and grazing industries.[107]

The House Resources Committee reported an ESA reauthorization bill, which amended section 10(j). The bill, which followed the American Farm Bureau Federation's recommendations, required the Secretary to limit predator reintroduction to national parks or wildlife refuges and strictly comply with state laws regarding the reintroduced species. The bill was not enacted.[108]

There is an ongoing debate regarding the interpretative significance of legislative inaction.[109] Legal scholars point out that legislative inaction should be attributed some significance in statutory interpretation. The failure of Congress to change administrative "building block" interpretations, those "authoritative, well-settled interpretations upon which public and/or private parties reasonably rely to carry out their roles under the statute," indicates that the interpretations are consistent with the "presumed intent" of Congress. The attribution of significance to legislative inaction improves horizontal coherence, keeping the law in harmony with current policies, and avoids the problems of vertical coherence, which stresses continuity over time. This weak presumption assumes that two other preconditions are met. First, those adversely affected by the interpretation have access to Congress. Second, the interpretation is consistent with the text, intent, and purposes of the statute.[110] Both of these preconditions were satisfied regarding NRM wolf reintroduction.

Congressional inaction is also significant when viewed through the lens of positive political theory, which perceives governmental institutions as rational actors competing to have their policy preference prevail. The constitutional system of separation of powers and checks and balances provides each institution with some authority over the other institutions. Each institution sends and responds to the signals sent by other institutions to avoid the reversal of its positions. Congressional inaction shows agreement with the agency's statutory interpretation because Congress can easily send signals to the agency.[111] Legislative inaction also provides support for Chevron because it demonstrates the reasonability of the administrative interpretation.

Chevron: Step Two

If the traditional tools of statutory interpretation do not provide the answer to the interpretative issue, the court must move to the second step of Chevron. The court must assume that Congress delegated interpretative authority to the agency and defer to the agency's legal interpretation if it is reasonable.[112] The Tenth Circuit appropriately followed congressional guidance and also found the FWS's decision was reasonable. Section 10(j) delegated broad discretionary authority to the Secretary regarding experimental populations. The definitions of population and current range, as well as the status of individual dispersers, were issues, which Congress intended for the agency to determine. These were also issues of scientific and technical expertise within the realm of agency expertise to which the courts generally defer.[113] Congress accepted and supported the FWS decision, which successfully reintroduced the gray wolf into the NRM.

National Environmental Policy Act (NEPA)

The FWS compliance with the NEPA was another issue raised in the litigation. The NEPA establishes a national commitment by the federal government to protect the environment and backs this commitment with requirements that force action. When a federal agency contemplates a major federal action that significantly affects the environment, the agency must prepare an EIS which discusses: "1) the environmental impact of the proposed action; 2) any adverse environmental effects, which cannot be avoided should the proposal be adopted; 3) alternatives to the proposed action; 4) the relationship between local short-term uses of man's environmental and the maintenance and enhancement of long-term productivity; and 5) any irreversible and irretrievable commitment of resources, which should be involved in the proposed action should it be implemented."[114] The EIS ensures that the federal decision makers have considered environmental factors in their decision-making process. The EIS also informs the public and other political actors about the potential consequences of the proposed federal activity.[115]

The courts view the NEPA as a procedural, rather than a substantive, statute.[116] The NEPA is an environmental full-disclosure law, which does not require a federal agency to choose the most environmentally benign course of action.[117] NEPA compliance is reviewed pursuant to the Administrative Procedures Act (APA) to determine if the agency's action is "arbitrary, capricious, an abuse of discretion, or otherwise not according to the law" or "without observance of the procedure required by law."[118] The Supreme Court explained that "the court must consider whether the decision was based on a consideration of the relevant factors and whether there has been a clear error of judgment. Although this inquiry into the facts is to be searching and careful, the ultimate standard of review is a narrow one. The court is not empowered to substitute its judgment for that of the agency." Furthermore, the agency's decision is entitled to a "presumption of regularity. But that presumption is not to shield [the agency's] action from a thorough, probing, in-depth review."[119]

The FWS determined that "no evidence exists that wolf populations persisted in the NRM of the U.S. since their extirpation in the 1930's to the present time, or that lone wild wolves occasionally reported in these areas are other than dispersing wolves from Canadian populations." The FWS also found that recent taxonomic research indicates that little genetic difference exists among North American wolves and suggests that gray wolves throughout North America are all one subspecies of *Canis lupus*.[120] As a result the EIS did not discuss any alleged impacts on indigenous wolves and wolf subspecies.

The Urbigkits, a couple who studied the wolves in Yellowstone, claimed that the failure of the EIS to discuss the impact of the reintroduction of the

Canadian gray wolves on the indigenous subspecies of natural wolves in the area, *Canis lupus irremotus*, violated the NEPA. The Tenth Circuit properly rejected the Urbigkit's NEPA claim. The Tenth Circuit explained that the NEPA only requires the agency to take a "hard look" at environmental consequences. The court cannot second guess the agency's ultimate decision. The Tenth Circuit found that the FWS adequately analyzed the claim regarding the existence of the subspecies of natural wolves and the supporting research. The existence of conflicting scientific evidence did not make the FWS decision wrong.[121]

DOWNLISTING PROPOSAL

While the litigation was under way, Secretary Babbitt began to consider downlisting the gray wolf to threatened species status. Section 4(a) of the ESA provides for the listing of endangered and threatened species based on the following five factors: "A) the present or threatened destruction, modification, or curtailment of its habitat or range; B) overutilization for commercial, recreational, scientific, or educational purposes; C) disease or predation; D) the inadequacy of existing regulatory mechanisms; or E) other natural or manmade factors affecting its continued existence." The same factors are utilized for downlisting and delisting species.[122] Delisting was a relatively new policy.

The Clinton administration sought to prove that the ESA was compatible with economic development and stressed that delisting would be the measure of success for species conservation.[123] The FWS and the NMFS published a joint policy regarding ESA implementation in 1994, which was designed to "promote healthy ecosystems" and required the use of the best scientific information in recovery planning.[124] The FWS in 1996 declared, "recovery is the cornerstone and ultimate purpose of the endangered species program. Recovery is the process by which the decline of an endangered or threatened species is arrested or reversed, and threats to its survival are neutralized, so that its long term survival in nature can be ensured. The goal of the process is to restore listed species to a point where they are secure, self-sustaining components of their ecosystems and, thus to all delisting."[125]

Secretary Babbitt in the summer of 1998 stated that "the recovery of the wolf is becoming an impressive conservation success story and a gift to future generations." Consequently, "it's time to stand back and take a close look at wolf populations throughout the country, and to carefully consider if all of the wolves still need the same level of species protection under the ESA."[126] Vice President Gore endorsed the new policy, stating "the return of the gray wolf is a testament to nature's resilience and also to the remarkable success of the ESA. In fact, we soon may be able to remove the populations of the gray wolf from the endangered species list."[127] In July 2000, Interior issued a Proposed Rule that established four distinct population segments in the Western Great Lakes, Northeast, West, and Southwest and downlisted the gray wolf from an endangered to threatened species throughout most of its historic range, except the Southwest.[128] The designation of a distinct population segment allows unique treatment for the discrete significant population.

Environmental groups were critical of the proposal. The National Wildlife Federation declared the proposal "reflects the success of wolf recovery programs," but "falls far short of a bolder vision for recovery of wolves" in the West. The Predator Conservation Alliance stated that it is "downright reckless to lower the goal posts in mid-game when what is at stake is the successful restoration of wolves to Northern Rockies."[129]

CONCLUSION

The first battle regarding the reintroduction of the gray wolf to the NRM occurred from the Carter through the Clinton administrations. There were struggles between the executive and Congress regarding wolf reintroduction. Democratic administrations supported wolf reintroduction, while Republican administrations procrastinated. The political conflict over wolf reintroduction became the focus of public law litigation. The livestock, hunting, and outfitting industries, supported by the western states, brought suit challenging the legality of reintroduction in Yellowstone and central Idaho pursuant to section 10(j) of the ESA. Federal courts had to interpret section 10(j) and determine if Interior's actions were consistent with the statute.

The Tenth Circuit correctly upheld the FWS decision and determined that the experimental populations of wolves were "wholly separate geographically" from the natural population and released outside the "current range" of the natural population. Furthermore, the treatment of the individual dispersers as part of the experimental population and the corresponding reduction in their status from endangered to threatened did not violate the ESA. The Tenth Circuit's decision was consistent with the text, intent, and purposes of the statute and reflected the current policy preferences. Furthermore, the Tenth Circuit properly determined that EIS complied with the NEPA.

Congress was aware of wolf reintroduction and did not act to halt the project. Congressional inaction demonstrated that the FWS statutory interpretation was consistent with the "presumed" legislative intent. Congress rejected several proposals that would have amended section 10(j). Furthermore, the failure of Congress to overturn the FWS's decision when viewed from the perspective of positive political theory lends further support to congressional acquiescence.

Neither judicial proponents nor skeptics would strongly criticize the Tenth Circuit's decision. Judicial skeptics would not object to the court granting standing to the interest groups representing the livestock industry, hunting and outfitters, which alleged harm to their common law interests, not general harm to the public. The Tenth Circuit employing the traditional tools of statutory interpretation upheld Interior's decision. Judicial skeptics would object to the use of legislative history, but applaud the court's deference to the FWS analysis. The Tenth Circuit's decision was consistent with the Ninth Circuit's decision in the McKittrick case, so there was no fragmentation of federal policy.

The Tenth Circuit's decision was important for all reintroduction efforts.[130] Wolf reintroduction was "truly an endangered species success story." By 2000, northwest Montana supported approximately 63 wolves in five packs. The central Idaho reintroduction area contained at least 141 wolves, including ten breeding packs. There were 118 wolves, including eight reproducing packs, in Yellowstone.[131]

Wolves did not decimate the livestock industry. The DOW maintained a one-hundred-thousand-dollar Wolf Compensation Trust, which compensated ranchers at fair market value for losses due to wolves and at half market value for other losses when the wolves were the likely culprits. The Trust, which was established in 1987, covered losses in Arizona and New Mexico, Yellowstone, central Idaho, and expanding areas where reintroduced wolves were beginning to disperse. As of September 2000, the total payments from the Trust were $138,475. In the Greater Yellowstone ecosystem, 110 sheep, 21 cattle, and 9 dogs had been killed by wolves, requiring $28,870 in compensation. In central Idaho, 154 sheep, 58 cattle, and 2 dogs had been killed, requiring $52,539 in compensation. In northwest Montana, 64 sheep, 78 cattle, and 1 dog had been killed, requiring $1,725 in compensation.[132] By comparison, 11,200 sheep were lost to coyotes, 500 to domestic dogs, and 11,600 to weather or disease in Idaho in 1998. The livestock industry in Montana annually lost 142,000 sheep and 86,000 cattle that were valued at forty-five million dollars.[133]

In light of the success, Interior issued a proposed regulation downlisting the gray wolf from endangered to threatened in some parts of the country. Secretary Babbitt stated, "[W]olves are a living symbol of the regard Americans have for things wild. We as a people have made the choice to do the right thing and bring these animals back from the brink of extinction. We have weighed the cost of saving an irreplaceable part of our world and found it to be worth our effort."[134]

NOTES

A version of this chapter originally appeared as an article: "*Wyoming Farm Bureau Federation v. Babbitt*: The Children of the Night Return to the Northern Rocky Mountains," 16 *Journal of Natural Resources and Environmental Law* 79 (2001–2).

1. 987 F. Supp. 1349 (D. Wyo. 1997); 199 F. 3d 1224 (10th Cir. 2000).
2. Bruce Hampton, *The Great American Wolf* (Henry Holt, 1997), 114–20.
3. Stanley P. Young and Edward A. Goldman, *The Wolves of North America* (Dover, 1944), 363.
4. Rick McIntyre, *War Against the Wolf: America's Campaign to Exterminate the Wolf* (Voyager Press, 1995), 118, 150.
5. Timothy B. Strauch, "Holding the Wolf By the Ears: The Conservation of the Northern Rocky Mountain Wolf in Yellowstone National Park," 27 *Land and Water Law Review* 33, 40–42 (1992). McIntyre, 120–21.
6. Jenks Cameron, *The Bureau of Biological Survey: Its History, Activities and Organization* (John Hopkins University, 1929), 315.
7. Inga Haagenson Causey, "The Reintroduction of the Wolf into Yellowstone," 11 *Tulane Environmental Law Journal* 461, 462 (1998).
8. 16 U.S.C. 21, 22.
9. Christopher J. Kirwan, "Wolves and Recovery Plans: The Difficult Road to Wolf Preservation in the Greater Yellowstone Ecosystem," 60 *University of Missouri Kansas City Law Review* 517, 521 (1992). Alston Chase, *Playing God in Yellowstone* (Harcourt Brace Jankovich, 1987), 132.
10. 16 U.S.C. 1–18f.
11. Strauch, 42–44. Paul Schullery (ed.), *The Yellowstone Wolf, A Guide and Sourcebook* (High Plans, 1996), 12–20.
12. Hampton, 143. Chase, 128.
13. Richard D. Lamm and Michael McCarthy, *The Angry West* (Houghton Mifflin, 1982).
14. 43 U.S.C. 1701 (1976).
15. Bruce Babbitt, "Federalism and the Environment: An Intergovernmental Perspective of the Sagebrush Rebellion," 12 *Environmental Law* 847 (1982); John D. Leshy, "Unraveling the Sagebrush Rebellion: Law, Politics and Federal Lands," 14 *University of California Davis Law Review* 317 (1980); Michael E. Shapiro, "Sagebrush and Seaweed Robbery: State Revenue Losses for Onshore and Offshore Federal Lands," 12 *Ecology Law Quarterly* 481 (1985).
16. A. Constandina Titus, "The Nevada 'Sagebrush Rebellion' Act: A Question of Constitutionality," 23 *Arizona Law Review* 264, 265 (1981). R. McGreggor Cawley, *Federal Land, Western Anger: The Sagebrush Rebellion and Environmental Politics* (University of Kansas, 1993), 101–11.
17. *Nevada v. U.S.*, 512 F. Supp. 166, 171–72 (1981).
18. Donald Snow, "The Pristine Silence of Leaving It All Alone," in Philip D. Brick and R. McGreggor Cawley (eds.), *A Wolf in the Garden: The Land Rights Movement and the New Environmental Debate* (Rowman & Littlefield, 1996), 28–29.
19. House Committee on Interior and Insular Affairs, 95th Congress, 2d Session, *Hearings: Fish and Wildlife Miscellaneous Part 4* (July 29, 1978), 238.
20. 16 U.S.C. 1533. *Fund for the Animals v. Babbitt*, 903 F. Supp. 96, 104–5 (D.D.C. 1995).
21. Kirwan, 521–25.
22. Richard M. Mollison and Richard W. Eddy, "Sagebrush Rebellion: A Simplistic Response to Complex Problems of Federal Land Management," 19 *Harvard Journal on Legislation* 97, 104–7 (1982). George C. Coggins and Doris K. Nagel, "'Nothing Besides Remains': The Legal Legacy of James G. Watts' Tenure as Secretary of Interior on Federal Land Law and Policy," 17 *Boston College Environmental Affairs Law Review* 473, 491–97 (1990).
23. Chase, 140.

24. Dale D. Goble, "Of Wolves and Welfare Ranching," 16 *Harvard Environmental Law Review* 101, 126–27 (1992). "Hunt May Cut Short Return of Wolves," *New York Times*, September. 9, 1987. "Wolf Pack Living In Rocky Mountains," UPI, April 18, 1986.

25. Kirwan, 523–25. Schullery, 240–47.

26. Goble, 110–26.

27. Julie S. Thrower, "Ranching with Wolves: Reducing Conflicts Between Livestock and Wolves Through Integrated Grazing and Wolf Management Plans," 29 *Journal Land, Resources, and Environmental Law* 319, 327–28 (2009).

28. Matthew H. Wilson, "The Wolf in Yellowstone: Science, Symbol, or Politics?" 10 *Society and Natural Resources* 453, 456–57 (1997).

29. House Committee on Resources, 104th Congress, 1st Session, *Introducing the Gray Wolf into Yellowstone and Idaho* (January 26, 1995).

30. Harry R. Bader, "Wolf Conservation: The Importance of Following Endangered Species Recovery Plans," 13 *Harvard Environmental Law Review* 517, 518 (1989).

31. "Wildlife Director Rolls Over for Sheep," *Caspar Star-Tribune*, November 23, 1987.

32. Strauch, 57–63.

33. "Congress Gets Involved," UPI, December 13, 1987. "Environmentalist, Politician Pledge to Bring Wolf Back to Yellowstone," AP, June 5, 1988.

34. *H.R. Conf. Rep. No.862*, 100th Cong., 2d Sess. 14–15 (1988).

35. Ron Arnold, "Overcoming Ideology," 15, 18, in Philip D. Brick and R. McGreggor Cawley, *A Wolf in the Garden: The Land Rights Movement and the New Environmental Debate* (Rowman & Littlefield, 1996); Karen Budd-Falen, "Protecting Community Stability and Local Economies: Opportunities for Local Government Influence in Federal Decision and Policy Making Process," 73–85, also in Brick and Calwey, 1996. Rene Erm II, "The 'Wise Use' Movement: The Constitutionality of Local Action on Federal Lands Under the Preemption Doctrine," 30 *Idaho Law Review* 631 (1993–1994).

36. Wilson, 454.

37. Strauch, 60–62.

38. *H.R. 2786*, 101st Cong., 1st Sess. (1989). "Return of the Wolves to Yellowstone urged," AP, June, 29, 1989. "National Park Service Opposed Yellowstone Bill," UPI, July 20, 1989. "Congress Moves to Speed Return of Wolves to Yellowstone," AP, July 21, 1989.

39. Strauch, 62.

40. Pub. L. No. 101–121 (1989).

41. Yellowstone Park et al., *Wolves for Yellowstone? A Report to the U.S. Congress* (1990).

42. "Studies Spur Calls for Government Decisions," *US Newswire*, May 21, 1990.

43. Patrick Impero Wilson, "Wolves, Politics, and the Nez Perce: Wolf Recovery in Central Idaho and the Role of Native Tribes," 39 *Natural Resources Journa*l 543, 545–49 (1999).

44. Pub. L. No. 101-512 (1990), cited at 1990 U.S.C.C.A.N 1915.

45. Wolf Management Committee, *Wolves in Yellowstone National Park and the Central Idaho Wilderness Area* (1991).

46. Brian Beisher, "Are Ranchers Legitimately Trying to Save Their Hides or Are They Just Crying Wolf," 29 *Land and Water Law Review* 417, 429 (1994). Robert B. Keiter and Patrick T. Holsher, "Wolf Recovery," 11 *Public Land Law Review* 19, 51 (1990).

47. "Environmentalists Attack Yellowstone Plan," AP, May 15, 1991.

48. "Proposal to Bring Wolf Back Ignites Northwest," *Christian Science Monitor*, May 24, 1991. "Bringing Wolves Back Is Stirring Howls," *Seattle Post*, July 9, 1991.

49. Pub. L. No. 102-154 (1991).

50. *DOW v. Lujan,* 792 F. Supp. 834, 835–36 (D.D.C. 1992).

51. *H.R. Conf. Rep. No. 256*, 102d Cong., 1st Sess. 16–17 (1991). Strauch, 67.

52. House Committee on Resources 19.

53. John Andrew Zuccotti, "A Native Returns: The Endangered Species Act and Wolf Reintroduction to the Northern Rocky Mountains," 20 *Columbia Journal Environmental Law* 329, 347–54 (1995).

54. 59 *Federal Register* 60252, 60253–56 (1994).

55. "Gray Wolf Wins New Future in National Park," *Guardian*, May 6, 1994."Yellowstone Will Shelter Wolves Again," *New York Times*, June 17, 1994. "Wolves set off Howling Debate," *Philadelphia Inquirer*, November 10, 1994.

56. "Interior Report Calls for Return," *States News Service*, May 4, 1994. "Five Senators Seek to Delay Reintroduction," *Greenwire*, December 5, 1994.

57. Ann Southworth, "Conservative Lawyers and the Contest Over the Meaning of Public Interest Law," 52 *UCLA Law Review* 1223 (2005). Karen O'Connor and Lee Epstein, "Rebalancing the Scales of Justice: An Assessment of Public Interest Law," 7 *Harvard Journal Law and Public Policy* 483 (1984).

58. "Wolves Come Home to Yellowstone," AP, January 13, 1995.

59. House Committee on Resources, 89. Robert C. Moore, "The Pack Is Back," 12 *Thomas Cooley Law Review* 647, 655, 678 (1995). Schullery, 283–334,

60. "Wolf Cost Doubles," *Denver Post*, January 26, 1995. "Babbitt Defends Reintroduction," *Denver Post*, January 27, 1995. "Wolf Reintroduction Process," *Congpress*, March 21, 1995. "U.S. Taking Chances With Wolves in Yellowstone," *Pittsburgh Post*, March 24, 1996.

61. "Wolves: Bring More to Park," *Idaho Falls*, January 23, 1996. "Wolves' Comeback Sparks Dispute," *Washington Times*, February 5, 1996.

62. "Yellowstone Pens Opened: Reactions," *Greenwire*, March 22, 1995.

63. 16 U.S.C. 1539(j)(2)(C).

64. 987 F. Supp., 1366-69, 71–76. Scott Youngblood, "Wildlife Restoration Projects: Hope for Life or a Death Sentence: A Look at Reintroduction of Wolves to the Northern Rocky Mountains," 40 *South Texas Law Review* 1045 (1999). Scott R. Cleere, "Wolf Reintroduction as an Experimental Population Under the ESA," 36 *Idaho Law Review* 83 (1999).

65. "Wolf Reintroduction Illegal," *Washington Post*, December 13, 1997. "Both Sides Howling," *Lewiston Morning Tribune*, December 13, 1997. "Federal jJudge Overturns Reintroduction Plans," *Greenwire*, December. 15, 1997. "Babbitt Yellowstone to Keep Wolves," AP, March 21, 1998.

66. 199 F.3d 1224, 1231–41 (10th Cir. 2000). Elizabeth Cowan Brown, "The 'Wholly Separate' Truth: Did the Yellowstone Reintroduction Violate Section 10(j) of the Endangered Species Act?" 27 *Boston College Environmental Affairs Law Review* 425 (2000).

67. "Babbitt Statement," *US Newswire*, January 13, 2000. "Wolves: Court Rules Can Stay," *Greenwire*, January 14, 2000.

68. 59 *Federal Register* 60, 252–62.

69. 199 F. 3d, 1234–36.

70. 16 U.S.C. 1532(15).

71. 50 C.F.R. 17.3. 199 F. 3d, 1234.

72. *U.S. v. Missouri Pacific Railroad*, 278 U.S. 269, 278 (1929).

73. Wildlife Society, *The Restoration of the Wolves in North America* 6–7 (1991), cited in House Committee on Resources, *Hearings: Introducing Wolves to Yellowstone and Central Idaho*, 104th Cong., 1st Sess. (1995), 217–18.

74. *U.S. v. McKittrick*, 142 F.3d 1170, 1175 (9th Cir. 1998).

75. Michael J. Bean and Melanie J. Rowland, *The Evolution of Natural Wildlife Law*, 3d ed. (Praeger, 1997), 233.

76. 142 F. 3d 1170, 1174–75 (9th Cir. 1998). Jennifer Li, "The Wolves May Have Won the Battle, But Not the War: How the West Was Won Under the Northern Rocky Mountain Wolf Recovery Plan," 30 *Environmental Law* 677 (2000). Daniel R. Dinger, "Throwing Canis Lupus to the Wolves: *United States v. McKittrick* and the Existence of the Yellowstone and Central Idaho Experimental Wolf Populations Under a Flawed Provision of the ESA," 2000 *Brigham Young Law Review* 377.

77. 142 F. 3d, 1175.

78. Frank B. Cross, "Shattering the Fragile Case for Judicial Review of Rulemaking," 85 *Virginia Law Review* 1243, 1249–50 (1999).

79. 59 *Federal Register* 60259.

80. 199 F. 3d, 1235–36.

81. *Webster's New World Dictionary*, Third College Edition (1988).

82. Wildlife Society, 6–7.

83. 16 U.S.C. 1532(15).

84. Brief for Plaintiffs-Appellants/Appellees, Predator Project, Sinapu, Gray Wolf Committee, *WYFB v. Babbitt*, 22.

85. 59 *Federal Register* 60261.

86. 199 F. 3d, 1236–37.

87. H.R. Conf. Rep. No. 835, 97th Cong., 2d Sess. 30, 34 (1982), reprinted 1982 U.S.C.C.A.N. 2871.

88. H.R. Rep. No. 412, 93d Cong., 1st Sess. (1973).

89. 40 *Federal Register* 31376 (July 28, 1975).

90. 40 *Federal Register* 44412 (Sept. 26, 1975).

91. 50 C.F.R. 17.11(i)(1977), revised 43 *Federal Register* 6233 (Feb. 14, 1978).

92. 43 *Federal Register* 9612 (March 9, 1978).

93. S. Rep. No. 151, 96th Cong., 1st Sess. 6–7 (1979).

94. 16 U.S.C. 1531, 1532.

95. 142 F. 3d, 1174.

96. 437 U.S. 184.

97. William N. Eskridge, "Interpreting Legislative Inaction," 87 *Michigan Law Review* 67 (1988).

98. *Grove City College v. Bell*, 465 U.S. 555, 568 (1984). *Bob Jones University v. U.S.,* 451 U.S. 574, 600 (1983).

99. Brief of Amicus Curiae, Environmental Defense Fund et al., *WYFB v. Babbitt*, 9.

100. 59 *Federal Register* 60261.

101. Neal E. Devins, "Regulation of Government Agencies Through Limitation Riders," 1987 *Duke Law Journal* 456.

102. "With the Return of the Wolves to the West, Predatory Habits Bring Back Fear and Anger," *New York Times*, December 29, 1995.

103. H.R. Rep. No. 483, 105th Cong., 2d Sess. 8–9 (1998). "Funding Increased, Host of GOP Riders Fall in $14.1 Billion Interior Bill," 1998 *Congressional Quarterly Almanac* 2:57–63.

104. H.R. Rep. No. 259, 104th Cong., 1st Sess. 26 (1995). S. Rep. No. 125, 105th Cong., 1st Sess. 18 (1995). S. Rep. No. 319, 104th Cong., 2d Sess. 16 (1996). S. Rep. No. 56, 105th Cong., 1st Sess. 21 (1997). S. Rep. No. 227, 105th Cong., 2d Sess. 17–18 (1998).

105. Eskridge, "Legislative Inaction," 84–89.

106. *NLRB v. Robbins Tire & Rubber Co.,* 437 U.S. 214, 248 (1978).

107. James E. Satterfield, "A Funny Thing Happened on the Way to the Revolution: The Environmental Record of the 104th Congress," 27 ELR 10019, 10032 (1997).

108. Satterfield, 10031–32.

109. John C. Grabow, "Congressional Silence and the Search for Legislative Intent: A Venture into 'Speculative Unrealities,'" 64 *Boston University Law Review* 737 (1985). Laurence H. Tribe, "Toward a Syntax of the Unsaid," 57 *Indiana Law Journal* 515 (1982).

110. Eskridge, "Legislative Inaction," 108–24. Eskridge, "New Textualism," 37 *UCLA Law Review*, 636–40.

111. William N. Eskridge, "Post-Enactment Legislative Signals," 57 *Law and Contemporary Problems* 75, 82 (1994). Daniel A. Farber and Philip P. Frickey, "Forward: Positive Political Theory in the Nineties," 80 *Georgetown Law Journal* 457, 462 (1992). Jonathan R. Macey, "Separated Powers and Positive Political Theory: Tug of War Over Administrative Agencies," 80 *Georgetown Law Journa*l 671, 700–703 (1992).

112. 467 U.S. 843–44.

113. H.R. Rep. No. 567, Part 1, 97th Cong., 2d Sess. 33–34 (1982). *IRS v. FLRA*, 494 U.S. 922, 933 (1990).

114. 42 U.S.C. 4321, 4332 (c).

115. *Calvert Cliffs' Coord. Comm. v. U.S. Atomic Energy Commission,* 449 F. 2d 1109, 1114 (D.C. Cir. 1971).

116. *Stryker's Bay Neighborhood Council v. Karlen,* 444 U.S. 233, 227–28 (1980); *Vermont Yankee Nuclear Power Corp. v. NRDC*, 435 U.S. 519, 558 (1978); *Kleppe v. Sierra Club*, 427 U.S. 390, 410 n.21 (1976).

117. *Robertson v. Methow Valley Citizens Council,* 490 U.S. 332, 350 (1989).

118. 5 U.S.C. 706(2) (A), (D).
119. *Citizens to Preserve Overton Park v. Volpe,* 401 U.S. 402, 415–16 (1971).
120. 59 *Federal Register* 60252–53.
121. 199 F. 3d, 1240–41.
122. 16 U.S.C. 1533 (c)(2)(B)(i). *Fund for Animals v. Babbitt,* 903 F. Supp. 96, 104–105 (D.D.C. 1995).
123. Frederico Cheever, "The Rhetoric of Delisting Species Under the ESA," 31 *Environmental Law Reporter* 11302, 11306 (2001).
124. 59 *Federal Register* 34272 (July 1, 1994). John Ruhl, "Congress?—An Agenda for Administrative Reform," 6 *New York University Environmental Law Journal* 368 (1998).
125. U.S. FWS, *Report to Congress on the Recovery Program for Threatened and Endangered Species* (1996), 2.
126. "Gray Wolves Make Strong Comeback," *M2 Presswire*, June 30, 1998.
127. "White House: Gore Statement," *M2 Presswire*, June 30, 1998.
128. 65 *Federal Register* 43450 (July 13, 2000).
129. "Interior Proposal Could Reduce Gray Wolf Population," AP, July 11, 2000. "Federal Proposal Would Change Wolf's Status in Wyoming," AP, February 28, 2000.
130. Craig E. Enochs, "Gone Today, Here Tomorrow," 4 *Hastings West-Northwest Law Review* 91, 92 (1997).
131. "Gray Wolves Rebound: U.S. Fish and Wildlife Service Proposes to Reclassify, Delist the Wolves in Much of the U.S.," U.S. FWS News Release, July 11, 2000.
132. Defenders of Wildlife, *Wolf Compensation Trust,* at www.defenders.org/wolfcomp.html.
133. "News Release," Defenders of Wildlife, January 14, 2000. "Wolves Reestablish Strong Roots in Rockies," *New York Times*, June 1, 1999.
134. "News Release," U.S. FWS, July 11, 2000.

Chapter Four

Dysfunctional Downlisting Defeated

Defenders of Wildlife v. Interior

The Bush administration modified the Clinton administration proposal and established three distinct population segments (DPS) that incorporated the entire historic range of the gray wolf and downlisted the wolf in the Eastern and Western DPS to a threatened species. Interior built on the success in three midwestern states (Minnesota, Michigan, and Wisconsin) and three western states (Montana, Idaho, and Wyoming) to downlist the wolf across much of its historic range in thirty states, despite its absence from 96 percent of its historic range. Environmental groups brought suit. The U.S. District Court for the District of Oregon in *Defenders of Wildlife (DOW) v. Secretary of Interior*[1] and the U.S. District Court for the District of Vermont in *National Wildlife Federation (NWF) v. Secretary of Interior*[2] held that Interior violated the Endangered Species Act (ESA). The gray wolf was missing from significant portions of its historic range, which could still support wolves. The designation of a distinct population segment could be employed to downlist a small discreet significant population from a larger population, but could not be used to downlist a larger population based on the success of the smaller population. Combining the Northeast and Western Great Lake DPSs into the Eastern DPS violated the ESA and Interior's DPS policy. This chapter examines the Bush administration's initial effort to delist the wolf across much of the United States, analyzes both federal district court decisions, and reviews the regulatory changes and congressional action following the litigation.

BUSH ADMINISTRATION

George W. Bush won seven of the eleven western states in the 2000 presidential election, losing only Washington, Oregon, California, and New Mexico. Gail Norton, an attorney with the Mountain States Legal Foundation, became Secretary of Interior from 2001 through 2006. Development interests praised the nomination as an "enormous victory" that would provide greater access to public lands and resource development and would preserve jobs and the rural culture. Environmental groups, who were skeptical, declared that "we are coming off the best year for land and wildlife conservation in 20 years, and it would be a colossal mistake to try to reverse this momentum. The last thing we need is a remake of the James Watt era."[3]

Secretary Norton appointed industry lobbyists to high administrative positions. She criticized the pro-environmental policies of the Clinton era and promised to consult with western states regarding public land policies. Her "new environmentalism," which relied on market-based methods, was based on four Cs: communication, consultation, and cooperation, all in service of conservation.[4]

Early battles demonstrated Secretary Norton's pro-western state and pro-development orientation. She began her tenure by canceling the reintroduction of grizzly bears into Idaho wilderness areas. Idaho Governor Dirk Kempthorne declared, "the new administration is changing tone in Washington. They care about state's rights and state inputs. We can tell the difference." The DOW noted, "Secretary Norton is essentially allowing a governor to veto a major conservation initiative in a way that undermines the ESA and that sets a very dangerous precedent."[5]

WOLF RECOVERY

Wolves were reintroduced into Yellowstone and central Idaho as a nonessential experimental population and naturally recolonized northwest Montana from Canada. The wolf population in the NRM continued to expand and exceeded recovery goals. There were approximately 663 wolves in 49 breeding pairs in 2002.

Wolves were returning to other regions. The gray wolf population in the Western Great Lakes region, which included Minnesota, Wisconsin, and Michigan, expanded and exceeded recovery goals. The existence and identity of wolves in the Northeast remained unknown. Mexican wolves were reintroduced into the Blue Range Wolf Recovery Area (BRWRA) in New Mexico and Arizona as a nonessential experimental population in 1998. The Mexican wolf population was expanding despite numerous obstacles.[6]

In light of this success, the FWS issued a Proposed Rule in July 2000 that established four DPSs in the Western Great Lakes, Northeast, West, and Southwest and downlisted the gray wolf from an endangered to threatened species throughout most of its historic range, except the Southwest.[7] The Final Rule issued in April 2003 established only three DPSs in the East, West, and Southwest and downlisted the wolves in the Eastern and Western DPSs. All the wolves in the Eastern DPS, including those in the Western Great Lakes and Northeast regions, were reclassified as a threatened species. Wolves in the NRM, including those in Montana and Idaho, were downlisted to threatened species, but the nonessential experimental population designations in Wyoming and Idaho remained in place. Gray wolves were downlisted in the remaining Western DPS states, including Washington, Oregon, California, Nevada, Utah, and Colorado. Downlisting the gray wolf to threatened species status permitted their taking pursuant to section 4(d)of the ESA, which allows the Secretary to "issue regulations as he deems necessary and advisable to provide for the conservation of the species." This moved the gray wolf one step closer to delisting. The gray wolf was delisted in fourteen southeastern states because the region was not part of its historic range. Gray wolves in the Southwest DPS retained their endangered species status.[8]

On the same day, Interior announced its intention to delist the gray wolf in the Eastern and Western DPSs and remove the nonessential population designations in the NRM.[9] Secretary Norton stated, "thirty years ago, the future of the gray wolf in the U.S. outside of Alaska was anything but certain. Today we celebrate not only the remarkable comeback of the gray wolf, but the partnerships, dedicated efforts, and spirit of conservation that have made this success story possible."[10]

DEFENDERS OF WILDLIFE V. SECRETARY OF INTERIOR

The DOW, representing nineteen environmental groups, brought suit challenging the downlisting of the gray wolf across much of its historic range in the Eastern and Western DPSs. The DOW established standing under the citizen suit provision in the ESA, which allows any person to "commence a civil suit on his own behalf to enjoin any person, including the U.S. and any other governmental instrumentality or agency . . . , who is alleged to be in violation of any provision of this chapter or regulation issued under the authority thereof."[11] The U.S. District Court for the District of Oregon in *DOW v. Secretary of Interior* properly rejected Interior's action. The court determined that the Secretary's interpretation of the "significant portion" of the gray wolf's range was contrary to the ESA and case law. The Secretary's implementation of the DPS policy violated Interior's own regulations and the ESA. Since the Secretary's analysis was limited to the gray wolf's current range, her conclusions regarding the five downlisting factors set forth in section 4(a) of ESA were erroneous. As a result, the gray wolf remained an endangered species in the continental United States, except in Minnesota and the experimental population areas located in Wyoming, Montana, Idaho, Arizona, New Mexico, and Texas where it was a threatened species.

Significant Portion of Its Range

The ESA defines species as "endangered" if it is "currently in danger of extinction throughout a significant portion of its range."[12] A species is "threatened" if it "is likely to become an endangered species within the foreseeable future throughout all or a significant portion of its range."[13] The FWS limited its analysis to the gray wolf's current range in the Western Great Lakes and NRM, even though wolves lived outside these core areas. The FWS defined "significant portion of its range" as "that area that is important or necessary for maintaining a viable, self-sustaining, and evolving representative population or populations in order for the taxon to persist into foreseeable future." The FWS concluded that "the presence or absence of gray wolves outside of core recovery areas is not likely to have a bearing on the long term viability of the three wolf populations," so threats outside core areas did not have to be evaluated.[14]

The Oregon federal district court rejected Interior's interpretation and found the gray wolf "extinct throughout a significant portion of its range [because] . . . there are major geographic areas in which it is no longer viable but once was." The court held that major geographic areas outside the Western Great Lakes and NRM in the historic range of the gray wolf still provided suitable habitat for the gray wolf. The FWS acknowledged the existence of extensive potential wolf habitat in the Northeast (Maine, New Hampshire, and New York) and Northwest (Washington and Oregon) and the dispersal of wolves into North and South Dakota. The court recognized that the Secretary had broad discretion regarding what constituted a significant portion of the range because the term was not defined in the statute. Nevertheless, the Secretary had to explain why potential wolf habitat within the wolf's historic range did not constitute a significant portion of the gray wolf's range. The existence of viable wolf populations in the Western Great Lakes and NRM did not render areas in the remainder of the gray wolf's historic range insignificant. The court found the Secretary's interpretation contrary to legislative history and case law.[15] The court's decision was consistent with the text, intent, and purposes of the ESA.

Legal Meaning of "Significant Portion of its Range"

The definition of "significant portion of its range" was a legal question, which required the court to employ the two-step Chevron framework. The court must first determine "whether Congress has directly spoken to the precise question at issue." If Congress has not addressed the issue, the court can "not simply impose its own construction on the statute." The court moves to the second step to decide "whether the agency's answer is based on a permissible construction of the statute."[16] Courts selectively employ Chevron in both a strong and weak manner. The strong reading mandates that the court defer to a reasonable agency interpretation, unless Congress has directly addressed the issue. The weak version instructs the court to utilize the traditional tools of statutory interpretation—text, intent, and purposes—to determine the congressional mandate. If there is no congressional guidance, the court must defer to a reasonable agency decision.

Judicial skeptics applaud Chevron. Skeptics argue that federal courts do not have supervisory authority over executive agencies, which are responsible to the president. Courts utilize statutory interpretation to interfere with executive policy making. Unelected judges substitute their judgment for that of the expert agency. Chevron counters this tendency and restores power to the executive.[17]

Judicial proponents are wary of Chevron. Proponents argue that Chevron delegates too much power to the executive and violates separation of powers and checks and balances. There is no reason to assume that Congress delegated interpretative authority to the federal agency, not to the court.[18] Citizen suit provisions presume judicial review. The court ensures that interest group deals negotiated in Congress are implemented. The court is more likely to faithfully carry out legislative bargains than the federal agency, which is accountable to the present administration.[19]

The court's inquiry begins with the text of the statute, which has been enacted into law through the constitutionally prescribed process.[20] The term "significant portion of its range" was ambiguous. The Ninth Circuit addressed this issue in *DOW v. Norton*, which dealt with the FWS refusal to list the flat-tailed horned lizard as an endangered species. The FWS determined that suitable habitat on public land ensured the lizard's viability, despite threats to the species on private land. The DOW argued that the lizard's private land habitat constituted a significant portion of its range where its survival was in jeopardy. The Ninth Circuit did not find the text illuminating. The Ninth Circuit determined that the phrase "significant portion of its range" to be an oxymoron because "extinction suggests total rather than partial disappearance." The statutory language was "inherently ambiguous, as it appears to use language in a manner in some tension with ordinary usage."[21]

The Ninth Circuit rejected the Secretary's interpretation that a species was only entitled to ESA protection if it "faces threats in enough key portions of its range that the entire species is in danger of extinction, or will be within the foreseeable future" because it rendered the "significant portion of its range language" superfluous. The court adopted "a natural reading . . . which would give effect to all of [the statute's] provisions." The Secretary, by equating "a significant portion of its range" with *all* of the gray wolf's range, violated the rule. The Ninth Circuit concluded that a species could be extinct "throughout . . . a significant portion of its range" if there are major geographic areas in which it is no longer viable but once was.[22] The Ninth Circuit indicated that a species can have a different status in different portions of its range.

If the text does not answer the interpretative question, the court must examine the legislative history to discover the legislative intent, which is how the enacting legislature would have resolved the interpretative question.[23] Studying the legislative history places the court in the proper deferential framework regarding Congress and establishes criteria of reliability that helps the court select and weigh elements of the language in the legislative context.[24]

There is an ongoing debate regarding the use of legislative history. Judicial skeptics are particularly critical of the court's use of legislative history to overrule administrative policies. Skeptics argue that legislative history is manufactured by lobbyists and committee staff to influence the court's statutory interpretations. The use of legislative history elevates the views of individual congresspersons and committees over the entire Congress and the executive, which represent the nation.[25]

Judicial proponents point out that the legislative history reflects how Congress conducts business. Specialized committees review potential legislation and delegate the writing of reports to staff. Committee reports inform members of Congress and the public of the content of the statute. Judge Patricia Wald notes that ignoring legislative history "is to second guess Congress's chosen form of organization and delegation of authority, and to doubt the ability to oversee its own constitutional functions effectively. It comes perilously close . . . to impugning the way a coordinate branch conducts its operations and, in that sense, runs the risk of violating the spirit if not the letter of the separation of powers."[26]

The two statutes preceding the ESA described endangered species as those facing complete extinction. The ESA of 1973 expanded the definition of endangered species to those facing "extinction throughout all or a significant portion of its range." The House Merchant Marine and Fisheries Committee stated that this major change represented "a significant shift in the definition in existing law which considers a species to be endangered only when it is threatened with worldwide extinction."[27] The new language was added to encourage greater federal-state cooperation and grant the secretary greater flexibility regarding wildlife management.

The FWS recognized that the ESA permits different populations of the same species to have different status in different parts of its range. For example, grizzly bears were listed as threatened species within the forty-eight contiguous states, but not in Alaska. Only the California, Oregon, and Washington populations of the marbled murrelet, whose range in North America extends from the Aleutian Archipelago in Alaska to Central California, are listed as threatened. The desert big horn sheep is only listed as an endangered species in peninsular ranges of Southern California, although its range extends into Baja California. The population of Steller sea lions occurring west of 144 degrees W. longitude are listed as endangered species, while the remaining population is listed as threatened. Only the Florida population of the Audubon crested caracara, a hawk that occurs from Florida, southern Texas and Arizona, and northern Baja California, south to Panama is listed as a threatened species. The piping plovers in the watershed of the Great Lakes are listed as endangered species, but are only a threatened species throughout the remainder of their range.[28]

There was an attempt to change the statutory text in 1978. The Senate passed an amendment, which defined "essential [as] that portion of the range necessary for the continued survival and recovery of the species."[29] The amendment was rejected by the conference committee.[30] The failure of Congress to adopt this amendment represented an explicit rejection of Interior's definition of "significant portion of its range."[31]

There was also language by the House Merchant Marine and Fisheries Committee in 1978 indicating that the term "range" refers to the "historical range" of the species. Section 4(c) (1) requires the Secretary to publish a list of endangered and threatened species and specify the portion of the range in which they are protected. The committee bill amended section 4(c) (1) to require the secretary to include critical habitat designations on endangered and threatened species lists. The committee stated that "the term 'range' is used in the general sense, and refers to the historical range of the species."[32] The amendment was adopted by the conference committee.[33]

The ESA Amendments of 1982 added section 10(j), which provides for the release of an experimental population of endangered or threatened species "outside the current range of such species if the Secretary determines that such release will further the conservation of such species."[34] This demonstrates congressional awareness of the difference between the current and historical range of the species.

Further guidance and clarification of statutory meaning are found in the statutory purposes.[35] While more abstract than the legislative intent, statutory purposes provide the overall statutory goals. Judicial skeptics argue that statutes contain many different purposes, which are stated in general terms. These aspirational commands are difficult to implement and provide federal courts with great discretion.[36] Judicial proponents argue that statutory purposes help the court to determine legislative intent, direct the court when legislative intent has not been manifested, and allow the court to keep the statute in harmony with contemporary values.[37] Furthermore, the court by following the stated public purposes of the statute mitigates the naked interest group deals negotiated in Congress.[38]

The ESA is concerned with the protection, conservation, and restoration of endangered and threatened species and the ecosystems on which they depend.[39] Congress was particularly concerned with the protection of ecosystems. Congress found "the two major causes of extinction are hunting and destruction of natural habitat." The most crucial was the destruction of natural habitat.[40] Congress recognized that the "critical nature of interrelationship of plants and animals between themselves and with their environment [demonstrated the] ecologist's short hand phrase that 'everything is connected to everything else' is nothing more than cold, hard fact."[41]

Congress mandated that ecosystems be preserved to protect endangered and threatened species. The House Merchant Marine and Fisheries Committee stated: "As we homogenize the habitats in which these plants and animals evolved, and as we increase the pressure for products that they are in a position to supply (usually unwillingly) we threaten their—and our own—genetic heritage. The value of this genetic heritage is, quite literally, incalculable."[42]

The ESA Amendments of 1982 stressed the importance of ecosystem conservation. The Senate Environment and Public Works Committee asserted that all taxonomic groups should receive equal treatment under the ESA because they "form the basis of ecosystems and food chains upon which all other life depends. The ESA stated purpose is to conserve ecosystems."[43] The conference committee noted that "individual species should not be viewed in isolation, but must be viewed in terms of their relationship to the ecosystem of which they form a constituent element." The conference committee declared that "the purposes and policies of the Act are far broader than simply providing for the conservation of individual species or individual members of listed species."[44]

The ESA is designed to protect ecosystems, which are defined as "community of organisms interacting with one another and with the chemical and physical factors making up their environment."[45] Ecosystems comprise individuals that are linked genetically with past, present, and future members of the same species. Individuals are members of a species that have adjusted to different environmental conditions and are a storehouse of information about how and why the species exists as the result of physical, chemical, and biological forces. Ecosystems provide the matrix for the interaction and preservation of species. Given the vast array of interactions between species, ecosystems are greater than the sum of their parts.

All organisms rely on a healthy ecosystem, which depends upon the viability of species whose interactions regulate the system. There is a hierarchy within the ecosystem. Keystone species, which link other species to the food chain above and below themselves, include predator, prey, plants, links, and modifiers. All species are interconnected, so the removal of one keystone species can lead to population changes or severe physical disturbances.[46] Disruptions in the ecosystem cause environmental instabilities that diminish nature's ability to establish food chains, cycle nutrients, maintain air and water quality, control the climate, maintain the soil, dispose of waste, pollinate crops, and control pests and disease.[47] Robert Costanza estimated the value of ecosystem services in the range of sixteen to fifty-four trillion dollars per year. He noted:

> Because ecosystem services are not fully captured in commercial markets or adequately quantified in terms comparable with economic services and manufactured capital, they are often given too little weight in policy decisions. This neglect may compromise the sustainability of humans in the biosphere. The economies of the Earth would grind to a halt without the services of ecological life support systems, so in one sense their total value to the economy is infinite.[48]

Ecosystem maintenance requires biodiversity, which relies on a diverse gene pool.[49] The degree of complexity necessary for healthy maintenance is unknown.[50] Paul Ehrlich equates the loss of species to the loss of structural rivets on an airplane—a dozen may never be missed, but the loss of the thirteenth might spell disaster.[51] Predators, like the wolf, play an important role by balancing the ecosystem, which is one of the central purposes of the ESA.[52] The wolf provides sustenance for the entire food chain. After the wolf makes a kill, other scavengers take their share, insects clean the carcass, and birds feed on the insects. The wolf also maintains the balance between predators. The wolf limits the coyote population, which expands in its absence. This replenishes the coyote's prey, mainly rodents, for predatory birds, such as hawks, eagles, and owls. The reduction in coyote numbers helps the fox, which coexists with the wolf. The wolf keeps its prey in check, affects prey behavior, and increases the supply and diversity of plant life. This "top-down" effect, which is known as a trophic cascade, varies across ecosystems because of food web complexity, diversity, productivity, and other factors.[53] A balanced ecosystem provides goods and service beneficial to man.[54]

FWS's Analysis

The FWS failed to assess the threats to the gray wolf across significant portions of its range, which included the suitable habitat within the gray wolf's historic range. The FWS analysis was limited to the gray wolf's current range. The federal district court did not have to defer to the FWS definition regarding the significant portion of the range. The FWS definition, which was developed at a Marymount University meeting in 2000, was not part of the Proposed or Final Rule. The definition appeared for the first time during the litigation as a post-hoc rationalization.[55]

Prior to the issuance of the Final Rule, the Ninth Circuit rendered its decision in *DOW v. Norton*, which defined the significant portion of the range as that area where the species once was but is no more. Despite the Ninth Circuit decision, the FWS maintained that the significant portion of the gray wolf's range was only its current range, not its historic range. Ron Refsnider, the author of the Final Rule, recognized problems with this approach. He noted that the gray wolf was listed "across forty-eight states, yet we are recovering it in only three portions of that listed range. Even if the recovery criteria for all three recovery plans are fully met, we'll only have viable gray wolf populations in 5–10 percent of the historical range. Can we delist such a species under the Ninth Circuit's interpretation? We might be able to delist only in Minnesota, Wisconsin, the Upper Peninsula of Michigan, and parts of the Rockies."[56] The FWS could not downlist the gray wolf across its historic range because it was absent from significant portions of its historical range.

Case Law

The Secretary's definition of "significant portion of its range" was contrary to the case law. Courts principally adopted a geographic or quantitative definition and secondarily a functional definition for the significant portion of the range.[57] Following precedent provides vertical coherence in the law, which entails predictability, replicability, and doctrinal stability. This enhances the legitimacy of the court's decision. Interest groups and political decision makers rely on precedent.[58] The FWS insistence that the key factor determining the significant portion of the range was its relevance to the survival of the taxon as a whole had been consistently rejected by the federal courts.[59]

For example, the Ninth Circuit in *DOW v. Norton* dealt with the Secretary of Interior's refusal to list the flat-tailed horned lizard because sufficient public land habitat ensured the viability of the species. According to the Secretary, a species can only be protected if it "faces threats in enough key portions of its range that the entire species is in danger of extinction, or will be in the foreseeable future." The Secretary "assumes that species endangered in a significant portion of its range only if endangered everywhere." The Ninth Circuit rejected Interior's position and held "that a species can be extinct 'throughout a significant portion of its range' if there are major geographic areas in which it is no longer viable but once was."[60] The FWS was required to analyze the status of the flat-tailed horn lizard on 34 percent of its historic range, which constituted a significant portion of its range.[61]

The U.S. District Court for the District of Columbia evaluated the FWS determination of the significant portion of the lynx range in *DOW v. Norton.* The historic range of the lynx comprised four regions: Northeast, Great Lakes, Northern Rockies, and Southern Rockies. After protracted litigation, the FWS listed the lynx as a threatened species in a contiguous U.S. DPS, but determined the "Northeast, Great Lakes, and Southern Rockies do not constitute significant portions of the range of the DPS." The federal district court, relying on the Ninth Circuit rationale, rejected the FWS decision to exclude a significant portion of the lynx range as "counterintuitive and contrary to the plain meaning of ESA phrase significant portion of the range." The court held that the absence of the lynx in three of the four regions, which comprise 75 percent of its historical range, was a "noticeably or measurably large amount" of species range. The court held that "FWS's exclusive focus on one region where lynx is more prevalent, despite its historic presence in three additional regions, [is] contrary to expansive protection intended by ESA."[62]

Other Significant Areas

There were other significant areas within the historical range of the gray wolf that could support gray wolves.[63] Scientific studies demonstrated that there is suitable wolf habitat in the Pacific Northwest. Gray wolves were sited in Washington and Oregon. The Northern Cascades and Selkirk Mountains in Washington have high potential for wolf re-colonization because of their close proximity to the Canadian and NRM wolf populations and their prevalence of public lands. Other potential areas include Washington's Olympic Peninsula, the Blue Mountains of southeastern Washington and northeastern Oregon, the Siskiyou Mountains of southern Oregon and northern California, and the northern Sierra Nevada Mountains in California. Studies demonstrated that 470 wolves can live in the complex of wild lands that include the Modoc Plateau of California and Oregon and the southern Oregon Cascades. Another study showed that Oregon could support 2,200 wolves.[64]

The southern Rocky Mountains (SRM), which extend from south-central Wyoming to northern New Mexico, contain some of the best wolf habitat in the United States. This forty-one-million-acre region includes twenty-five million acres of public lands and has abundant elk and deer populations. The SRM region contains one and half times more public land than is available in the Greater Yellowstone Ecosystem, almost twice as much land as available in central Idaho, and six times the amount of public land available in the BRWRA in Arizona and New Mexico. The region contains 1.7 to 25 times more public land than other sites considered for wolf restoration. The region contains roadless areas and wilderness, which equals 70 percent of the wilderness available to wolves in the Yellowstone area. It is equivalent to the amount of wilderness available to the wolves in central Idaho and about four times the amount of wilderness available to Mexican wolves in the BRWRA.

Roadless areas are important for wolf recovery. Road development leads to negative regional and local impact on the wolves. Roads fragment habitat, which isolates wolves and their prey. This is particularly dangerous for wolves that exist in low density and have a large home range. Roads affect the behavior of prey, which avoid areas near open roads and regions with high road density. Road development increases human access, which discourages the presence of prey and leads to greater wolf mortality.[65]

The absence of wolves in the SRM region represented a significant gap in the taxon. Since the region is equidistant from the NRM and the BRWRA, the establishment of an SRM wolf population would create "a spatially segregated population of wolves that extended from the Arctic to Mexico." David Mech, a noted wolf expert, declared that "[SRM] restoration could connect the entire North American wolf population from Minnesota, Wisconsin, Michigan through Canada and Alaska, down the Rocky Mountains into Mexico. It would be difficult to overestimate the biological and conservation value of this achievement."[66]

FWS studies showed the SRM area can support 1,100 wolves. Potential gray wolf restoration sites include Vermejo Park Ranch/Carson National Forest complex, the San Juan Mountains, Rocky Mountain National Park, and the Gunnison National Recreation Area. There was public support for wolf restoration in the region. A 1994 public opinion poll revealed about 71 percent of the registered voters in Colorado supported the restoration of gray wolves to the state. The SRM were described as "the mother lode for wolves."[67]

There were additional areas in the Southwest that are amenable for wolves. These areas include the Sky Islands ecosystem in southern Arizona and New Mexico, the Apache Highlands (White Mountain and San Carlos Apache Reservations), and Big Bend National Park and Big Ben State Park in Texas.[68]

The Northeast was another major geographic area that contains suitable habitat to support wolves. The population of wolves across the Canadian border in Quebec and Ontario could serve as a source population for recovery in the Northeast. There were unconfirmed reports of wolf sightings in the Northeast that were suspected to be Canadian wolves. The FWS suggested the establishment of a separate Northeast DPS in the proposed rule. All of the peer reviewers, who commented on the issue, supported the establishment of the Northeast DPS.[69] Researchers estimated that the region can support as many as one thousand wolves.

Distinct Population Segment (DPS)

The definition of "species" in the ESA includes "any subspecies of fish or wildlife or plants, and any distinct population segment of any species of vertebrate fish or wildlife which interbreeds when mature."[70] The ESA does not define "distinct population segment." In 1996, the FWS and NMFS adopted a joint DPS policy for purposes of listing, reclassifying, and delisting vertebrate species under the ESA. A DPS is a group of vertebrate animals that is both discrete from and significant to the taxon as whole. The population is discrete if it is "markedly separate from other populations of the same taxon by physical, physiological, ecological, or behavioral factors or by an international boundary that coincides with differences in the control of exploitation, management of habitat, conservation status, or regulatory mechanisms." Complete isolation from other populations of its parent taxon is not a necessary condition of discreteness. State or other intranational boundaries can't be used in determining the discreteness of a potential DPS. The state boundary, however, can be utilized for the demarcation of the DPS when it incidentally separates two DPSs that are considered to be discrete on other grounds.

The significance of the DPS is determined by its importance to the taxon as a whole. Such indicators include, but are not limited to, "the use of any unusual or unique ecological setting; a marked difference in genetic characteristics; or occupancy of an area that, if devoid of the species, would result in a significant gap in the taxon." If the population is both discrete and significant, it can be evaluated pursuant to the five criteria of section 4(a)(1) for listing, downlisting, or delisting. The FWS and NMFS recognized that the establishment of a DPS "may allow protection and recovery of declining organisms in a more timely and less costly manner, and on a smaller scale than the more costly and extensive efforts that might be needed to recover an entire species or subspecies."[71]

The FWS in the Final Rule established the Eastern,[72] Western,[73] and Southwestern DPSs,[74] which encompassed the historic range of the gray wolf. The FWS determined that the areas were discrete because the current populations were separated from one another by large unoccupied areas. There was no evidence of wolves migrating from one DPS to another DPS. The three DPSs were significant because the loss of any DPS would cause a significant gap in the taxon. In addition, gray wolf populations in the three DPSs did not share the same genetic characteristics, so they represented different reservoirs of genetic diversity.

The federal district court found the three DPSs inconsistent with the DPS policy and the ESA. The court determined that the DPS policy was designed to encapsulate a population whose conservation status differed from other populations of the same species. The FWS inverted this purpose to downlist large geographic areas. The FWS established three DPSs, but acknowledged that only the gray wolf populations in the Western Great Lakes and NRM had recovered. Other populations in the Northeast and Pacific Northwest were "tenuous or nonexistent." Instead of isolating the distinct populations in the Western Great Lakes and NRM, the FWS extended the boundaries of these two core areas to include the entire historic range of the gray wolf. As a result, the conservation status of the population within each DPS varied from recovered to extinct.[75]

The Secretary's implementation of the DPS policy was a policy question, which involves a mix of legal and factual determinations. Generally, the court upholds the agency's policy decisions, which generally "reflect political choices—accommodation of competing interests, application of value choices, and responsiveness to the electorate—methods of decision making thought to be sharply distinguishable from the chief business of the courts, and hence owed great deference."[76] Nevertheless, the court must perform a "through, probing, and in-depth review" of agency action. The "hard look" doctrine requires the court to examine the agency action "to satisfy itself that the agency has exercised reasoned discretion with reasons that do not deviate from or ignore the ascertainable legislative intent."[77] The court does not owe any deference to the agency when there is no "rational connection between facts found and choices made." The agency relies on factors Congress did not intend for it to consider or fails to consider an important part of the problem. Rigorous judicial review "ensures that the agency's decision was a reasoned exercise of discretion and not merely a response to political pressures."[78] This is particularly important when the agency changes existing policy.[79]

Judicial skeptics oppose the hard-look doctrine, which allegedly is selectively employed to delay a project that the court disagrees with. Skeptics argue that the court is not aware of the political constraints facing the agency, which has to balance competing factors in its decision-making process. Agency decision-making is essentially a political process. Judicial oversight ossifies agency action. The agency must address marginal issues and compose a massive record to satisfy potential judicial oversight. This costly and indefinite process misallocates scarce agency resources, limits agency flexibility, delays and often precludes agency action. The court should defer to the agency's decision, which reflects the policy priorities of the current administration.[80]

Judicial proponents point out the agency has its own agenda, which includes the protection of turf, satisfying the demands of the president, Congress, interest groups, and adherence to standard operating procedures. Judicial review is necessary to ensure the agency considers the relevant factors and makes its decision based on these factors, not political concerns. The court ensures that the agency carries out the congressional mandate.[81]

The federal district court decision was correct. The FWS establishment of three DPSs, which encompassed the historic range of the gray wolf, was inconsistent with the legislative history, the DPS policy, and case law.

Legislative History

The FWS interpretation of the DPS policy was inconsistent with the legislative history, which demonstrates a narrowing of the focus of ESA protection from species, to subspecies, to discrete population segments. The Endangered Species Preservation Act of 1966 provided limited protection for certain species of fish and wildlife threatened with extinction. There was no concern with subspecies or populations. The Endangered Species Conservation Act of 1969 protected species and subspecies of wildlife threatened with worldwide extinction. Congress became concerned with the limited scope of prior statutes. The ESA of 1973 protected endangered and threatened species through all or a significant portion of their range. Species were defined as "subspecies of fish or wildlife or plants and any other group of fish or wildlife of the same species or smaller taxa in common spatial arrangement that interbreed when mature."[82]

The ESA Amendments of 1978 established the current definition for a species as "any subspecies of fish or wildlife or plants, and any distinct population segment of any species of vertebrate fish or wildlife which interbreed when mature."[83] Other definitions that excluded subspecies and populations were offered, but rejected in the floor debates.[84]

The ESA Amendments of 1979 did not change the definition of species. The legislative history is informative because the DPS listing was the subject of debate. The General Accounting Office (GAO) suggested that the DPS listing should be terminated because it could "result in the listing of squirrels in a specific city park, even though there is an abundance of squirrels in other parks in the same city, or elsewhere in the country." The Senate rejected the proposal.[85] The definition was not changed in the ESA Amendments of 1982 and 1988.[86]

DPS Policy

The FWS action was inconsistent with its own policy. The DPS policy focuses on discrete population segments, which are "markedly separate . . . as consequence of physical, physiological, ecological, or behavioral factors [or] delimited by international governmental boundaries."[87] The DPS must be based on best available scientific evidence, which includes dispersal distances and other limiting factors, such as significant mountain ranges, bodies of water, deserts, or major urban areas. The use of state boundaries to establish the DPS is expressly prohibited. The three DPSs were not based on science. The FWS just aggregated all of the states in the gray wolf's historic range and divided them into three DPSs. Each DPS was too large and encompassed more territory than the gray wolves in the cores areas would ever be able to reach or inhabit. The DPS boundaries were based on politics, not biology. The FWS believed that this was "the best and quickest way to get the policy and legal framework greased for wolf delisting."[88]

In the Western DPS, the core wolf populations in three states—Montana, Wyoming, and Idaho—were on the way to recovery. Six other states in the Western DPS had few, if any, wolves. The FWS utilized the success in three core states to downlist the gray wolf in the other six states where its endangered status had not changed. FWS experts noted that the Western DPS was too large. The boundaries of the Western DPS were not based on natural limitations or dispersal distances, which are generally 250 miles. FWS Western Regional Coordinator Ed Bangs acknowledged the massive size of the Western DPS when he declared there was no way that any gray wolf in the Western DPS was going below I-70. Doug Smith, the leading wolf biologist for Yellowstone National Park, criticized the FWS for overstating the amount of wolf dispersal among three NRM wolf populations.[89]

The FWS argued that all the areas in the gray wolf's historic range must be included in the three DPSs. Neither the ESA nor the implementing regulations supported the FWS position. The ESA contemplates a national species listing and a DPS for the unique treatment of smaller populations of gray wolves.[90] The DPS can be separated from the historic range of the species for unique treatment, but it is not a vehicle for downlisting the entire species.

Case Law

Federal courts did not support the FWS position. The Ninth Circuit in *DOW v. Norton* (flat-tailed horned lizard) recognized that the ESA provided different levels of protection for different populations of the same species, such as the alligator, grizzly bear, marbled murrelet, desert big horn sheep, Steller sea lions, Audubon crested caracara, and piping plover.[91]

The U.S. District Court for the District of Oregon in *Friends of the Swan (FS) v. FWS* rejected the FWS attempt to utilize the DPS policy as the means for avoiding ESA requirements. FS petitioned to have the bull trout listed as an endangered species. Initially, the FWS determined that a national listing was warranted, but later changed its position. The FWS created five DPSs and entered into a Conservation Agreement, so the bull trout was not granted a national listing. The federal district court held that the FWS failure to list the bull trout and explain its adoption of five DPSs, which decreased the protection of the species, was arbitrary and capricious. The court noted that the DPS "is a proactive measure to prevent listing over larger range—not a tactic for subdividing a larger population that FWS already determined warrants listing through its entire range."[92]

The Oregon federal district court in *DOW v. Interior* recognized that the establishment of three DPSs for the gray wolf was similar to that of the bull trout. According to the court, the three DPSs "decreased protection to species, even though the population status of wolf was not improved outside core areas." The establishment of three gray wolf DPSs, like those for the bull trout, "appears to be a tactic to downlisting areas the FWS has already determined warrants listing, despite unabated threats and low to non-existent populations outside core areas."[93]

Section 4(a): Five Factor Analysis

Section 4(a) of the ESA provides for the listing and delisting of endangered and threatened species based on the following five factors: "A) the present or threatened destruction, modification, or curtailment of its habitat or range; B) overutilization for commercial, recreational, scientific, or educational purposes; C) disease or predation; D) the inadequacy of existing regulatory mechanisms; or E) other natural or manmade factors affecting its continued existence."[94] Interior asserted that the reclassification of the gray wolf in the Eastern and Western DPSs from endangered to threatened species status was based on the gray wolves' progress under their recovery plans and the FWS evaluation of the five-factor threat analysis.

The federal district court, rejecting Interior's contention, determined that the downlisting of the gray wolf in the Eastern and Western DPSs was based solely on success in the two core regions. The FWS by limiting its analysis to the gray wolf's current range and failing to conduct the five-factor analysis over much of the gray wolf's historic range violated the ESA.[95]

The FWS only analyzed the five factors with respect to core populations that were present in six states: Minnesota, Wisconsin, Michigan, Montana, Idaho, and Wyoming. Thirty states in the Eastern and Western DPSs did not have viable wolf populations. The FWS should have analyzed the five factors across a significant portion of the gray wolf's historic range, rather than its current range. There was much habitat suitable for viable wolf populations outside of the core six states where the gray wolf still faced danger. The change in status from endangered to threatened decreased the protection afforded to the gray wolf.

The Final Rule retained threatened species status in Minnesota and downlisted the gray wolf in Michigan and Wisconsin to a threatened species. Gray wolves in Montana were downlisted to a threatened species, while the gray wolves in the experimental population regions in Wyoming and Idaho retained their threatened species status. The major problem posed by the Final Rule was the downlisting of the gray wolf beyond the two core areas of recovery. The FWS should have considered the creation of two smaller DPSs encompassing the Western Great Lakes and NRM, then downlisted the gray wolf to a threatened species in the two smaller DPSs. The FWS analysis, which was based exclusively on the Western Great Lakes and NRM wolf populations, demonstrated that the gray wolves could be downlisted to a threatened species pursuant to section 4(a) of the ESA. The FWS was too aggressive in downlisting the gray wolf across a significant portion of its historic range.

Environmental groups applauded the decision. The Center for Biodiversity (CBD) declared, "Interior Secretary Norton tried to gerrymander the entire contiguous 48 states so that wolves in a few areas would make up for the absence of wolves in much larger regions. Now instead of drawing lines on a map based on political considerations, any future lines must be based on science."[96]

NATIONAL WILDLIFE FEDERATION V. NORTON

The FWS abandoned the Northeast DPS because the existence and identity of the wolf in the region were unknown. There was also a lack of state support for the wolf in the region. The FWS simply aggregated the northeast region into the Eastern DPS.[97] Environmental groups criticized the proposal. The NWF declared that "the howl of the wolf has been missing too long from the Northern forests and our national wolf recovery efforts cannot be declared complete while that gap remains."[98] Former FWS official, Paul Nickerson, stated "to leave out the whole Northeast and say they're recovered, I think we're kind of kidding ourselves, from a biological basis."[99] The FWS responded that, "our job is to keep animals from going extinct. . . . Having wolves in the Northeast might be desirable, but it's not the purpose of ESA to get more wolves in more places."[100]

The National Wildlife Federation (NWF), which did not join the DOW litigation, and four other plaintiffs[101] filed suit in the U.S. District Court for the District of Vermont, challenging the FWS abandonment of wolf recovery efforts in the Northeast. The Vermont federal district court correctly rejected the FWS decision on several grounds: First, the court held that the Final Rule must be the logical outgrowth of the Proposed Rule; otherwise, "affected parties will be deprived of notice and opportunity to respond to the proposal." The FWS abandonment of the Northeast DPS in the Final Rule deviated too much from the Proposed Rule. Even the FWS acknowledged that the Final Rule constituted a major departure. Ron Refsnider, the author of the Final Rule, proposed publishing "a 6-month extension for the gray wolf proposal in July [2001], based on internal FWS disagreement. . . . The extension notice would open a comment period and ask for information on 8 or so of the issues that would help with [FWS's] decision on the NE DPS." Nevertheless, the FWS proceeded without additional comment.[102]

Second, the court held that the FWS violated the DPS policy and the ESA. In the Proposed Rule, the FWS determined that the four proposed DPSs were discrete because "each is being repopulated by wolves of distinct morphological character which may represent different gray wolf subspecies." In the Final Rule, the FWS declared that the northeast wolves could be a different subspecies from the midwest wolves. Nevertheless, the FWS combined the two subspecies into a single DPS, which was based on geography, not biology. This geographic approach, which used "intranational boundaries as a basis for recognizing discrete entities for delisting," was rejected by the FWS in the 1996 DPS policy.[103]

Third, the court held that the designation of the Eastern DPS violated the DPS policy and the ESA. The court rejected the FWS assertion that a "non-DPS remnant" could not remain outside the DPS. The Secretary could establish a "non-DPS remnant" designation, particularly when the remnant area was already listed within the historic range of the endangered species. Interior could maintain a national listing and establish a DPS where necessary for management flexibility. The FWS could not simply "lump[s] together" the core population with low to non-existent population outside the core area and downlist or delist the entire area. The FWS implementation of the DPS policy was "inconsistent with the statute under which the regulation was promulgated."[104]

Finally, the court held that the Secretary did not analyze the five downlisting factors across a significant portion of the gray wolf's range. The FWS determined that the existence of the western Great Lakes wolf population rendered the remainder of the Eastern DPS insignificant, even though "extensive and significant gaps" in range would be created without the Northeast DPS. The Final Rule rendered all areas outside the core area irrelevant. This contradicted the meaning of "significant portion of the range" set forth by the Ninth Circuit dealing with the flat-tailed horned lizard and the federal district court dealing with the lynx.[105] The NWF declared the ruling a "major victory for wolves and for all people who care so much about preserving America's natural heritage."[106] The FWS did not appeal the decision.

Judicial skeptics would criticize the decision because it focused on procedural compliance, rather than substantive criteria. Skeptics assert that the courts overemphasizes formal procedures at the expense of scientific analysis. The focus on legalistic concerns detracts from the development of sound policy. Furthermore, judicial decisions divert scarce resources and disrupt the agency's agenda.[107]

POST-LITIGATION DEVELOPMENTS

Regulatory Changes

There were regulatory changes following the litigation. Despite the failure of early efforts to develop a regional plan among NRM states, Interior approved Idaho and Montana state management plans in 2004. Secretary Norton declared, "Idaho and Montana have developed the appropriate balance in their wolf management plans between the necessary protections for the wolves and the management tools critical to protect children, property, pets and livestock."[108]

In January 2005, Interior granted Montana, Idaho, and Indian tribes with approved wolf management plans expanded authority over the nonessential experimental populations of wolves within their boundaries.[109] The new rule permitted taking, without authorization, wolves that were attacking livestock, guardian animals, and dogs on private land; permittees attacking the aforementioned on public land grazing allotments without authorization; and causing harm to wildlife according to state and tribal officials. The new rule also allowed states and tribes with wolf management plans to enter into cooperative agreements for the management of experimental populations on public land. Wyoming was not granted expanded authority because its management plan had not been approved.[110]

Threatened and Endangered Species Recovery Act of 2005

Judicial decisions are "political resources" that are "best viewed as the beginning of a political process."[111] Congress is well aware of judicial decisions regarding statutory interpretations and their implications.[112] Judicial decisions can stimulate congressional action. Positive political theory asserts that government institutions behave as rational actors and attempt to have their policy preferences prevail.[113]

The ESA was due for reauthorization. The Bush administration's hostility to the ESA was evidenced by few listings, no critical habitat designations, and no funding requests.[114] Congressmen in the NRM region hoped that the wolf litigation would herald a call to circumscribe the ESA. Representative Mike Simpson (R. Id.) stated that no interest "is well served by a process that allows the courts to manage our natural resources. This decision provides yet another glaring example of why we must work harder than ever to reform ESA. The proper influence of sound science, commonsense, and fairness needs to be restored to its proper role in our nation's public lands and resource management laws." Representative Butch Otter (R. Id.) noted, "the ESA is driven by lawsuits and advocacy science. Too many decisions that influence the lives and livelihoods of most of us in Idaho are being made in Washington, D.C. and—even worse—in courtrooms. We need to change the law to ensure that only the best peer-reviewed science is used as the basis for public policy."[115]

Following the litigation, the House passed the Threatened and Endangered Species Recovery Act of 2005. Environmental groups criticized the bill as "the dream of every irresponsible developer out there."[116] Nevertheless, the bill did not expressly change any of the statutory provisions involved in the litigation. The "significant portion of the range" language in the definition of endangered and threatened species was not altered. The Secretary was instructed to utilize the DPS designation "only sparingly." Listing, downlisting, and delisting decisions continued to be based on the five factors enumerated in section 4(a) of the ESA.[117] The failure of the Republican House to alter any of the relevant statutory provisions represented its implicit agreement with the federal district court's interpretation of the ESA in the DOW and NWF cases. The Supreme Court noted that congressional failure to address a controversial judicial interpretation when it was considering the reenactment of the statute "is itself evidence that Congress affirmatively intended to preserve the interpretation."[118]

CONCLUSION

The Bush administration established three DPSs and downlisted the gray wolf to a threatened species in a significant portion of its historic range in the Eastern and Western DPSs. The gray wolf retained endangered species status in the Southwest DPS. The gray wolf, however, had only recovered in 4 percent of its historic range. The remaining 96 percent of its historic range was inhabited by phantom wolves. Environmental groups brought suit challenging Interior's action in this public law litigation.

The U.S. District Court for the District of Oregon in *DOW v. Secretary of Interior* correctly invalidated Interior's dysfunctional downlisting of the gray wolf. The court rejected Interior's interpretation of the legal meaning of "significant portion of its range," which was not consistent with the text, intent, and purposes of the ESA. The court took a hard look and invalidated Interior's implementation of its own DPS policy, which provides different populations of the same species different levels of protection in different portions of their historic range. The court determined that Interior failed to assess the five factors of section 4(a) across significant portions of the gray wolf's historic range. Interior only assessed the five factors across the current range of the gray wolf.

The U.S. District Court for the District of Vermont in *NWF v. Secretary of Interior* appropriately found the FWS amalgamation of the Western Great

Lake and Eastern DPSs violated the notice and comment requirements and the DPS policy and failed to assess the ESA downlisting criteria across a significant portion of the gray wolf's range. Similar holdings by the Oregon and Vermont federal district courts precluded the balkanization of national policy feared by judicial skeptics.

Wolf recovery was promoted by active judicial involvement. Interior simply downlisted phantom wolves, when it should have been creating conditions for the return of the gray wolf to significant portions of its historic range. Gray wolves were on the road to recovery in the two core areas, but still needed the protection of threatened species status. Gray wolves were absent from significant portions of their historic range, creating significant gaps in the taxon that would jeopardize recovery. Gray wolves dispersing from the core areas into other sectors of their historic range required the full ESA protection. This would assure their recovery and restoration as vital components of the ecosystems across their historic range. Furthermore, the abandonment of recovery efforts was premature. Interior should have heeded the warning of Professor Holly Doremus:

> Delisting is an aspirational goal, the achievement of which will require substantial regulatory and societal changes, rather than a short term expectation. The primary purpose of the ESA is not delisting; rather it is the protection of species against ill-considered human activity while society works toward the kind of fundamental mechanisms of regulating economic development that might support widespread delisting. The ESA can encourage progress towards such changes, both by making society aware of the shortcomings of its current regulatory efforts and by providing an incentive for improvements in other regulation, but it serves its purpose if it simply provides a safety net against extinction until those changes arrive.[119]

Edward O. Wilson warned that the "loss of genetic and species diversity by the destruction of natural habitats . . . is the folly our descendants are least likely to forgive us."[120] The ESA is explicitly concerned with protection of species and the restoration of ecosystems on which they depend. The gray wolf helps to preserve biodiversity and maintain ecosystem balance by keeping prey in check; improving their genetic stock; stopping environmental dislocations; promoting the survival of other species; and allowing plant communities to flourish. Interior's obligation under the ESA is to ensure that gray wolves, not their phantoms, stalk the land. The howl of the wolf in the night signals that all is well for man.

NOTES

A version of this chapter originally appeared as an article: *"Defenders of Wildlife v. Secretary of Interior*: Dysfunctional Downlisting Defeated," 34 *Boston College Environmental Affairs Law Review* 37 (2007).

1. 354 F. Supp. 2d 1156 (D. Or. 2005).
2. 386 F. Supp. 2d 553 (D. Vt. 2005).
3. "Clinton Betrayed West," *USA Today*, January 16, 2001. "Battle over West's Land May Take New Tack," *Christian Science Monitor*, January 2, 2001. "Libertarian Belle," *Village Voice*, February 6, 2001. "Bush Choosing Industry Insiders to Fill Environmental Positions," *New York Times*, May 12, 2001.
4. "Environmental Groups: Free Market Enviros Gaining Ground," *Greenwire*, June 4, 2001.
5. "Idaho Officials Applaud Report of Norton's Grizzly Intentions," AP State & Local Wire, April 25, 2001. "Grizzlies: Westerners Polarized on Reintroduction," *Greenwire*, June 22, 2001.
6. Edward A. Fitzgerald, "Lobo Returns from Limbo: *New Mexico Cattlegrowers Assoc. v. U.S. FWS*," 46 *Natural Resources Journal* 9 (2006).
7. 65 *Federal Register* 43450 (July 13, 2000).
8. 68 *Federal Register* 15804 (April 1, 2003).
9. 68 *Federal Register* 15876 (April 1, 2003). 69 *Federal Register* 43664 (July 21, 2004).
10. "Norton Announces Proposal to Remove Eastern Population of Gray Wolves From Endangered Species List," FWS Press Release, July 16, 2004.
11. 16 U.S.C. 1540 (g).
12. 16 U.S.C. 1532(6).
13. 16 U.S.C. 1532(20).
14. 68 *Federal Register* 15825.
15. 354 F. Supp. 2d, 1167–68.
16. 467 U.S. 837, 842–45 (1984).
17. Kenneth W. Starr, "Judicial Review in the Post-Chevron Era," 3 *Yale Journal on Regulation* 283, 307–9 (1986).
18. Cynthia Farina, "Statutory Interpretation and the Balance of Power in the Administrative State," 89 *Columbia Law Review* 452 (1989).
19. William Landes and Richard Posner, "The Independent Judiciary in an Interest-Group Perspective," 18 *Journal Law & Economics* 875, 878–85 (1975).
20. Thomas W. Merrill, "Textualism and the Future of the Chevron Doctrine," 72 *Washington University Law Quarterly* 351, 355–63 (1994). Abner J. Mikva & Eric Lane, "The Muzak of Justice Scalia's Revolutionary Call to Read Unclear Statutes Narrowly," 53 *Southern Methodist University Law Review* 11, 123, (2000). Charles Tiefer, "The Reconceptualization of Legislative History in the Supreme Court," 2000 *Wisconsin Law Review* 205, 212–21.
21. *DOW v. Norton*, 258 F.3d 1136, 1141 (9th Cir. 2001). Linda C. Maranzana, "*Defenders of the Wildlife v. Norton*: A Closer Look at the 'Significant Portion of Its Range' Concept," 29 *Ecology Law Quarterly* 263, 265 (2002). Ryan Jennes, "*Defenders of Wildlife v. Norton*: 'Extinction' Under the ESA Construed Favorably to Conservation Efforts," 15 *Tulane Environmental Law Journal* 143 (2001).
22. 258 F.3d, 1141–42.
23. Max Radin, "Statutory Interpretation," 43 *Harvard Law Review* 863 (1930), Reed Dickerson, *The Interpretation and Application of Statutes* (Little Brown, 1975), 68–69. William N. Eskridge, "The New Textualism," 37 *UCLA Law Review* 621, 643–50 (1990).
24. Eskridge, "New Textualism," 630. Robert Weisberg, "The Calbresian Judicial Artist: Statutes and the New Legal Process," 35 *Stanford Law Review* 213, 246–47 (1983). Martin H. Redish & Theodore T. Chung, "Democratic Theory and the Legislative Process: Mourning the Death of Originalism in Statutory Interpretation," 68 *Tulane Law Review* 803, 813–15 (1994).
25. Abner Mikva and Eric Land, *An Introduction to Statutory Interpretation and the Legislative Process* (Aspen Law, 1997), 27–41.

26. Patricia Wald, "The Sizzling Sleeper: the Use of Legislative History in Construing Statutes in the 1988–89 Term of the U.S. Supreme Court," 39 *American University Law Review* 277, 306–7 (1990).
27. H.R. Rep. No. 412, 93d Cong., 1st Sess. (1973).
28. 258 F. 3d, 1144–45.
29. Senate, Committee on Environment and Public Works, A Legislative History of the ESA of 1973, as Amended in 1976, 1977, 1978, and 1980, 97th Cong., 2d Sess. 1126–1130 (1982) [hereinafter Legislative History].
30. H.R. Rep. No. 1804, 95th Cong., 2d Sess. (1978), cited in Legislative History, 1192.
31. *INS v. Cardozo-Fonseca*, 480 U.S. 421, 442–443 (1987). William N. Eskridge, "Interpreting Legislative Inaction," 87 *Michigan Law Review* 67, 84–89 (1988).
32. Legislative History, 742, 946–48.
33. Legislative History, 1205.
34. 16 U.S.C. 1539.
35. Henry M. Hart and Albert M. Sacks, *The Legal Process* (Foundation Press, 1994), 1124, 1374–80.
36. Michael S. Greve, *The Demise of Environmentalism in American Law* (American Enterprise Institute, 1996), 8.
37. Vincent Wellman, "Dworkin and the Legal Process Tradition," 29 *Arizona Law Review* 413, 463 (1987).
38. Jonathan Macey, "Promoting Public-Regarding Legislation Through Statutory Interpretation, An Interest-Group Model," 86 *Columbia Law Review* 223, 261–67 (1990).
39. 16 U.S.C. 1531(b), (c).
40. S. Rep. No. 307, 93d Cong., 1st Sess. 2 (1973). *TVA v. Hill*, 437 U.S. 179.
41. H.R. Rep. No. 412, 93d Cong., 1st Sess. 6 (1973).
42. Legislative History, 144–45.
43. Sen. Rep. No. 418, 97th Cong., 2d Sess. 14 (1982).
44. H.R. Rep. 835, 97th Cong., 2d Sess. 30 (1982). See also, Daniel J. Rohlf, "Six Biological Reasons Why the ESA Doesn't Work—And What to Do About It," 5 *Conservation Biology* 273, 275 (1991).
45. Jacqueline Lesley Brown, "Preserving Species: The Endangered Species Act versus Ecosystem Management Regime," 12 *Journal Environmental Law & Litigation* 151, 228–29 (1997).
46. Marty Bergoffen, *ESA Reauthorization: A Biocentric Approach* (American Bar Association, 1995), 5–15. John C. Nagle, "Playing Noah," 82 *Minnesota Law Review* 1171, 1210 (1998).
47. Paul Ehrlich & Anne Ehrlich, *Extinction: The Causes and Consequences of the Disappearance of Species* (Random House, 1981), 86–95. Patrick Parenteau, "Rearranging the Deck Chairs: Endangered Species Act Reforms in the Era of Mass Extinctions," 22 *William & Mary Environmental Law & Policy Review* 227, 236–44 (1998).
48. Robert Costanza et al., "The Value of the World's Ecosystem Services and Natural Capital," 387 *Nature* 253, 259 (1987).
49. Robert S. Steneck, "An Ecological Context for the Role of Large Carnivores in Conserving Biodiversity," in Justina C. Ray, Kent H. Redford, Robert S. Stenneck, Joel Berger (eds.), *Large Carnivores and the Conservation of Biodiversity* (Island Press, 2005), 8, 13.
50. Keith Saxe, "Regulated Taking of Threatened Species Under the Endangered Species Act," 39 *Hastings Law Journa*l 399, 407–8 (1988).
51. Ehrlich and Ehrlich, xii–xiii.
52. Oliver A. Houck, "Why Do We Protect Endangered Species," 80 *Iowa Law Review* 297, 301 (1995). William S. Boyd, "Federal Protection of Endangered Wildlife Species," 22 *Stanford Law Review* 1289, 1291 n.12 (1970).
53. Craig R. Enochs, "Gone Today, Here Tomorrow: Policies and Issues Surrounding Wildlife Reintroduction," 4 *West-Northwest Journal of Environmental Law & Policy* 91, 99 (1997). Mark Hebblewhite et al., "Human Activity Mediates a Trophic Cascade Caused By Wolves," 86 *Ecology* 2135 (2005). John Terborgh et al, "The Role of Top Carnivores in Regulating

Terrestrial Ecosystems," in Michael E. Soule and John Terborgh (eds.), *Continental Conservation: Scientific Foundation of Regional Reserve Networks* (Island Press, 1999), 39–65.

54. Mark A. Urbanski, "Chemical Prospecting, Biodiversity Conservation, and the Importance of International Protection of Intellectual Property Rights in Biological Materials," 2 *Buffalo Journal International Law* 131, 134–35 (1995). Eric Christensen, "Genetic Ark: A Proposal to Preserve Genetic Diversity for Future Generations," 40 *Stanford Law Review* 279, 285–88 (1987). George Cameron Coggins & Anne Fleishel Harris, "The Greening of American Law?" 27 *Natural Resources Journal* 247, 253–55 (1987). Douglas O. Heiken, "The Pacific Yew and Taxol," 7 *Journal Environmental Law & Litigation* 175, 185–86 (1992).

55. 258 F.3d, 1145 n.11.

56. Plaintiffs' Response Memorandum, *DOW v. Interior*, 10–11.

57. Maranzana, 273.

58. K. M. Gebbia-Pinetti, "Statutory Interpretation: Democratic Legitimacy and Legal System Values," 21 *Seton Hall Legislation Journa*l 233, 243–47 (1997). Richard J. Pierce, "Reconciling Chevron and Stare Decisis," 85 *Georgetown Law Journal* 2225, 2237–48 (1997).

59. *Southwest Center for Biological Diversity v. Norton,* Civil Act No. 98-934 (RMU/JMF) (D.D.C. 2002). *Environmental Protection Information Center (EPIC) v. NMFS,* No. C-02-5401 EDL (D.D.C. 2004)

60. 258 F.3d, 1145.

61. Other cases cited that addressed whether the loss of a percentage of habitat constituted a significant portion of the species range included *Federation of Fly Fishers v. Daley*, cited 131 F. Supp. 2d 1158 (D. N.D. Cal. 2000), and *ONRC v. Daley*, cited 6 F. Supp. 2d 1139 (D. Ok. 1998).

62. *DOW v. Norton*, 239 F. Supp.2d, 9, 14–19 (D.D.C. 2002).

63. 354 F. Supp. 2d, 1166–69.

64. Defenders of Wildlife, *State of Wolf 2004*, 7.

65. Letter from Earthjustice to Ed Bangs, Comments on the Proposal to Designate the Gray Wolf Northern Rocky Mountain DPS and to Remove this DPS from the Federal List of Endangered and Threatened Wildlife (May 8, 2007), 11–12.

66. Michael K. Phillips, Rob Edward, and Tina Arapkiles, "Restoration of the Gray Wolf to the Southern Rocky Mountains: Anatomy of a Campaign to Resolve a Conservation Issue," in Nina Fascione, Aimee Delach, and Martin E. Smith (eds.), *People and Predators: From Conflict to Coexistence* (Island Press, 2004), 240, 243–246.

67. Michael Robinson, Dave Parsons, and Rob Edward, "South From Yellowstone, What Remains to Be Done," *International Wolf* (Spring 2006) 8, 9.

68. Defenders of Wildlife, *State of Wolf 2004*, 9–10.

69. 68 *Federal Register* 15820.

70. 16 U.S.C. 1532.

71. 61 *Federal Register* 4722, 4725 (February 7, 1996). Katherin M. Hausrath, "The Designation of 'Distinct Population Segments' Under the ESA In Light of *National Association of Homebuilders v. Norton*," 80 *Chicago Kent Law Review* 449, 456–65 (2005).

72. The Eastern DPS consisted of wolves in twenty-one states: North Dakota, South Dakota, Nebraska, Kansas, Minnesota, Iowa, Missouri, Wisconsin, Illinois, Michigan, Indiana, Ohio, Pennsylvania, New Jersey, New York, Connecticut, Rhode Island, Massachusetts, Vermont, New Hampshire, and Maine. In 1978, prior to the DPS policy, the FWS established a DPS for the Minnesota wolf population. 68 *Federal Register* 15818–20.

73. The Western DPS included California, Idaho, Montana, Nevada, Oregon, Washington, Wyoming, Utah north of Highway 50, and Colorado north of Highway 70. Ibid.

74. The Southwest DPS consisted of Arizona, New Mexico, Utah south of Highway 50, and Colorado south of Highway 70. 68 *Federal Register* 15818–20.

75. 354 F. Supp. 2d, 1170.

76. Christopher F. Edley, *Administrative Law, Rethinking Judicial Control of Bureaucracy* (Yale University, 1990), 33–34.

77. *Greater Boston Television Corp. v. FCC,* 444 F.2d 841, 850–51 (D.C. Cir. 1970). *National Ass'n of Home Builders v. Norton,* 340 F.3d 835, 841(9th Cir. 2003).

78. Cass R. Sunstein, "Deregulation and the Hard-Look Doctrine," 1983 *Supreme Court Review* 177, 181–184. William H. Rogers, "A Hard-Look at Vermont Yankee: Environmental Law Under Close Scrutiny," 67 *Georgetown Law Journal* 699, 704–706 (1979).
79. *Motor Vehicle Mfrs. Ass'n v. State Farm Mutual Auto Ins. Co.*, 463 U.S. 29, 43 (1989).
80. Thomas O. McGarity, "Some Thoughts on the 'Deossifying' the Rulemaking Process," 41 *Duke Law Journal* 1385 (1992). Mark Seidenfeld, "Demystifying Deossification: Rethinking Recent Proposals to Modify Judicial Review of Notice and Comment Rulemaking," 75 *Texas Law Review* 483, 485–87 (1997).
81. Thomas O. Sargentich, "The Critique of Active Judicial Review of Administrative Agencies: A Reevaluation," 49 *Administrative Law Review* 599, 605–10 (1997).
82. H.R. Rep. No. 93-740, 93d Cong., 1st Sess. (1973), reprinted Legislative History, 426, 429.
83. H.R. Rep. No. 1804, 95th Cong., 2d Sess. (1978), reprinted Legislative History, 1192, 1193.
84. Legislative History, 881–884, 1080–1107.
85. Legislative History, 1396–97.
86. Karl Gleaves, Michele Kuruc, Patricia Montanio, "The Meaning of "Species" Under the ESA," 13 *Public Law Review* 25, 27–36 (1992).
87. 61 *Federal Register* 4725.
88. Plaintiffs Memorandum in Support of Summary Judgment, *DOW v. Interior*, 44–45.
89. Plaintiffs Memorandum in Support of Summary Judgment, *DOW v. Interior*, 37.
90. *National Association of Homebuilders,* 340 F.3d, 342.
91. *DOW v. Norton*, 258 F.3d, 1144–1145.
92. *Friends of Swan v. U.S. FWS*, 12 F. Supp. 2d 1121, 1133 (D. Or. 1997).
93. 354 F. Supp. 2d, 1171.
94. 16 U.S.C. 1533. *Fund for Animals v. Babbitt*, 903 F. Supp. 96, 104–5 (D.D.C. 1995).
95. 354 F. Supp. 2d, 1164–66, 1172–74.
96. "Judge: Government Wrong to Downgrade Wolf from Endangered to Threatened," AP State & Local Wire, February 1, 2005.
97. 68 *Federal Register* 15835–36.
98. "NWF Files Law Suit over Wolf Plan," NWF Press Release, December 17, 2003.
99. "Court: Federal Wolf Plan Not Based on Science," *Union Leader*, February 6, 2005.
100. "FWS Faces Lawsuit for Downlisting Western Population to Threatened," *Land Letter*, October 9, 2003.
101. The other plaintiffs were the Maine Wolf Coalition, Maine Audubon Society, Vermont Natural Resources Council, and Environment Advocates of New York.
102. 386 F. Supp. 2d, 561–63.
103. 386 F. Supp. 2d, 562–64.
104. 386 F. Supp. 2d, 564–65.
105. 386 F. Supp. 2d, 565–67.
106. "Judge Orders Feds to Promote Wolf Restoration in Northeast," AP State & Local Wire, August 20, 2005.
107. Frank B. Cross, "Pragmatic Pathologies of Judicial Review of Administrative Rulemaking," 78 *North Carolina Law Review* 1013, 1046–48 (2000).
108. "Interior Proposes Broader Gray Wolf Management," *States News Service*, March 3, 2004.
109. Martin Nie, "State Wildlife Governance and Carnivore Conservation," in Nina Fascione, Aimee Delach, and Martin E. Smith (eds.), *People and Predators: From Conflict to Coexistence* (Island Press, 2005), 197, 210–215.
110. 70 *Federal Register* 1286 (January 6, 2005). See also U.S. FWS, "Rocky Mountain Wolf Recovery 2004 Annual Report," 37–40.
111. Stuart Shiengold, *The Politics of Rights: Lawyers, Public Policy and Political Change* (Yale University, 1974), 85.
112. James L. Walker & Michael E. Solomine, "The Next Word: Congressional Response to Supreme Court Statutory Decisions," 65 *Temple Law Review* 425 (1992).

113. Daniel A. Farber & Phillip P. Frickey, "Forward: Positive Political Theory in the Nineties," 80 *Georgetown Law Journal* 457, 475 (1992).

114. "Pushed to the Brink: ESA Not a Cure-All, Critics Say," *Contra Costa Times*, December 28, 2003. "Species Slip Away," *Tampa Tribune*, December 21, 2003.

115. "Reps. Simpson, Otter Call Court Rulings More Evidence of Need for ESA Reform," *US Fed News*, February 2, 2005.

116. "House Guts Endangered Species Act," DOW Press Release. September 29, 2005.

117. "Analysis of Richard Pombo's Threatened and Endangered Species Recovery Act of 2005," DOW Press Release, October 12, 2005. Nancy Kubasek, "Proposed Changes to ESA In the Spotlight Again," 34 *Real Estate Law Journal* 235, 241–43 (2005).

118. *Merrill Lynch, Pierce, Fenner & Smith v. Curran,* 456 U.S. 353, 381–82 (1982). Eskridge, "Legislative Inaction," 71–84, 108–122.

119. Holly Doremus, "Delisting Endangered Species: An Aspirational Goal, Not a Realistic Expectation," 30 *Environmental Law Reporter* 10435 (2000).

120. Janice Goldman-Carter, "Federal Conservation of Threatened Species: By Administrative Discretion or By Legislative Standard?" 11 *Boston College Environmental Affairs Law Review* 63, 94–95 (1983).

Chapter Five

The Northern Rocky Mountain Distinct Population Segment

Defenders of Wildlife v. Hall

Following the Oregon and Vermont federal court decisions, Interior approved Wyoming's wolf management plan, which only protected wolves in the northwest corner of the state. Interior then created a smaller Northern Rocky Mountain (NRM) Distinct Population Segment (DPS) and delisted the wolves therein. Environmental groups brought suit. The U.S. District Court for the District of Montana in *Defenders of Wildlife v. Hall*[1] issued a preliminary injunction halting this effort. The court found that there was not yet a functioning metapopulation in the NRM DPS, which the U.S. Fish and Wildlife Service (FWS) declared was a necessary pre-condition for delisting. Furthermore, Interior should not have approved Wyoming's wolf management plan because it manifested the same problems as the earlier Wyoming plan, which had been rejected in 2004. Wyoming enacted a new management plan, but Interior rejected the amended plan in 2009. This chapter examines the Bush administration's delisting effort, analyzes the 2008 litigation, and reviews subsequent events.

BUSH ADMINISTRATION DELISTING

The FWS announced in February 2006 that it was considering establishing a NRM DPS and delisting that wolf population. The proposal, however, was contingent on the approval of Wyoming's wolf management plan. FWS Director Dale Hall stated that "potential delisting cannot be finished until Wyoming's wolf management plan has been approved. We are hopeful that Wyoming will be able to develop a state law and management plan which meets the service criteria for approval."[2] Environmental groups criticized the proposal, arguing that "the Bush administration is planning to turn back the clock on wolf recovery by prematurely passing management responsibility to states such as Idaho that has expressed a clear intention of immediately exterminating all of the wolves in the state."[3]

After the proposal was announced, Idaho governor Dirk Kempthorne became Secretary of Interior. President Bush stated that Kempthorne would "work closely with state and local leaders to ensure wise stewardship of our resources." Environmental groups criticized the nomination. The Sierra Club declared, "President Bush nominated someone who has consistently opposed protecting public health and public lands." The Center for Biodiversity (CBD) stated, "the ESA has been in Kempthorne's cross hairs for a long time. I would expect him to even more aggressively undermine endangered species protections than Gale Norton." Earthjustice announced that "Kempthorne was chosen to keep pushing the same Bush agenda we know so well."[4] At his confirmation hearings, Governor Kempthorne complained that the ESA was hampered by litigation and promised to resolve the impasse with Wyoming over wolf management.

The FWS, acting as a rational agency seeking to fulfill the goals of the new Secretary, stopped demanding that Wyoming establish a statewide trophy game designation. Instead, Wyoming only had to establish a trophy game designation for wolves in the northwest corner of the state. The FWS in January 2007 reiterated its intent to create and delist the wolves in the NRM DPS. The FWS declared that "the management of the wolf population is best accomplished by the states. . . . We don't have a long history of delisting species, and we've been learning as we go."[5]

Environmental groups were divided on the proposal. The National Wildlife Federation (NWF) praised the decision "as a true example of the ESA potential." The Defenders of Wildlife (DOW) criticized the proposal for "hand[ing] wolf management over to at least two states whose main goal seems to be to eradicate wolves. It's like snatching defeat from the jaws of victory." Further, 230 scientists wrote to Interior, asserting that the FWS was not employing science objectively and questioning the administration's commitment to conservation.[6]

Montana and Idaho, recognizing Wyoming's intransigence, requested that their wolves be delisted, but Interior refused to consider a state-by-state delisting. Environmental groups opposed piecemeal delisting. The DOW noted, "Idaho, Montana, Wyoming share one population of wolves that is very interdependent. If you take away protection from one part of the population and you manage them different than the other part—that's a problem." Negotiations with Wyoming continued.[7]

Wyoming in 2007 enacted a statute that outlined state wolf management. In November 2007, the Wyoming Game and Fish Commission (WGFC) submitted a revised wolf management plan that designated wolves as "trophy game" in the twelve-thousand-square-mile area in northwest Wyoming, including Yellowstone and Grand Teton National Parks, after delisting. The trophy area constituted 70 percent of suitable wolf habitat in Wyoming; 91 percent of the area was public land. This area, excluding national parks, supported 175 wolves in twenty-five packs with fifteen breeding pairs in 2006. The trophy area could support fifteen breeding pairs and 150 wolves.[8] The WGFC promised to manage fifteen breeding pairs in the state, but only protect seven breeding pairs outside of the national parks. "Breeding pairs" were defined according to FWS recovery standards. Furthermore, the Wyoming law declared that the WGFC "shall manage the gray wolf population as necessary to ensure the long-term health and viability of any big game animal herd that is being threatened in this state."[9]

The wolf was classified as a predator in the remainder of the state, where it could be killed on sight. Wyoming encouraged the killing of predators. Each county in Wyoming was designated a "predator management district." The Board of Directors for each district consisted of livestock owners, hunters, and sportsmen. Districts were required to "devise and put in operation those methods that best manage or control damage caused by predatory animals" and were authorized to pay bounties. Wyoming law also created animal damage management board, which provided assistance "to prevent and mitigate damage by predators."[10]

In December 2007, Secretary Kempthorne fulfilled his promise and approved Wyoming's wolf management plan.[11] This permitted the NRM DPS delisting to move forward, but the decision faced opposition in Congress. Members of the House Resources Committee, including Representatives Nick Rahall, the chair (D. N.J.), George Miller (D. Cal.), Norman Dicks (D. Wash.), Fred Gilchrist (R. Md.), and Jim Saxton (R. N.J.), wrote to Secretary Kempthorne pointing out that states "hostile to wolf conservation" could reduce the number of wolves in the region from 1500 to 300. Senator John Barrasso (R. Wy.) responded that these congressmen, "who don't even live in our time zone . . . have no concept of the damage gray wolves do. This is a Wyoming concern that requires a Wyoming solution. It does not require interference from Washington."[12]

In February 2008, Interior issued the Final Rule designating and removing the wolves in the NRM DPS from the list of endangered and threatened species.[13] The NRM DPS included Montana, Idaho, and Wyoming, eastern Washington, eastern Oregon, and north-central Utah. Only northwest Montana, central Idaho, and Greater Yellowstone Area (GYA) were known to have wolf packs. Interior stated that "the wolf population of the Northern Rockies has far exceeded its recovery goal and continues to expand its size and range.

States, tribes, conservation groups, federal agencies and citizens of both regions can be proud of their roles in this remarkable conservation success story."[14]

Senator Mike Crapo (R. Id.) applauded the delisting, stating Idaho "has followed strict scientific monitoring guidelines to ensure that all the benchmarks have been met for delisting this animal, and the announcement that the wolf no longer is an endangered is a welcome one for wildlife conservationists, ranchers, and sportsmen alike." Earthjustice cautioned that "the enduring hostility to wolves still exists. We are going to have hundreds of wolves killed under state management."[15]

Earthjustice proved to be prophetic. After ESA protection was removed, four wolves were killed immediately. Within one month, twenty wolves were killed in the NRM. Thirteen of the wolf deaths occurred in Wyoming, where wolf hunting was permitted. The CBD proclaimed that "the wolf population is being gunned down right now." Wyoming Game and Fish Department (WGFD) countered that "wolves reproduce prodigiously. You could take 80 in Wyoming and still have as many as you started with in the beginning of the year."[16]

DEFENDERS OF WILDLIFE V. HALL

The DOW, representing ten environmental groups,[17] brought suit, seeking a preliminary injunction to stop Interior's action. Injunctions are important components of public law litigation.[18] The court begins its analysis with the presumption that the statute embodies public values and must provide relief that realizes the public values. To obtain a preliminary injunction, "the plaintiffs must establish (1) that they are 'likely to succeed on the merits,' (2) that they are 'likely to suffer irreparable harm in the absence of preliminary relief,' (3) that the 'balance of equities tips' in their favor, and (4) that such an injunction is in the 'public interest.'"[19]

Judicial skeptics argue that Congress enacts statutes with transcendent values that can't realistically be implemented. Broadly worded statutes delegate implementing authority to executive agencies with few directions or priorities. Congresspersons claim electoral credit for the statutory enactment, then blame administrators for not implementing the public values. The court is granted too much authority to carry out the aspirational goals embodied in these statutes.[20]

In July 2008, the U.S. District Court for the District of Montana issued a preliminary injunction, which restored ESA protections to the wolves in NRM DPS. The court held that the FWS acted arbitrarily and capriciously because there was no genetic connectivity between the wolves in the DPS area, which the FWS declared was necessary for the maintenance of a viable wolf population. The court also invalidated Interior's approval of the 2007 Wyoming wolf management plan, which suffered the same defects as the Wyoming plan rejected in 2004. At least thirty-seven wolves were killed in the six-month interim between the Final Rule and the court's decision.[21]

Standard of Review

The FWS implementation of the DPS policy involved a mixture of legal and factual determinations. The court reviews an agency's policy determinations to ensure that they are not "arbitrary and capricious, an abuse of discretion, or otherwise not in accordance with law."[22] Generally, the court defers to an agency's policy decisions, which involve "accommodation of competing interests, application of value choices, and responsiveness to the electorate," because of agency expertise.[23] Nevertheless, the court must perform a "through, probing, in-depth review" of agency action.[24] The hard-look doctrine requires the court to examine the agency action "to satisfy itself that the agency has exercised a reasoned discretion, with reasons that do not deviate from or ignore the ascertainable legislative intent."[25] Rigorous judicial review "ensures that the agency's decision was a 'reasoned' exercise of discretion and not merely a response to political pressures."[26]

Judicial skeptics oppose the hard-look doctrine, which imposes too great a burden on the agency to defend its decision. Skeptics argue that administrative decision making is based on technocratic-bureaucratic rationality, which acknowledges "the limitations that inadequate data, unquantifiable values, mixed societal goals, and political realities place on the capacity of structured rational thinking, and it does the best that it can with what it has." This differs from the comprehensive analytical reasoning that underlies judicial analysis, which breaks down and evaluates choices based on the goals of the statute. The agency must adopt a defensive position and do extensive paperwork to survive judicial scrutiny. The court by employing such synoptic reasoning can always find some flaw in the agency's analysis and delay a project it does not agree with.[27] Judicial involvement disrupts the agency's agenda, forces the agency to focus on judicial priorities, and misallocates scarce agency resources.[28]

Judicial proponents support hard-look review, which checks administrative discretion and ensures the public values in the statute are implemented. The agency has its own agenda, which includes the protection of turf, following standard operating procedures, and satisfying interest group, presidential, and congressional demands. Judicial review is essential to ensure that the public values acknowledged in the halls of Congress are not lost in the administrative corridors. Courts must check agency power.[29]

Connectivity

The court found that there was no connectivity between the three wolf populations in the NRM DPS.[30] The FWS conceded that there was no genetic exchange between the wolves in Yellowstone and those in Idaho and Montana, but argued that such exchanges were likely given the wolf's fertility and mobility. Potential, not actual, exchange, was all that was required. Even if there was no dispersal, the Yellowstone wolf population had sufficient genetic diversity that would preclude any genetic problems over the next one hundred years. Other wolf populations existed with less diversity. For example, the Isle Royale wolf population only had two founders and experienced no genetic problems.[31]

The court determined that the FWS did not follow its own recovery standards.[32] The FWS in 1994 identified the NRM DPS recovery criteria as "thirty or more breeding pairs comprising some 300+ wolves in a metapopulation (a population that exists as partially isolated sets of subpopulations) with genetic exchange between populations." The FWS stated that "it is fairly clear that ten breeding pairs in isolation will not comprise a viable population (i.e., have a high probability of survival for a long period of time without human intervention.)" The FWS stressed that "the importance of movement of individuals between subpopulations cannot be overemphasized." The court determined that the FWS reliance on likely future genetic exchanges contradicted its earlier stated position. The FWS failed to recognize that more wolves would be killed under state management, creating a lower probability of genetic exchange. Future problems would be exacerbated, not alleviated. Furthermore, the FWS was aware of the genetic diversity of the Yellowstone wolf population and the success of smaller isolated wolf populations, but still insisted that genetic exchange was required. No new evidence justified the FWS change in position.[33]

Judicial proponents assert that courts must scrutinize an agency's change in policy. The agency expended resources to implement the congressional mandate. Others have relied on the position. When the agency changes its position, the court must be sure that change is based on statutory, not political, factors.[34] Judicial skeptics counter that judicial review ossifies the agency, which needs flexibility to change policy to meet current circumstances, the presentation of new data, or the reconceptualization of old data. The agency should not be accountable to the old congressional coalition, but should follow present administration policy.[35]

The court's decision was correct. The ESA mandates that the Secretary of Interior make decisions "solely on the basis of the best scientific and commercial data available."[36] Justice Scalia noted that this requirement is designed "to ensure that the ESA not be implemented haphazardly, on the basis of speculation or surmise."[37] Professor Holly Doremus argued that the best available science mandate "is generally intended to ensure objective, value-neutral decision making by specially trained experts." The mandate promotes more accurate decisions; increases public trust and builds political credibility; and encourages "hard look" judicial review.[38]

Scientific studies demonstrated that there was no connectivity, which would create genetic problems for the wolves in the NRM DPS. Connectivity of the wolf populations in the NRM DPS was essential because "small isolated populations of animals [are] vulnerable to accidents of demography and genetics and to environmental fluctuations and catastrophe." Connectivity provides for "generic and demographic rescue and for viability of wide-ranging species," like the wolf.[39]

Studies demonstrated that there was not a functioning metapopulation of wolves, nor was such a metapopulation likely in the NRM DPS.[40] Oakleaf's study pointed out that there was little interchange among the wolf populations in the three NRM recovery areas. The Greater Yellowstone Area (GYA) was isolated from the other populations. Only one wolf entered the GYA from Idaho and did not reproduce; five of the other "documented dispersals between the GYA and other recovery areas resulted in either death, disappearance or relocation of the disperser." This indicated that dispersal corridors were inadequate and continuous habitat was lacking. Oakleaf stressed that "for the Northern Rocky Mountain wolf population to effectively function as a metapopulation, it will be desirable to prioritize the protection and perhaps restoration of dispersal linkages between the GYA and other recovery areas."[41]

Carroll's study stressed that connectivity was important for wolf recovery, but landscape changes in the West "can quickly result in a loss of connectivity." There was adequate wolf habitat in the NRM DPS, but this was premised on the existing habitat not degrading. The projected increase in the NRM human population from 62 million to 88 million people by 2025 and expanded road development on public and private land, which fragments habitat and increases human access, would decrease dispersal corridors and habitat suitability.[42] Carroll concluded that "the loss of such high proportions of potential wolf habitat as result of landscape change in the western United States over the next quarter-century suggests . . . many western landscapes will become unsuitable for the species."[43]

VonHoldt's 2007 study, which was commissioned by the FWS, found the wolves in the GYA remained isolated. VonHoldt concluded that "if the Yellowstone wolf population remains relatively constant at 170 individuals (estimated to be Yellowstone's carrying capacity), the population will demonstrate substantial in-breeding effects within 60 years." There will be an "increase in juvenile mortality from an average of 23–40 percent, an effect equivalent to losing an additional pup in every litter." To prevent such in-breeding effects, "migration will be needed, including translocation of wolves from elsewhere or the development of specific habitat corridors." Only low-quality corridors connected the GYA wolves with other wolf populations "exposing dispersers to high human-associated mortality risks." VonHoldt concluded that "the genetic impact of isolation may take decades to accumulate but can be delayed if gene flow with other populations is established and maintained."[44]

The FWS argued that the vonHoldt study was not "the best scientific...data available" for several reasons: First, vonHoldt only examined 30 percent of the Yellowstone wolves and only sampled until 2004. Genetic exchange might have occurred after 2004. Second, vonHoldt only looked at wolves in Yellowstone, not the GYA. Dispersal from central Idaho and northwest Montana into the GYA was very likely. Third, genetic exchange was difficult to determine because of the genetic similarity of the wolves in the NRM DPS. Fourth, vonHoldt's predictions were based on erroneous assumptions that underestimated the carrying capacity of Yellowstone National Park.[45] The court rejected the FWS arguments and found the vonHoldt study to be of sufficient size and statistical significance. Evidence indicated that there had been only four to twelve dispersals from or into other areas.[46]

The FWS asserted that human intervention would solve any connectivity problems. Montana and Wyoming were committed to population dispersal and continued to work on connectivity, including open and ranch space maintenance and relocation in the event of genetic risk. As a fall-back position, the FWS declared that "complications from a potential lack of natural habitat connectivity could be quickly resolved by agency management, such as relocations."[47] One manager stated "connectivity could happen by a ride in the back of the truck."[48]

The FWS reliance on human intervention was dubious. The ESA foresees recovery of a functioning ecosystem, not the maintenance of a captive population. The FWS's "Interagency Cooperative Policy for Ecosystem Approach to the ESA" states that agency policy is "to develop and implement recovery plans . . . in a manner that restores, reconstructs, or rehabilitates the structure, distribution, connectivity and function upon which those listed species depend."[49] Even if the FWS relied on human relocation, there was no relocation program in existence. The courts have held that future speculative efforts do not comply with the ESA.[50]

WYOMING'S WOLF MANAGEMENT PLAN

The federal district court determined that Interior's acceptance of Wyoming's 2007 plan was arbitrary and capricious because it suffered from the same defects as the earlier rejected plan. The FWS in 2003 demanded that the wolf be declared trophy game across the state. Wyoming's 2007 wolf management plan retained predator status over 90 percent of the state. Trophy-area boundaries in the plan were malleable. The WGFC could allow unrestricted wolf killing even in trophy areas. In 2003, the FWS declared that Wyoming must commit to managing fifteen breeding pairs. Wyoming's 2007 wolf management plan committed to manage fifteen breeding pairs in the state, but only seven breeding pairs outside national parks. Wyoming relied on federal management of eight breeding pairs on public land.[51]

The history of Wyoming's wolf management plan supports the court's decision. Wyoming in 2003 passed a law, which treated wolves once delisted as trophy game in Yellowstone National Park, Grand Teton National Park, J. D. Rockefeller Parkway and U.S. Forest Service wilderness areas. Most of the area was useless to wolves because of unsuitable habitat, including high elevation, deep snow, and low ungulate productivity. Wolves in other parts of Wyoming would only be considered trophy game if there were less than seven packs outside of national parks and fewer than fifteen packs in the state. In this case, the WGFC could readjust the trophy area to ensure that there were seven packs in Wyoming outside public land at the end of the calendar year. Packs were defined as "five or more gray wolves travelling together," or, if the group had more than ten members travelling together, "the number of packs within such a group to be equal to the number of reproductive mature females bearing young found within that group."

The management of trophy game in Wyoming was more regulated than predatory animals. A trophy-game designation allowed the WGFC and WGFD to regulate the method, season, and number of wolves taken. The taking of a wolf in the trophy area without a license was a misdemeanor, subject to exceptions. State law mandated that whenever there were more than seven packs on the public lands and fifteen packs in Wyoming, the wolf would be designated as a predator outside national parks and wilderness areas. Predators fell under the jurisdiction of the Wyoming Department of Agriculture and could be taken anywhere without limit by any means without a license. This posed a significant risk to many packs south and east of Yellowstone, which leave the park in the winter. These packs would be subject to unregulated killing as predators.[52]

Montana and Idaho submitted state wolf management plans. In July 2003, WGFD submitted a wolf management plan, which followed the dictates of the state law. Interior approved the Montana and Idaho wolf management plans,[53] but all state plans had to be considered together because they comprised the Western DPS. Interior in January 2004 rejected the Wyoming plan for several reasons: First, the FWS objected to Wyoming's insistence on defining the wolf as a predatory animal, stating "the predatory animal status for wolves must be changed. The unregulated harvest and inadequate monitoring plan, and unit boundaries proposed by the state's management plan do not provide sufficient management controls to assure [FWS] that the wolf population will remain above recovery goals." The FWS suggested that "the designation of wolves as 'trophy game' statewide would allow Wyoming to devise a management strategy that provides for self-sustaining populations above recovery goals, regulated harvest and adequate monitoring of that harvest."

Second, the FWS questioned Wyoming's commitment to managing at least fifteen breeding pairs. Under the Wyoming plan, the WGFC's authority to manage wolves as trophy game would end when there were more than fifteen packs in the state or more than seven packs outside national parks and wilderness, even if there were less than fifteen packs in the state. After the wolf population exceeded the minimum level, wolves would be classified as predators and subject to unregulated killing that would bring the population below the minimum level. The continual shift in status from trophy game to predator would make management impossible. Other factors, such as predator control and disease, would further jeopardize Wyoming's ability to meet recovery goals.[54]

Even the Wyoming Attorney General (WAG) recognized problems with the plan. The WAG determined that the plan was internally inconsistent and in conflict with the legislative goal of delisting the wolf. The WAG identified several inconsistencies with the plan and law regarding the goal of seven packs outside public land. The first inconsistency would occur if there were ten packs on public land and five packs outside public land. Wolves would be classified as predators because there would be fifteen packs in the state, but less than seven packs outside public land. The second inconsistency would occur if there were three packs on public lands and ten packs outside public land. Wolves would be classified as predators because there would be at least seven packs outside public land. Both scenarios undermined the goal of fifteen packs in the state and the maintenance of seven packs outside public land. The WAG suggested that the state law not be interpreted strictly, but according to its purposes.[55]

Third, the FWS determined that Wyoming's definition of a pack must be consistent with the other states and be biologically based. The essential unit for wolf recovery is a breeding pair, which is defined as an adult male and female producing two pups per breeding season that survive until December 31. Wyoming law and management plan defined a pack as five or more wolves traveling together. If there were more than ten wolves, packs would be defined as the number of reproducing females bearing young found within the group. The FWS declared that "state law must define pack size as at least six wolves travelling together in the winter. At the current time, biological monitoring and analyses indicate that this pack size is expected to include at least one breeding pair."[56]

The FWS found Wyoming's definition of a pack inconsistent with wolf biology and the criteria for measuring wolf recovery. Wolf packs only breed and produce pups once per year in April, so the wolf population can only increase at that time. If the pack's breeding adults were killed between February and April, no pups would be born for at least a year. If the pups were killed, no more pups would be produced for another year. Wyoming's pack definition would lead to greater predator designations and a minimal population going into summer when mortality from disease and human killing was more likely. For example, if fifteen groups of five wolves went into the summer and experienced the normal rate of mortality, the wolf population could fall below the recovery goal when the only opportunity to replenish the population in that year had passed. In addition, fifteen groups of five wolves of unknown status traveling together in winter only constituted 8.4 breeding pairs. Wyoming's own data showed that five wolves traveling together in the winter had only .56 percent probability of being a breeding pair.[57]

Wyoming filed suit in May 2004, alleging that Interior's rejection of its plan violated the ESA and Administrative Procedures Act (APA) by ignoring the best scientific and commercial data available and relying on "litigation risk management" and political concerns. The Wolf Coalition, which consisted of several groups including state and local governments, agricultural advocates, environmental and outdoor sporting groups, filed a similar suit. The Wolf Coalition alleged that Interior violated the National Environmental Policy Act (NEPA) by failing to prepare a Supplemental Environmental Impact Statement to address the impact of wolf populations outside of the GYA and requiring Wyoming to adopt a plan that would necessitate the management of gray wolves outside the recovery area identified in the Revised Plan, the Final EIS, and the Final Rule.

The case was dismissed by the U.S. District Court for the District of Wyoming in February 2005.[58] The court found Wyoming's complaint was premature because the state never filed a petition requesting a change in the wolf's status. Interior's rejection of the Wyoming plan was merely advisory, not final agency action. Interior then announced that it was ready to delist the wolves in the NRM once Wyoming's management plan was completed. Wyoming Governor David Freudenthal accused Interior of engaging in "political blackmail" that was designed to pressure Wyoming into capitulating to the federal government's management plan, "a move he says the state doesn't intend to make."[59] Governor Freudenthal was facing reelection in 2006. Wyoming's "shoot on sight" policy was supported by 65 percent and opposed by 27 percent of Wyoming's citizens. This was a winning issue for the Democratic governor in the Republican state.[60]

The Tenth Circuit upheld the dismissal of Wyoming's suit in April 2006.[61] Environmental groups were pleased. Earthjustice declared that "this ruling confirms that Wyoming has been wasting time and energy in a frivolous lawsuit. If Wyoming is serious about delisting, it should make a plan to protect wolves in Wyoming instead of fighting for the right to exterminate them." The Sierra Club noted that "Wyoming wants to throw away a huge investment in wolf recovery and bring back the bad old days of poisoning, trapping, and shooting wolves on site. That's no way to ensure a healthy wolf population."[62]

Wyoming petitioned Interior to establish the NRM DPS and delist the wolves therein in July 2005.[63] Wyoming made several requests: First, the lethal taking of wolves should be permitted as long as the population exceeded recovery goals. Second, uniform standards regarding an "unacceptable impact" on wildlife should be established on the basis of sound science. Third, wolves harassing elk on or near feeding grounds should be terminated. Finally, livestock owners should be reimbursed for depredation loss. Governor Freudenthal stated that "there is unambiguous evidence that the species has met the federal recovery goals, and the state of Wyoming has a good plan for managing wolves into perpetuity." The federal government should "relinquish control over how wolves in Wyoming are managed."[64]

Interior in August 2006 rejected Wyoming's petition, citing continued problems with the Wyoming wolf management plan.[65] Interior declared that Wyoming's plan "really doesn't provide enough assurance for us to move forward with delisting at this time." Environmental groups were pleased. The DOW stated that "Wyoming's wolf management plan to nearly eliminate restrictions on killing wolves in the state could jeopardize the future of the wolf in the region." Furthermore, "as large carnivores, wolves play an enormously important role in maintaining a healthy ecosystem that benefits us all. Suggestions that they take a huge toll on human activities like ranching and hunting are simply not true."[66]

Wyoming again brought suit. Governor David Freudenthal stated, "it seems to me that we have a plan that satisfies the scientific obligation that they have imposed on us." Wyoming officials accused the FWS of "delaying the delisting process by selectively using data and references that seem to support its case while ignoring other data and the preponderance of evidence that Wyoming's plan will ensure a recovered population of Wyoming." The FWS rejection was based "on unrealistic assumptions, misinterpretation of data, misrepresentation of Wyoming's wolf plan under Wyoming state law and hypothetical examples that are infeasible or highly unrealistic under Wyoming management plan."[67] The U.S. District Court for the District of Wyoming dismissed Wyoming's suit.[68]

Subsequent events demonstrated that Interior was correct to reject the 2003 and 2006 Wyoming management plans. First, Wyoming was not able to meet the recovery goal of seven breeding pairs outside public lands and fifteen breeding pairs in the state. The 2004 wolf population in Yellowstone National Park (YNP) (171 wolves in sixteen breeding pairs) would have triggered a predator designation outside public lands and allowed all of the wolves outside the public lands (89 wolves and eight breeding pairs) to be terminated. In 2005, disease decreased the wolf population in the YNP to 118 wolves and seven breeding pairs. This was the only time packs outside public land (134 wolves and nine breeding pairs) constituted a greater portion of the Wyoming wolf population than Yellowstone (118 wolves, seven breeding pairs). If all the wolves outside public lands had been exterminated in 2004 and early 2005, Wyoming's wolf population would have fallen to seven breeding pairs in 2005, which was below the ten breeding pair recovery limit.[69]

Second, Wyoming's pack definition would have skewed the breeding pair numbers and interfered with the management strategy. Few pups survived in 1999 and 2005. Five wolves traveling together in the winter would not have constituted a breeding pair of male and female producing two pups. From 2002 to 2005, many wolves in Montana and Wyoming did not survive because they were infected with mange. Five wolves traveling together with mange would not constitute a breeding pair because they were unlikely to survive until December 31. At the end of 2004,[70] there were sixteen breeding pairs in Wyoming according to the FWS definition, but twenty-four packs would have been counted as breeding pairs under Wyoming's definition, an overestimate of 50 percent. If Wyoming only managed fifteen packs, there would have been fewer than ten actual breeding pairs in Wyoming.

Third, Wyoming's ability to meet recovery goals was dependent on eight breeding pairs being found in Yellowstone National Park. This was unrealistic. Breeding pairs in YNP were reduced from sixteen (171 wolves) in 2004 to seven (118 wolves) in 2005. If each group of five wolves was counted as a pack pursuant to Wyoming law, there would have been twenty-four packs in Wyoming, thirteen outside and eleven inside YNP in 2005. This would have triggered a predator designation, which would have significantly reduced the number of wolves in Wyoming even though there were only seven breeding pairs in the state.[71]

Finally, Wyoming's predator control law could frustrate the state's ability to meet recovery goals. Wyoming allowed landowners to take wolves "doing damage to private property" without a permit, and game wardens could take trophy animals "doing substantial damage" to property. There were no limits on the number of wolves that could be taken to protect property or prevent depredation. State wildlife officials lacked authority to stop this. Wyoming's predator control law was not identical to the section 10(j) experimental population regulation, which only allowed the killing wolves caught in the act of predation. Wyoming allowed the killing of wolves that were, in the subjective view of the property owner, damaging property. Predator control was not limited regardless of its effect on wolf recovery. This was particularly egregious in light of Wyoming's lack of commitment to protect fifteen breeding pairs. Furthermore, the cumulative impacts of unlimited predator control in

Wyoming would result in greater genetic isolation of the GYA wolves because dispersers would likely be killed at the edge of the trophy-game area.[72]

Wyoming Revised Plan

Wyoming in October 2008 submitted a revised wolf management plan, which maintained the dual classification of trophy game in northwest Wyoming and predator in the remainder of the state. Wyoming committed to managing fifteen breeding pairs consisting of at least 150 wolves. Seven breeding pairs would be maintained outside national parks and public lands in northwest Wyoming. If there were less than eight breeding pairs inside national parks for two consecutive years, the WGFC would manage additional breeding pairs to meet fifteen breeding pairs and the 150-wolf population goal. Property owners in northwest Wyoming could still take wolves "doing damage to private property." The WGFC was committed to managing wolves "so that genetic diversity and connectivity issues do not threaten the gray wolf population." Such actions included "encouraging the incorporation of effective migrants into the gray wolf population" and "working with other states to promote natural dispersal . . . and, if necessary, by relocation or translocation."[73]

During the waning days of the Bush administration in January 2009, Interior again rejected Wyoming's state management plan. Interior admitted that "in hindsight, we were probably too optimistic about what the law really committed Wyoming to and what could be accomplished by regulations alone. We should also have evaluated the potential for genetic connectivity more closely, when we determined that the 2007 plan was sufficient."[74] Interior determined that Wyoming's regulatory framework did not guarantee that the state would be able to manage its share of the wolf population in the NRM DPS. Wyoming must commit to managing 150 wolves in fifteen breeding pairs in mid-winter and 70 wolves in seven breeding pairs in mid-winter outside the national parks. Wyoming was instructed to manage its wolf population to maintain high levels of genetic diversity and facilitate genetic exchange. The current framework limited natural genetic connectivity. Genetic exchange between the three wolf populations in the NRM DPS would be more likely if dispersers had safe passage through the entire state. This would be promoted by a statewide trophy game designation, which would also help Wyoming to devise more flexible management strategies. Furthermore, Wyoming should authorize the taking of wolves in the defense of property in a manner similar to the current regulations and consider all sources of mortality, including hunting and the defense of property, in its total statewide mortality limits. Wolf management in Wyoming remained subject to the 1994 experimental population regulations.[75] The court remanded the case to the FWS to revise the regulation.

THE LAST GASP

In January 2009, the outgoing Bush administration attempted an eleventh hour delisting of the wolves in Montana and Idaho, while retaining threatened species status for the wolves in Wyoming. Environmental groups accused the "FWS of playing politics and prolonging the conflict." The FWS's piecemeal approach abandoned its commitment to recover the NRM wolf population; divided the population into separate populations based on political boundaries; and deprived Wyoming of the opportunity to fix its management plan. The proposal was viewed as "a giant step backwards" that would generate litigation for years.[76]

CONCLUSION

Following the federal district court decisions in 2005, the Bush administration established the NRM DPS, approved Wyoming's wolf management plan, and delisted the NRM wolves. There was no evidence that judicial review deterred the FWS. Environmental groups brought suit requesting an injunction to halt the premature downlisting of the NRM DPS. Injunctions are an important tool in public law litigation because they acknowledge the public values in the statute. The U.S. District Court for the District of Montana correctly halted Interior's premature delisting, which violated the best available science mandate in the ESA. Studies demonstrated that there was not a functioning metapopulation in the NRM DPS, which the FWS asserted was a necessary condition for delisting. The court was also required to examine Interior's change in policy to ensure it was based on statutory, not political, factors. The federal court properly invalidated Interior's approval of Wyoming's wolf management plan, which manifested the same defects as the earlier plan rejected in 2004. Wyoming's revised management plan was rejected by Interior in 2009. Before the Bush administration left office, Interior sought to subdivide the NRM DPS and delist all of the wolves therein except in Wyoming. This set the stage for the incoming Obama administration.

NOTES

1. 565 F. Supp.2d 1160 (D. Mont. 2008).
2. "FWS Announces Intent to Remove Northern Rocky Mountain Wolves from Endangered Species List," *US FedNews*, February 2, 2006.
3. "DOW Denounces Norton's Delisting Plan," *PR News*, February 1, 2006.
4. "Idaho Governor Picked for Interior," *Denver Post*, March 17, 2006.
5. "Proposal to Delist Western Great Lakes and Northern Rocky Mountains," *Interior Documents*, January 29, 2007.

6. "Northern Rocky Mountain Population Faces Uncertain Future," *Land Letter*, February 1, 2007. "Endangered Species: Even Success Breeds Controversy for ESA Listings," *Land Letter*, May 17, 2007.

7. "Montana, Idaho Still Seek Delisting of Wolves," *Billings Gazette*, July 28, 2006. "Interior Pushes for Speedier Delisting," *Land Letter*, September 8, 2005. "Freudenthal Outlines Plan for Wolf Bill," *Caspar Star Tribune*, February 16, 2007. "State-Federal Wolf Talks Could Revive," *Caspar Star Tribune*, February 20, 2007.

8. 73 *Federal Register* 10514, 10549 (February 27, 2008). The hunting of trophy game is regulated by license. Wyo. Stat. 23-1-302(a) (xxix). The WGFC can establish zones "in which trophy game animals may be taken . . . in the same manner as predatory animals without a license," Wyo. Stat. 23-1-302(a)(ii) 23-3-103(a). The WGFC can reduce the trophy boundary for wolves if it "does not impede the delisting of wolves and will facilitate Wyoming's management of wolves," Wyo. Stat. 11-6-302(a) (x)(B)(I), 23-1-101(a)(xii)(B)(I).

9. Wyo Stat. 23-1-304 (a), (c), (e), (n).

10. Wyo. Stat. 11-6-201(a), 202(a), 205 (a), 302, 304. 72 *Federal Register* 6106, 6129 (February 8, 2007).

11. "State, Feds Note Wolf Concessions," *Caspar Star Tribune*, May 25, 2007. "State, Feds Strike Wolf Deal," *Caspar Star Tribune*, May 25, 2007.

12. "Barrasso Takes Issues with K on Wolves," AP, January 16, 2008.

13. 73 *Federal Register* 10514 (February 27, 2008).

14. "Interior Removes Northern Rocky Mountain Wolves from Endangered Species List," *States News Service*, February 21, 2008.

15. "Crapo Applauds Wolf Delisting," *Capitol Hill Press*, February 21, 2008.

16. "Wolf Kills in Rockies Cause Activist Alarm," *USA Today*, April 18, 2008. "Wolf Gets Fresh Start as Managed Species," *Spokesman Review*, April 6, 2008.

17. Natural Resources Defense Council, Sierra Club, Humane Society of US, Center for Biological Diversity, Jackson Hole Conservation Alliance, Friends of the Clearwater, Alliance for the Wild Rockies, Oregon Wild, Cascadia Wildlands Project, Western Watersheds Project, and Wildlands Project.

18. Abram Chayes, "The Role of the Judge in Public Law Litigation," 89 *Harvard Law Review* 1281, 1292–96 (1976).

19. *Winter v. NRDC*, 129 S. Ct. 365, 374 (2008).

20. Frank B. Cross, "Pragmatic Pathologies of Judicial Review of Administrative Rulemaking," 78 *North Carolina Law Review* 1013, 1057–67 (2000).

21. Plaintiffs Memorandum in Support for Motion Preliminary Injunction, *DOW v. Hall*, 16–17.

22. 5 U.S.C. 706.

23. Christopher F. Edley, Jr., *Administrative Law, Rethinking Judicial Control of Bureaucracy* (Yale University, 1990), 34.

24. *Nat'l Ass'n of Homebuilders v. Norton*, 340 F.3d 835, 841 (9th Cir. 2003).

25. *Greater Boston Television Corp. v. F.C.C.*, 444 F.2d 841, 850–51 (D.C. Cir. 1970).

26. Cass R. Sunstein, "Deregulation and the Hard Look Doctrine," 1983 *Supreme Court Review* 177, 182. William H. Rodgers Jr., "A Hard Look at Vermont Yankee: Environmental Law Under Close Scrutiny," 67 *Georgetown Law Journal* 699, 704–7 (1979).

27. Thomas O. McGarity, "The Courts and Ossification of Rulemaking: A Response to Professor Seidenfeld," 75 *Texas Law Review* 525, 536–41 (1997).

28. Cross, 1027–36.

29. Thomas O. Sargentich, "The Critique of Active Judicial Review of Administrative Agencies: A Reevaluation," 49 *Administrative Law Review* 599 (1997).

30. 565 F. Supp.2d, 1169–70.

31. 73 *Federal Register* 10553–54. The Isle Royale population is currently under stress. Tracy O'Connell, "Now What? Two Views Address the Declining Wolf Population at Isle Royale," 23 *International Wolf* (Spring 2014), 4.

32. 72 *Federal Register* 6106–7, 6121 (February 8, 2007).

33. 565 F. Supp.2d, 1168–72.

34. Merrick Garland, "Deregulation and Judicial Review," 98 *Harvard Law Review* 505, 553–61 (1985).
35. Garland, 553–61. Cross, 1039–44.
36. 16 U.S.C. 1533 (b). Daniel J. Rohlf, "Science, Law, and Policy" in Karen Arabas and Joe Bowersox (eds.), *Forest Futures: Science, Politics, and Policy for the Next Century* (Rowman and Littlefield, 2004), 127, 128–29
37. *Bennett v. Spear,* 520 U.S. 154, 176–77 (1997).
38. Holly Doremus, "The ESA's Best Available Science Mandate," 34 *Environmental Law* 397, 417–19, 449 (2004).
39. Michael Soule and Reed Noss, "Rewilding and Biodiversity, Complementary Goals for Continental Conservation," 8 *Wild Earth* 18, 22 (Fall 1998).
40. 72 *Federal Register* 6116, 6119. 73 *Federal Register* 10536. 74 *Federal Register* 15157–58.
41. John K. Oakleaf, Dennis L. Murray, James R. Oakleaf, Edward E. Bangs, Curt M. Mack, Douglas W. Smith, Joseph A. Fontaine, Michael D. Jimenez, Thomas J. Meier, Carter C. Niemeyer, "Habitat Selection by Recolonizing Wolves in the Northern Rocky Mountains of the United States," 70 *Journal Wildlife Management* 554, 560–61 (2006).
42. 74 *Federal Register* 15160.
43. Carlos Carroll, Michael K. Phillips, Carlos A. Lopez-Gonzalez, and Nathan Schumaker, "Defining Recovery Goals and Strategies for Endangered Species: The Wolf as a Case Study," 56 *BioScience* 25, 34–35 (2006).
44. 565 F. Supp.2d, 1168–69, citing Bridgett vonHoldt, Daniel Stahler, Douglas Smith, Dent Earl, Johan Pollinger, Robert Wayne, "The Genealogy and Genetic Variability of Reintroduced Yellowstone Wolves," 17 *Molecular Ecology* 252 (2007).
45. 74 *Federal Register* 15133–34.
46. 565 F. Supp.2d, 1169–71.
47. 73 *Federal Register* 10533–34.
48. Plaintiff's Memorandum in Support of Motion for Preliminary Injunction, *Defenders of Wildlife v. Hall*, 8.
49. 59 *Federal Register* 34273, 34274 (July 1, 1994).
50. *Oregon NRC v. Daley*, 6 F. Supp.2d 1139, 1154–55 (D. Or. 1998); Fed'n of *Flyfishers v. Daley*, 131 F. Supp.2d 1158, 1165 (N.D. Cal. 2000); *NWF v. NMFS*, 481 F.3d 1224, 1241 (9th Cir. 2007); *Arizona Cattlegrowers v. FWS*, 273 F.3d 1229, 1244 (9th Cir. 2001).
51. 565 F. Supp.2d, 1172–76.
52. 71 *Federal Register* 43427–28. *Wyoming v. Interior*, Case No. 04-CV-0123-J (March 23, 2005), 15–16.
53. 74 *Federal Register* 15166.
54. *Wyoming v. Interior*, 16–17.
55. 71 *Federal Register* 43428–29.
56. *Wyoming v. Interior,* 16–17.
57. 71 *Federal Register* 43428–29.
58. *Wyoming v. Interior*, 65–67. County to Join State of Wyoming in Appealing Wolf Decision, AP State & Local Wire, April 14, 2005.
59. "Wyoming Fights U.S. on Wolf Management," *Denver Post*, February 5, 2006.
60. "Commission: Shoot on Sight Isn't Worth Fight," *Wyoming Tribune*, March 16, 2006.
61. 442 F.3d 1262 (10th Cir. 2006).
62. "Federal Appeals Court Tosses Wyoming Wolf Lawsuit," *US Fed News*, April 6, 2006.
63. 74 *Federal Register* 15124.
64. "Wyoming Petitions to Remove Gray Wolf from List," AP, July 14, 2005.
65. 71 *Federal Register* 43410 (August 1, 2006).
66. "FWS Denies Wyoming's Petition," *US Fed News*, June 25, 2006.
67. "Wyoming Responds to FWS Refusal to Delist," *US State News*, October 6, 2006.
68. Wyoming District Court Case Number 2-06-CV-00245 (Feb. 27, 2008).
69. 71 *Federal Register* 43428.
70. For the discrepancy in numbers, 71 *Federal Register* 43413.
71. 71 *Federal Register* 43428–30.

72. 565 F. Supp.2d, 1175–77. 74 *Federal Register* 15170–71. 73 *Federal Register* 10540.

73. Wyoming Game and Fish Commission, *2008 Draft Revision, Wyoming Gray Wolf Management Plan* (October 28, 2008), 1–3.

74. 74 *Federal Register* 15149.

75. 74 *Federal Register* 15125, 15419, 15172, 15179, 15182–83.

76. "Bush Administration's Eleventh Hour Wolf Delisting Proposal Fails," *Yellowstone Coalition*, January 16, 2009.

Chapter Six

Premature Delisting

Defenders of Wildlife v. Salazar

The Obama administration revived the Bush administration's proposal to delist the wolves in the Northern Rocky Mountain Distinct Population Segment (NRM DPS), which comprises Montana, Idaho, eastern Oregon, eastern Washington, and north-central Utah, while retaining threatened species status for the wolves in Wyoming. Environmental groups brought suit challenging Interior's implementation of policy. The U.S. District Court for the District of Montana halted Interior's action in *Defenders of Wildlife (DOW) v. Salazar.*[1] The court determined that piecemeal delisting violated the text of the Endangered Species Act (ESA), which treats the DPS as the smallest unit for ESA analysis, and prior Interior policy, which precluded the subdivision of the DPS and use of state lines to determine DPS boundaries. Subsequently, additional variables were introduced. A new study demonstrated there was connectivity between the three wolf populations in the NRM DPS. The U.S. District Court for the District of Wyoming invalidated Interior's rejection of Wyoming's wolf management plan in 2009. The judicial decisions regarding the NRM wolves generated a congressional response. Congress enacted section 1713, a rider to a Defense Department appropriation bill, which delisted wolves in NRM DPS, except Wyoming, and precluded judicial review of the provision. This chapter analyzes the federal court decisions, the subsequent political reactions, and the status of the wolf in other states in the NRM DPS.

OBAMA ADMINISTRATION

Barack H. Obama won the presidency in 2008 and 2012. He lost Idaho, Montana, Utah, and Wyoming, but carried Washington and Oregon in both elections. Senator Kenneth Salazar (D. Colo.) became Secretary of Interior. Environmental groups were split on the appointment. Some praised the selection, pointing to Senator Salazar's stellar environmental record in 2008. Others were skeptical, highlighting his earlier opposition to numerous environmental initiatives.[2]

In January 2009, the outgoing Bush administration attempted an eleventh-hour delisting of the wolves in the NRM DPS, while retaining threatened species status for the wolves in Wyoming. Environmental groups described the proposal as "a giant step backwards" that would generate litigation for years.[3] The incoming Obama administration put a freeze on all pending regulations, including the NRM wolf delisting.

The Obama administration initially appeared sympathetic to the concerns of environmental groups. President Obama in March 2009 rescinded the Bush administration regulation that allowed federal agencies to determine whether their actions would harm endangered species and returned this authority to the Fish and Wildlife Service (FWS) and National Marine Fisheries Service (NMFS). President Obama pledged to "restore the scientific process to its rightful place at the heart of the ESA, a process undermined by past administrations."[4]

The president's decision returning authority to the FWS and NMFS received mixed reviews in Congress. Representative Nick Rahall (D. W.Va.), chair of the House Natural Resources Committee, supported "the President's proposal to restore the protections for endangered species that the Bush administration spent so many years trying to undermine." Republicans were angry. Representative Doc Hastings (R. Wash.), the ranking minority member on the House Resources Committee, warned that the change would lead "to endless bureaucratic regulation and lawsuits by special interest groups." Ironically, Representative Hastings was particularly critical of the removal of the regulations through language in the Interior appropriation bill. He noted that "Democratic leaders have slipped dangerous language into the $410 billion spending bill to withdraw two ESA rules without any public input or public comment period. This type of secret, backdoor maneuver is not how the public expects their government to operate."[5]

Three days later Secretary Salazar announced that the wolves in the NRM DPS would be delisted and ESA protections for the wolves in Wyoming would be retained. Secretary Salazar stated that "the recovery of the gray wolf throughout significant portions of its historic range is one of the great success stories of the ESA." Interior restored the Bush administration regulation in April 2009.[6]

Judicial skeptics assert that judicial involvement ossifies the bureaucracy. Federal agencies are reluctant to change policy because of fear of judicial override.[7] After the Montana federal district court invalidated the earlier delisting proposal, both the Bush and Obama administrations pursued piecemeal delisting as the means to circumvent the earlier federal court decision.

Montana and Idaho officials applauded the decision. Senator John Tester (D. Mt.) stated, "I have always supported delisting, and this is good news." Representative Denny Rehberg (R. Mt.) explained, "as a rancher, I know firsthand the frustrations many Montanans have felt over the continued unnecessary federal management of wolves, and that's why I asked the President to uphold the previous delisting decision." Idaho governor Butch Otter declared that "we know that well-intentioned but narrowly focused interest groups will challenge this decision, but we in Idaho are determined to continue our policy of responsibly managing wolves for a viable, sustainable population that can coexist with our ungulate herds, our livestock and our people."

Wyoming officials were disappointed. Governor David Freudenthal stated, "Unfortunately the Obama administration adopted the same approach as the Bush Administration. . . . The more things change, the more they stay the same." Senator Mike Enzi (R. Wy.) declared, "Wyoming exceeded by leaps and bounds the number of wolves in the original recovery plan. It's time to let the states, all the states, have their shot at managing the wolves." Senator John Barrasso (R. Wy.) asserted that "delisting the wolf in Montana and Idaho but not Wyoming simply does not make sense. Wolves don't check for state boundaries."[8]

Environmental groups were angry. The DOW stated that President Obama pledged to "restore the science process to its rightful place at the heart of the ESA," but did not follow up on the pledge regarding gray wolves in the NRM. The Center for Biodiversity (CBD) declared, "This is clearly unlawful, and we will go to court."[9]

Despite the delisting, state legislatures in the region took action. The Idaho legislature enacted a bill, which offered to give wolves to any state that would accept them. The Montana Senate considered a bill, which terminated all federal-state wolf agreements and compelled the state attorney general to seek compensation for any damage caused by wolves. The Wyoming House studied a bill that would put into law the provisions of the recently revised state wolf management plan.[10]

There was positive action by the federal government. The Gray Wolf Livestock Loss Mitigation Act, which was sponsored by Senators Tester and Barrasso, was enacted. The bill authorized one million dollars per year over five years for demonstration projects by the states and Indian tribes that are designed to assist livestock producers in undertaking proactive nonlethal measures to decrease the risk of livestock loss due to wolf predation and compensate owners for such livestock loss.[11]

States and Indian tribes planned wolf hunts that allowed the killing of 75 wolves in Montana (15 percent of the state population), 220 wolves in Idaho (25 percent of the state population), and 35 wolves on Nez Pearce lands.[12] Environmental groups brought suit, seeking a preliminary injunction to halt the wolf hunts. The plaintiffs had to establish (1) that they are "likely to succeed on the merits," (2) that they are "likely to suffer irreparable harm in the absence of preliminary relief," (3) that the "balance of equities tips" in their favor, and (4) that the injunction is in the "public interest."[13]

The U.S. District Court for the District of Montana refused to issue an injunction halting the hunt in September 2009. The court found that there was no showing of irreparable harm. Experts pointed out that a 30 percent reduction of the wolf population in the region would not jeopardize the wolf population. The maximum projected killing of 330 wolves in the hunts would only reduce the wolf population by 20 percent, which was well within acceptable limits.[14] The court did provide encouragement to the environmental plaintiffs. The court held that the plaintiffs were likely to prevail in the full trial on the merits because the Secretary could not subdivide the NRM DPS by retaining endangered species status for the wolves in Wyoming. The balance of the equities and public interest also favored the plaintiffs because the ESA prioritized the recovery of endangered and threatened species.[15]

Environmental groups criticized the decision. The DOW stated, "We are disappointed in the short-term that the hunting season is going to be allowed to go forward but it is clear the judge felt the (FWS) has violated the ESA and delisting may be considered illegal in the long-term." Wolf opponents applauded the decision. Idaho governor Otter declared, "Judge Molloy did the right thing. Idaho has met and exceeded the criteria agreed upon by all parties for recovery." Wyoming governor Freudenthal stated he "was encouraged to see the judge recognize that hunting, essentially management, of the wolf population was probably necessary."[16]

By the end of the 2010 season, hunters in Montana killed 72 wolves, and wildlife agents terminated another 145 wolves for depredation. In Idaho, hunters killed 134 wolves, and wildlife agents killed 93 wolves. In Wyoming, wildlife agents killed 32 wolves. This left 525 wolves in Montana, 843 wolves in Idaho, 320 wolves in Wyoming, 5 wolves in Washington, and 14 wolves in Oregon in the spring of 2010.[17]

Environmental groups, who were critical of the Obama administration's overall wildlife policy,[18] pursued another strategy. The CBD petitioned Interior to establish a national recovery plan for wolves. The CBD stated, "Interior's failure to develop a national recovery strategy for the wolf . . . has led to tremendous confusion and hampered true wolf recovery. Wolves have been an integral part of the North American landscapes for millions of years and are cherished, iconic animals that deserve a certain future in this country."[19] A similar effort by the National Resource Defense Council (NRDC) in 2008 had been unsuccessful.[20]

DEFENDERS OF WILDLIFE V. SALAZAR

The DOW, representing numerous environmental groups,[21] brought suit. In August 2010, the U.S. District Court for the District of Montana rejected Interior's delisting proposal on the grounds that the NRM DPS cannot be subdivided on a state-by-state basis. The court found that the text of ESA defines the units for listing and delisting as species, subspecies, or DPS. The NRM DPS must be treated as a single unit. The "significant portion of the range" language cannot be utilized to change the definition of an endangered or threatened species. Since Wyoming constitutes "a significant portion of the range," wolves in the NRM DPS cannot be delisted until Wyoming develops an adequate state management plan.[22]

Standard of Review

The differential treatment of the Wyoming wolf population in the NRM DPS delisting posed a legal question. The court, employing a weak version of Chevron, examined the text, intent, and purposes of the ESA.[23]

Judicial skeptics applaud Chevron because it prevents the court from imposing its own views on the agency. Chevron grants the agency flexibility to deal with new circumstances and carry out the policies of the current administration. Skeptics argue that vague congressional delegations of authority to the executive reflect voter preference every four years in the presidential election. If the law is too specific, it will constrain the president, who will not be able to respond to the demands of the electorate. Congress delegates broad power to the president, who is accountable to the electorate.[24]

Judicial proponents argue that Chevron is inconsistent with the evolution of the non-delegation rule, which prohibits Congress from delegating unfettered authority to the executive.[25] The non-delegation rule supports the separation of powers and prevents the concentration of power in the Executive. Congress delegates power to executive agencies to make policy within statutory limits, but not to define those statutory limits.[26]

Piecemeal Delisting

The Secretary of Interior (Secretary) delisted the wolves in the NRM DPS, but the wolves in Wyoming retained their threatened species status. Interior claimed that greater protection can be accorded to the wolves in Wyoming, which constitutes a significant portion of the range.[27] The court correctly determined that the ESA does not allow the piecemeal delisting of the NRM

DPS. The court refused to accord Chevron deference because the FWS position contradicted earlier agency decisions, the legislative history, and was not reasonable.[28]

The text of the ESA is clear. The ESA only permits the listing, reclassification, and delisting of species, subspecies, and DPS.[29] Once designated, ESA protections apply to the entire DPS. Regulations establish the DPS as a single unit because of its discreteness and significance. Interior determined that Wyoming, which lacked an approved state management plan, constituted a significant portion of the range of the NRM DPS, so delisting was not permitted.

Interior's interpretation conflicted with the "agency's earlier interpretation" that the DPS is a single unit.[30] In 2003, Interior declared that "delisting can only occur when a species (or subspecies or DPS) is recovered."[31] In 2005, Interior stated that "at this time the Act does not allow wolves to be delisted on a State-by-State basis."[32]

Interior's altered position was based on a 2007 memo by Interior's solicitor, which focused on the current range of the species. The memo asserted that the "significant portion of the range" language can be used to change the status of wolves in the different regions of the DPS.[33] Since the wolf had recovered in Montana and Idaho, it could be delisted in these states, and ESA protections should only be retained in Wyoming.

The memo changed the delisting process, allowing Interior to create another distinct population segment within the NRM DPS. This contradicted the text of section 4(c)(1), which indicates that the only relevant units of analysis are species, subspecies, and DPS. The legislative history indicates that the DPS is the means for providing differential treatment for a species.[34] Furthermore, Interior previously determined that state lines cannot be used in designating DPS boundaries, unless the state lines incidentally separate two DPSs.[35]

Interior cited the reclassification of wolves in Minnesota from endangered to threatened species in 1978 to demonstrate its regulatory flexibility to revise a species status pursuant to section 4(c)(1). The reclassification in 1978 was not analogous to subdividing the DPS. Treating a DPS whose conservation status is different from a species or subspecies listing is acceptable.[36] The DPS is a single unit that is distinguishable from its constituent elements. Interior recognized the wolf population in the NRM DPS as a single unit. Section 4(c)(1) only allowed Interior to revise the status of the entire DPS.

Interior's decision also contradicted earlier federal court decisions, which consistently found the DPS to be a single unit for ESA analysis. In *National Wildlife Federation v. Norton*, the U.S. District Court for the District of Vermont held that "the FWS cannot exclude portions of a DPS from listing a species. Once a DPS is formed, it is treated uniformly throughout the DPS."[37] The U.S. District Court for the District of Oregon in *Alsea Valley*

Alliance v. Evans noted that "listing distinctions below that of subspecies or a DPS of species are not allowed under the ESA."[38] The Ninth Circuit supported this interpretation in *Trout Unlimited v. Lohn.*[39]

POST-LITIGATION DEVELOPMENTS

Subsequent developments generated a conflict between the two federal district court decisions. The U.S. District Court for the District of Wyoming in 2010 determined that Interior's rejection of the Wyoming wolf management plan in 2009 was arbitrary and capricious. This contradicted the 2008 U.S. District Court for the District of Montana's decision in *Defenders of Wildlife v. Hall*, which found Interior's acceptance of a similar Wyoming plan in 2007 arbitrary and capricious. Furthermore, a recent scientific study determined that there was genetic connectivity in the NRM DPS. This contradicted the findings of an earlier study by many of the same authors relied upon by the Montana federal district court in its 2008 decision.

Wyoming v. United States

Following the Montana federal district court in *Defenders of Wildlife v. Hall*, Wyoming submitted a revised management plan, which maintained the dual classification of trophy game in northwest Wyoming and predator in the remainder of the state. Interior rejected Wyoming's state management plan in January 2009.[40] Wyoming brought suit, challenging Interior's decision.

The U.S. District Court for the District of Wyoming in 2010 invalidated Interior's dismissal of Wyoming's 2008 wolf management plan. The court held that Interior offered no new scientific evidence to support its insistence on a statewide trophy game designation. The court, relying on Interior's approval of the Wyoming plan in 2007, determined that the plan's malleable trophy game area did not pose any risk to genetic connectivity and diversity in the near future. The court was confident that the trophy game area would not be reduced to keep the wolf population at a minimum because Wyoming was committed to maintaining its recovery obligations. The court conceded that state predator control was more stringent than the section 10(j) experimental population rule, but its impact must be analyzed in terms of a larger trophy game area. Interior was instructed to reconsider the Wyoming plan and determine whether a larger trophy game area, not the entire state, would achieve genetic connectivity.[41]

Judicial skeptics caution that judicial review of administrative implementation of the law poses the danger of policy fragmentation. There are ninety-four federal district courts and thirteen circuit courts, which can render different decisions on the same legal issue. A single federal court can stop agency policy. The Supreme Court can resolve these conflicts, but only has a very limited ability to address numerous conflicts.[42] Policy fragmentation occurred in this case.

The Wyoming federal district court examined Interior's rejection of Wyoming's plan as a policy question, which involves a mixture of legal and factual determinations. The court was required to take a "hard look" and scrutinize the agency's action "to satisfy itself that the agency has exercised a reasoned discretion, with reasons that do not deviate from or ignore the ascertainable legislative intent."[43]

Judicial skeptics criticize the hard-look doctrine, arguing that the court evaluates a policy question Congress left to the agency. The court attempts to separate law and politics, but the question is essentially political. The court, which lacks the agency's subject matter expertise, is simply second-guessing agency policy that it disagrees with under the rubric of law.[44] Skeptics argue that agency decisions should be upheld as long as there is "some plausible public purpose that the rule might further."[45]

The Wyoming federal district court substituted its judgment for that of Interior. The court focused exclusively on Interior's acceptance of the state plan in 2007, but ignored Interior's prior and subsequent rejections that stressed the need for a statewide trophy game designation. Interior's acceptance of Wyoming's plan in 2007, which fulfilled Secretary Kempthorne's confirmation promise, was the aberration. Following the Montana federal district court decision in 2008, Interior reaffirmed its long-held position, stating:

> We were probably too optimistic about what the law really committed Wyoming to and what could be accomplished by regulations alone. We also should have evaluated the potential for genetic connectivity more closely. . . . The very specific and deliberate intent, tone, and working of Wyoming law clearly continues to be the major impediment to Wyoming developing and implementing a wolf management plan the Service can approve. In the past Wyoming has . . . almost without exception encouraged wolf take to drive the wolf population down to minimum recovery levels. We believe that the best way for Wyoming to provide adequate regulatory mechanisms would be to develop a statewide trophy game management designation as the basis for any revised regulatory framework.[46]

The court substituted its judgment for that of Interior under the guise of the "best available science," which can be used to both support and attack administration policy.[47] The Wyoming federal district court failed to acknowledge that Wyoming's plan only protected the wolf in 12 percent of the state. Wolves in Wyoming leave the national parks and trophy game area to seek food and establish new territory. Wyoming maintained twenty-two winter elk feeding stations, twelve of which were in predator control areas, which attract wolves. History indicated that wolves leaving the trophy game area would be terminated in predator control areas. After the 2008 delisting, most of the wolves in the predator control area (seventeen of the twenty-eight) were killed within a few weeks.

Wolves dispersing from Montana and Idaho need access to Greater Yellowstone Area (GYA). Physical barriers, such as mountains and high elevation, discourage dispersal from the north and west. Dispersing wolves have greater access to GYA from the east and south. Limited social opportunities in Yellowstone National Park will cause some dispersers to avoid the park. Wolves travelling to the GYA will have to traverse Wyoming, where they face death in the predator control areas.

The Wyoming federal district court believed that Wyoming would not adjust the trophy game area to keep the wolf population at a bare minimum. Interior admitted it did not consider the possibility of reduced trophy game area when it approved the Wyoming plan of 2007. Subsequently, Interior expressed concern that any reduction in the trophy game area would increase the predator control area and endanger dispersal and connectivity.

The Wyoming district court determined there was no danger to wolf recovery because Wyoming promised to manage fifteen breeding pairs and 150 wolves. Interior consistently demanded statewide trophy game designation as the best means to attain wolf recovery. This would allow Wyoming "to regulate the methods of taking, hunting season, types of allowed takings, and number of wolves killed." Wyoming's plan only met the minimum recovery goals, if there were less than eight breeding pairs in national parks for two years. Only then would additional wolves be permitted outside the national parks until the recovery goal was met. Such a reduction of the population for two years could jeopardize recovery. Interior demanded a margin of safety in state wolf management.[48]

A recent scientific study found genetic connectivity between the three NRM wolf populations. This occurred under federal statewide wolf management in Wyoming. The study warned that a population of sufficient size must be maintained and dispersal corridors must be protected to ensure adequate dispersal and genetic connectivity in the future.[49] The findings supported Interior's insistence on statewide management.

Wyoming's plan was deficient when compared to the Montana and Idaho federally approved plans.[50] Montana and Idaho provided wolves with statewide protection under state statutes and established hunting seasons with quotas. Montana and Idaho regulations on the taking of depredating wolves were consistent with the section 10(j) experimental population regulations. By comparison, Wyoming only provided trophy game protection in 12 percent of the state. Wolves were classified as predators that could be shot on sight in the remaining 88 percent of the state. Wyoming was committed to keeping wolf numbers at a bare minimum. Wyoming's predator control law was more severe than the section 10(j) regulations. The Obama administration decided not to appeal the decision but to negotiate with Wyoming for a revised plan.

Connectivity

The ESA requires Interior to utilize the "best available science" in delisting decisions. The Montana federal district court in 2008 found that there was no connectivity between the three wolf populations in the NRM DPS. A prominent study demonstrated that there was not a functioning metapopulation of wolves in the NRM DPS.[51] A 2010 study by many of the same authors found that there was genetic connectivity between the populations in the three recovery areas. During the course of the ten-year study, the wolf population increased from 101 to 846. The authors concluded that the high genetic diversity evidenced during the first decade of reintroduction, resulting from an average 5.4 migrations per generation, was sufficient to avoid any future genetic problems. The authors, however, cautioned that successful conservation will depend on management decisions that promote natural dispersal and minimize factors that reduce genetic connectivity, such as hunting and predator control. A sufficient size population and adequate dispersal corridors must be maintained to ensure connectivity.[52]

Successful genetic connectivity in the region occurred with a wolf population of 846. The existing wolf population was 1,650. Interior conceded that the population would be reduced after delisting. A wolf population above 1,500, which is the carrying capacity of the region, would be difficult to maintain because packs would compete for habitat and generate conflicts with livestock owners. Interior estimated that there would be at least 600 wolves, probably more than 1,000 wolves in the NRM DPS. The NRM DPS population would never go below 300 and would probably fluctuate between 973 and 1,302 wolves with 77–104 breeding pairs. Montana and Idaho would have between 673 and 1,002 wolves with 52–79 breeding pairs, and Wyoming would have 300 wolves with 22 breeding pairs. Interior asserted that the post-delisting decline would have a negligible impact on dispersal and connectivity among subpopulations. Dispersal would continue even if the wolf population decreased by 23 percent. Dispersal would only be impacted if the wolf population was reduced below 150 in any state.[53]

Given the hostility to the wolf in the region, these projections seemed overly optimistic. Idaho, Montana, and Wyoming are only each required to maintain fifteen breeding pairs and 150 wolves. Wyoming and Idaho are committed to strictly adhering to this minimum number. Reducing the current wolf population to 450 will threaten dispersal and genetic connectivity. Interior acknowledged that a strong core population is necessary "to provide a steady influx of dispersing wolves" into suitable habitat. A small wolf population will lack the ability and incentive to leave the core areas and move into suitable habitat. Greater isolation of the wolf population will decrease the genetic diversity within each area and preclude repopulation in outside areas.[54]

WOLF HYSTERIA

Events demonstrated that the NRM states were committed to managing wolves at minimum levels. Following the 2010 Montana federal court decision, Montana and Idaho sought permission to conduct conservation hunts. Montana wanted to reduce its population to 439 by the end of 2010. Idaho sought to decrease its wolf population from 843 to 500 by the end of 2010.[55] The Montana and Idaho management plans suggest that their wolf populations can safely be reduced by human-caused mortality rates of 28 to 50 percent, which is consistent with literature on wolf harvesting.[56] A 2010 Montana State University study, however, concluded that these thresholds are too high and will have an adverse long-term impact on the wolf population.[57] Interior denied the states' request for conservation hunts in October 2010. Senator Tester (D. Mt.), chair of the Congressional Sportmen's Caucus, disagreed, stating, "Allowing a regulated hunt will expand the state's management options for this predator and restore balance to the system."[58]

Montana and Idaho also sought permission for smaller hunts pursuant to the section 10(j) regulation, which allows the killing of wolves by states and tribes when wolf predation is having an "unacceptable impact" on the wild ungulate populations. Prior to approval Interior must find that the proposal is scientifically based; will not contribute to reducing the wolf population in the state below twenty breeding pairs and two hundred wolves; and will not impede wolf recovery.[59] Interior approved Idaho's request to kill wolves in the Lolo district and Montana's proposal to decrease the wolf population in the Bitterroot region.[60]

Idaho's Memorandum of Understanding (MOU) with Interior regarding wolf management expired in March 2010. Governor Otter began negotiations for a new MOU. After permission for the conservation hunt was denied, the governor terminated the state's participation in wolf management. State officials were ordered not to arrest poachers, investigate illegal wolf kills, monitor the state's wolf population, or investigate livestock predation. Governor Otter stated that "everything the (federal government) has promised us, they've not kept. . . . It's time to draw the line somewhere."[61]

In February 2011, prior to approval for the Bitterroot hunt, Montana's Democratic governor, Brian Schweitzer, declared rebellion. The governor urged land owners in northern Montana, where wolves are an endangered species, to kill wolves harassing livestock, which is similar to the 10(j) rule in southern Montana where wolves are a threatened species. Hunters were also encouraged to kill wolves threatening elk herds in the Bitterroot area. Governor Schweitzer defended his illegal exhortation, stating he was "going to take additional necessary steps to protect the interests of Montana's livestock producers and hunters to the extent that I can within my authorities as governor." Several days later the governor backtracked, stating that "I think the ESA in this case has been poorly managed, but I don't think we need to get rid of the ESA. There are a lot of endangered species in Montana." Nevertheless, the spirit for rebellion among Republicans in the Montana legislature was ignited. The Montana House passed a symbolic bill nullifying the ESA and a resolution urging the removal of ESA protections from the wolf.[62]

The spirit of rebellion spread to Idaho in April 2011. The Idaho legislature enacted a bill granting the governor the power to declare a wolf emergency in the state because "the introduction of the Canadian gray wolves . . . have caused and continue to threaten vast devastation of Idaho's social culture, economy and natural resources." The emergency can be triggered by potential wolf conflict with humans, livestock, and big game, particularly if there are more than one hundred wolves in the state. The emergency will end when the wolf is delisted statewide or the threat subsides. Governor Otter signed the bill as a precautionary measure, declaring that the new law can be useful if wolves are ever relisted under the ESA.[63]

CONGRESS RESPONDS

The NRM wolf controversy moved to Congress. The courts, executive agencies, and Congress are involved in a dynamic relationship regarding public policy. Positive political theory posits that branches of government act as rational actors and compete with each other regarding policy preferences.[64] Congress reacts to judicial decisions. Studies show that Congress is aware of judicial decisions, devotes significant time to analyzing their policy implications, and frequently overrides statutory interpretations. Studies stress the importance of political factors in congressional reversals of judicial statutory decisions.[65]

John W. Kingdon in *Agendas, Alternatives, and Public Policies* explains why policies are adopted when they are and what problems with the existing policies made such changes possible. Kingdon's model envisions three independent streams. The problem stream brings problems to the attention of people in and around government. In the policy stream, a community of specialists generates proposals that interact with each other. The national mood, public opinion, election results, changes of administration, shifts in partisan or ideological distributions in Congress, and interest group campaigns affect the political stream.

The three streams develop and operate largely independent of each other. New problems emerge. Solutions are proposed. The political stream is constantly changing whether or not the policy community is ready or the problems facing the country have changed. The key to understanding agenda setting and policy formulation is coupling. At critical times, the separate streams come together. A problem is recognized; a solution is available; and the political climate is favorable. These "policy windows" open for a short time, then close. Policy entrepreneurs, who are willing to invest political capital, play a major role in the coupling at the open policy window. There are often spillovers in which the appearance of one item on the government agenda establishes the subsequent prominence of conceptually adjacent items.[66]

Following the 2010 Montana federal district court decision, bills were introduced by western senators and congressmen that delisted the wolf in Montana and Idaho, but retained ESA protection in the remainder of the NRM DPS; delisted the wolf in the NRM DPS except in Wyoming; and delisted the wolf nationally. The bills arrived late in the session. No action was taken in the Democratic House, but there was an effort to move the national delisting bill in the Democratic Senate by unanimous consent. Senator Ben Cardin (D. Mary.) objected, so the bill died.[67]

Wolf opponents renewed their efforts in 2011. Similar bills were introduced with bipartisan support, but there were major changes in the political stream.[68] Republicans gained the majority in the House (241R, 193D), and the Democratic majority in the Senate (51D, 47R, 2I) was reduced.

Wolf opponents pursed another tactic. A provision sponsored by policy entrepreneurs, Senator Tester and Representative Mike Simpson, reviving the 2009 regulation and precluding its judicial review, was attached to the continuing resolution keeping the federal government funded through fiscal year 2011. The provision was included in both the House passed and proposed Senate version of the continuing resolution.[69] An effort by Representative Cynthia Lummis (R. Wy.) to include Wyoming was defeated because it constituted a substantive change in legislation not permitted in an appropriation measure. This indicated congressional skepticism regarding Wyoming's wolf management plan.[70]

PROPOSED SETTLEMENT

Fear of congressional action generated a settlement proposal, which provided for the following: ESA protections for wolves in Montana and Idaho would be removed. Negotiations with Wyoming would continue, and a new delisting regulation would be promulgated. ESA protections for wolves in eastern Washington, eastern Oregon, and north-central Utah would be retained.

Interior would withdraw the 2007 solicitor's memo on the meaning of "significant portion of the range." A scientific panel would reexamine recovery goals according to the best available science. Interior would monitor the wolves in the region for four years. Environmental groups promised not to pursue new relisting proposals in the region until 2013, and no further litigation until 2016. Some environmental plaintiffs felt this was the best of the bad alternatives. The CBD stated that "this agreement is necessary to preserve long term recovery potential and head off a terrible precedent that would invite conservative congresspersons to push legislation to delist endangered species all over the country. It was a difficult and heart-wrenching decision, but one that we feel is the best course in this very difficult and dangerous situation."[71]

Ten of the environmental plaintiffs agreed to the settlement, but four were opposed.[72] Earthjustice, which represented the environmental plaintiffs, was forced to withdraw from the suit because the split created a conflict of interest.[73] The settling parties requested Judge Molloy to stay his earlier decision and accept the settlement.

The Montana federal court rejected the proposal in April 2011. Judge Molloy noted that the court must follow the law, not policy, and stressed the need to protect the interests of all parties in the litigation. The court determined that the proposed settlement would place wolves in Montana and Idaho at greater risk. The court could not use its equitable powers to allow a substantive violation of the ESA. The settling parties previously argued that state management was inadequate, wolf numbers were too low for delisting, and the DPS could not be subdivided. If the stay was granted, many of these issues would not be resolved. The court found the withdrawal of the solicitor's 2007 memo insignificant because its conclusions were erroneous. Balancing the equities, the court refused to stay its earlier order.[74]

CONGRESSIONAL FINALE

After Judge Molloy rejected the proposed settlement, Congress enacted section 1713 in the Defense Department Continuing Appropriation Act that delisted the wolf in the NRM, except Wyoming, and precluded its judicial review. Interior was also ordered to reconsider Wyoming's wolf management plan in light of Judge Johnson's decision and determine if a statewide trophy game designation is warranted.[75]

There were various reactions to the congressional finale. Senator Tester, who was in a tough reelection battle, argued that "we didn't amend the ESA. We asked that a recovered species—a species that FWS projected at 300 when it was reintroduced and now is 1,700, be taken off and managed just how we manage elk and mule deer and everything else." Representative

Lummis stated that "this language removes obstacles that would have otherwise hindered discussions on the status of the fully recovered gray wolf in Wyoming." Environmental groups acknowledged that Senator Tester was given "a powerful political pelt to hang on his wall," but promised to focus on state legislatures where there will be great pressure to kill wolves.[76]

The premature delisting of the wolves in the NRM DPS was only a symbolic victory for the state and federal government. The NRM states constantly complained about funding for their wolf management programs.[77] Wyoming estimated that it costs $2.27 million per year for wolf management.[78] Idaho was spending $720,000 per year on wolf management.[79] Wolf management cost Montana between $913,000 and $954,000 per year. The governors of the three states sought to have Congress establish the Northern Rocky Mountain Grizzly Bear and Gray Wolf National Management Trust to provide a source of funding for state management of recovered endangered and threatened species.[80] If the wolf retained protected status under the ESA, the states would continue to receive federal funds for wolf management.[81] Montana and Idaho received $637,000 per year from the federal government pursuant to the federal-state cooperative agreement.[82] Furthermore, studies demonstrated that the wolf brings thirty-five to seventy million dollars of new funds into Montana, Idaho, and Wyoming, which will offset any losses.[83]

IMPACT ON OTHER STATES IN THE NRM DPS

The April 2009 regulation also removed ESA protection from wolves in eastern Washington, eastern Oregon, and north-central Utah. Wolves in these areas are subject to state law. None of these states have federally approved state management plans because Interior did not establish recovery criteria for these areas. The regulation did not delist wolves in Wyoming.

Wolves in western Washington are federally protected as endangered species. There are currently thirty-eight wolves in ten packs and three breeding pairs in the state.[84] After federal delisting the wolf will remain an endangered species under state law until statewide conservation objectives are met. The state wolf management plan calls for the presence of fifteen breeding pairs in three regions for three consecutive years or eighteen packs in one year before state delisting. The hunting and livestock industries oppose the plan, arguing that too many breeding packs are permitted. Hunters and cattlemen have petitioned the Washington Department of Fish and Wildlife to strip state endangered species protection from gray wolves in the eastern third of the state. Conservation groups oppose any removal of ESA protections. The Washington Department of Fish and Game allows the killing of wolves caught in acts of predation in the northeast region.[85]

Wolves in western Oregon remain under federal protection, and their management is governed by the 2007 "Federal/State Coordination Strategy for Implementation of Oregon's Wolf Plan." Wolves in the eastern third of Oregon have been delisted, but all of the wolves in Oregon are classified as endangered species under the Oregon ESA and are managed under the 2005 "Wolf Conservation and Management Plan." Once the wolf is federally delisted, Oregon will consider state delisting when there are four breeding pairs for three consecutive years. The objective of the plan is for seven breeding pairs in the state. There are currently sixty-one wolves in eight packs and four breeding pairs in Oregon.[86] After delisting the wolf will be considered a "special status mammal" under state law.[87]

Wolves in Utah are federally protected except in the north-central part of the state. There are currently no wolves in the state. The Utah Wildlife Board developed a state management plan in 2005, which permits two breeding pairs in the state.[88] Utah enacted a statute in 2010, which prevents the establishment of packs in the delisted area until the entire state is delisted. After statewide delisting, the state plan will be activated. Wolves in north-central Utah are considered a fur-bearing animal under state law, but rifle permits cannot be issued. Utah considered proposals to reclassify wolves and allow their hunting in the delisted area.[89] Utah was particularly worried about Interior's proposal to reclassify the Mexican wolf as a distinct subspecies and grant it full protection in southern Utah and Colorado.[90] Interior did not pursue this option, but has proposed to recognize the Mexican wolf as a distinct subspecies and establish the Southwest DPS where the Mexican wolf will have ESA protection.[91]

CONCLUSION

The Obama administration resurrected the Bush administration proposal to subdivide and delist the wolves in the NRM DPS. Interior was not reluctant to pursue a policy previously rejected by the court. The Montana federal district court correctly rejected the Obama administration proposal, which was inconsistent with the text of ESA and prior agency interpretations. Judicial skeptics would be critical the court's decision, arguing that the court substituted its judgment for that of Interior.

Subsequent events complicated the conflict. The Wyoming federal district court found Interior's rejection of Wyoming's 2008 wolf management plan to be arbitrary and capricious. The court, realizing the fear of judicial skeptics, simply substituted its view for the agency. In addition, a new study by the authors of an earlier study, which was relied on by Montana federal district court in 2008, found there was connectivity between the three wolf populations in the region, so the NRM metapopulation existed.

Judicial decisions generated congressional action. Congress enacted section 1713, a rider to the Defense Department Appropriation bill that delisted the NRM DPS and precluded its judicial review. This was contrary to the ESA text and federal court decisions that a DPS cannot be subdivided. Congress overruled Interior's rejection of the Wyoming wolf management plan and supported the decision of the Wyoming federal district court. The rider established a bad precedent.[92] This was the first time Congress delisted a specific species. The rider undermined the ESA because it was not based on science, but politics. It may endanger wolf recovery in the NRM, if wolf populations are driven down to 150 wolves per state as result of wolf hysteria. No protection was provided for the nascent recovering wolf populations in Washington, Oregon, and Utah, which do not have federally approved state plans. The stage was set for the next round of public law litigation regarding the constitutionality of section 1713.

NOTES

A version of this chapter originally appeared as an article: "*Defenders of Wildlife v. Salazar*: Delisting the Children of the Night in the Northern Rocky Mountains, 31 *Public Land & Resources Law Review* 1 (2010).

1. *Defenders of Wildlife v. Salazar*, 729 F. Supp. 2d 1207 (D. Mt. 2010).

2. "Ken Salazar Disappointing Choice as Secretary of Interior," *CBD*, December 16, 2008. "Green Groups Divided over Salazar for Secretary of Interior," *Grist*, December 17, 2008.

3. "The Bush Administration's Eleventh Hour Wolf Delisting Proposal Fails," *Greater Yellowstone Coalition*, January 16, 2009.

4. Jamie Rapport Clark, "An Interior Decision Imperils More Than Wolves," *Washington Post*, January 1, 2010.

5. "Obama Restores Scientific Consultation to ESA," *Environment News Service*, March 3, 2009.

6. 74 *Federal Register* 15123 (April 2, 2009).

7. Frank B. Cross, "Pragmatic Pathologies of Judicial Review of Administrative Rulemaking," 78 *North Carolina Law Review* 1013, 1020–27 (2000).

8. "Reaction to Wolf Delisting Decision," AP State & Local Wire, March 6, 2009.

9. Matthew Brown and John Flesher, "Salazar OKs Wolf Removal for Endangered List," AP State & Local Wire, March 7, 2009.

10. "State Gets No Takers for Idaho Wolves," AP State & Local Wire, August 10, 2009. Kahrin Deines, "Montana Bill Seeks to Wrest Wolf Control from Feds," AP State & Local Wire, February 20, 2009. Matt Joyce, "Wyoming Legislature Ops Against New Wolf Rules," AP State & Local Wire, February 12, 2009.

11. Senate Committee on Energy and Natural Resources, *Hearings: Current Public Lands and Forests Legislation,* 110 Cong., 2d Sess. (July 9, 2008). Pub. L. 111-11, section 6201 (2009). Lee Iwanski, "Lands Bill Includes Federal Wolf-kill Compensation," AP State & Local Wire, March 30, 2009.

12. Eric Baker, "Wolf Hunting Heads Back to Court," *Lewiston Morning Tribune*, August 21, 2009.

13. *Winter v. NRDC,* 555 U.S. 7, 20 (2008).

14. "Returning Wyoming's One-finger Salute," *Lewiston Morning Tribune*, September 13, 2009.

15. *Defenders of Wildlife v. Salazar*, Case 9:09-CV-00077-DWM (September 8, 2009), 5-14.

16. Sven Berg, "Judging Both Sides," *Idaho Falls Post Register*, September 10, 2009. Ben Neary, "Wyoming Governor Hails Judge's Ruling on Wolf Hunts," *Lewiston Morning Tribune*, September 17, 2009.

17. "Report: Wolf Population Rose Last Year in Northern Rockies, but at Slower Rate," *Lewiston Morning Tribune*, March 12, 2010.

18. Paul Rogers, "Obama Decisions on Wildlife Raising Environmentalists' Ire," *San Jose Mercury News*, February 21, 2010. Jamie Rapport Clark, "An Interior Decision Imperils More than Wolves," *Washington Post*, January 1, 2010.

19. Kelly Zito, "Group Wants Wolves Back in California," *San Francisco Chronicle*, December 29, 2010.

20. Matt Brown, "Wolves: Biologists File Petition Seeking Nationwide Recovery," *Lewiston Morning Tribune*, July 21, 2010.

21. The plaintiffs included NRDC, Sierra Club, Humane Society of the United States, Center for Biological Diversity, Jackson Hole Conservation Alliance, Friends of the Clearwater, Alliance for the Wild Rockies, Oregon Wild, Cascadia Wildlands, Western Watersheds Project, Wildlands Network, and Hells Canyon Preservation Council.

22. *DOW v. Salazar,* 729 F. Supp. 1207 (D. Mt. 2010).

23. *INS v. Cardoza-Fonseca*, 480 U.S. 421, 446–49 (1987).

24. Jerry L. Mashaw, "Why Administrators Should Make Political Decisions," 1 *Journal Law, Economics, and Organization* 95–99 (1985).

25. *Schecter Poultry Corp. v. U.S.,* 295 U.S. 495 (1935). *Panama Refining Co. v. Ryan,* 293 U.S. 388 (1935).

26. Cynthia Farina, "Statutory Interpretation and the Balance of Power in the Administrative State," 89 *Columbia Law Review* 452 (1989).

27. 74 *Federal REgister* 15153, 15182–83, 15187.

28. 729 F. Supp.2d, 1222–28.

29. 16 U.S.C. 1532 (6), (16), (20).

30. 729 F. Supp.2d, 1222–25.

31. 68 *Federal Register* 15804, 15825 (April 1, 2003).

32. 70 *Federal Register* 1286, 1296 (Jan. 6, 2005).

33. Department of Interior, Office of Solicitor, *The Meaning of "In Danger of Extinction Throughout All or a Significant Portion of its Range"* (March 16, 2007).

34. *Trout Unlimited v. Lohn,* 559 F.3d 946, 949–57 (9th Cir. 2009). 729 F. Supp.2d, at 1226–29.

35. 61 *Federal REgister* 4723–24.

36. Fitzgerald, 31 *Public Land & Resources Law Review*, 25–38.

37. 386 F. Supp.2d, 564 n.9.

38. *Alsea Valley Alliance v. Evans,* 161 F. Supp. 2d 1154, 1162 (D. Or. 2001).

39. 559 F.3d, 960–61.

40. Wyoming Game and Fish Commission, *2008 Draft Revision, Wyoming Gray Wolf Management Plan* (October 28, 2008), 1–3. 74 *Federal REgister* 15125, 15149, 15172.

41. *Wyoming v. Interior,* Case No. 09-CV-118J (D. Wy. Nov. 18, 2010).

42. Frank B. Cross, "Shattering the Fragile Case for Judicial Review of Rulemaking," 85 *Virginia Law Review* 1243, 1249–57 (1999).

43. *Greater Boston Television Corp. v. F.C.C.*, 444 F.2d 841, 850–51 (D.C. Cir. 1970).

44. Cross, 1262–66.

45. Richard J. Pierce, "Seven Ways to Deossify Agency Rulemaking," 47 *Administrative Law Review* 59, 95 (1995).

46. 74 *Federal REgister* 15149.

47. Holly Doremus, "The Purposes, Effects, and Future of ESA's Best Available Science Mandate," 34 *Environmental. Law* 397, 429–32 (2004).

48. 74 *Federal REgister* 15170–72, 76.

49. Bridgett M. vonHoldt et al., "A Novel Assessment of Population Structure and Gene Flow in the Grey Wolf Populations of the Northern Rocky Mountains of the United States," 19 *Molecular Biology* 4412 (2010).

50. 74 *Federal REgister* 15167–70.

51. Bridgett M. vonHoldt et al., "The Geneaology and Genetic Variability of the Reintroduced Yellowstone Grey Wolves," 17 *Molecular Ecology* 252 (2007). 74 *Federal REgister* 15157–58, citing John K. Oakleaf et al., "Habitat Selection by Recolonizing Wolves in the Northern Rocky Mountains of the United States," 70 *Journal Wildlife Management* 554 (2006) and Carlos Carroll et al., "Defining Recovery Goals and Strategies for Endangered Species: The Wolf as a Case Study," 56 *BioScience* 25 (2006).

52. Bridgett M. vonHoldt et al., 19 *Molecular Biology* 4412 (2010). Mark Hebblewhite, Marco Musiani, and L. Scott Mills, "Restoration of Genetic Connectivity Among Northern Rockies Wolf Populations," 19 *Molecular Biology* 4383 (2010).

53. 74 *Federal REgister* 15130–38, 15142.

54. 72 *Federal REgister* 6119.

55. Matt Brown, "Idaho, Montana Seek OK for Hunting of Endangered Wolves," *Lewiston Morning Tribune*, September 1, 2010.

56. L. David Mech, "Managing Minnesota's Recovered Wolves," 72 *Journal of Wildlife Management* 89 (2001). L. G. Adams et al., "Population Dynamics and Harvest Characteristics of Wolves in the Central Brooks Range, Alaska," 170 *Wildlife Monograph* 1 (2008).

57. Scott Creel and Jay Rotella, "Meta-Analysis of Relationships between Human Offtake, Total Mortality and Population Dynamics of Gray Wolves," *PLoS ONE,* September 2010. Dennis L. Murray et al., "Death from Anthropogenic Causes is Partially Compensatory in Recovering Wolf Populations," 143 *Biological Conservation* 2514 (2010).

58. "Feds Deny Montana's Wolf Hunt Request," *Lewiston Morning News*, October 8, 2010. "Tester Pushes Interior to Allow Montana Wolf Hunt," Congressional Documents, January 26, 2011.

59. 50 C.F.R. 17.84 (n).

60. "FWS Publishes Draft Environmental Assessment of Idaho's Request to Manage Gray Wolves in Lolo Elk Management Zone," Interior Dept. Documents, February 10, 2011. Matt Brown, "Feds Give Early Approval to Wolf Kills in Idaho," AP State & Local Wire, February 11, 2011. "FWS Issues Notice About Availability of Draft Environmental Assessment of Montana Dept. Fish, Wildlife, and Parks Proposal," *US Fed News*, March 30, 2011. "Governor Schweitzer Statement on Draft EIS," *States News Service*, March 28, 2011.

61. Becky Kramer and Betsy Russell, "Idaho Pulling Back on Wolves," *Spokesman Review*, October 19, 2010.

62. "Governor Notifies Interior of New Wolf Management Directives," *States News Service*, February 16, 2011. Matt Brown, "Montana Isn't Planning Any Big Wolf Kills," *Lewiston Morning Tribune*, February 19, 2011. Matt Gouras, "Montana Eyes Nullification of the ESA," *Lewiston Morning Tribune*, February 20, 2011.

63. Idaho House of Representatives, House Bill No. 343. Katherine Wutz, "A Day of Reckoning," *Idaho Mountain Express*, April 8, 2011. Ben Botkin, "Idaho Prepares for Renewed Hunts," *Times-News*, April 16, 2011. "Gov. Otter Signs Wolf Disaster Bill into Law," AP State and Local Wire, April 19, 2011.

64. Daniel Farber and Philip Frickey, "Foreward: Positive Political Theory in the Nineties," 80 *Georgetown Law Journal* 457, 458–463 (1992).

65. William N. Eskridge Jr., "Overriding Supreme Court Statutory Interpretation Decisions," 101 *Yale Law Journal* 331 (1991). James L. Walker and Michael E. Solomine, "The Next Word: Congressional Response to Supreme Court Statutory Decisions," 65 *Temple Law Review* 425 (1992).

66. John W. Kingdon, *Agendas, Alternative, and Public Policy,* 2d ed. (Harper Collins, 1995), 19–20, 113–15, 143–44, 162–64, 194–95.

67. H.R. 6028, S. 3825, S. 3919, S. 3864, 111th Cong, 2d Sess. Eve Byron, "Wolf Management Hot Topic in D.C.," *Independent Record*, December 3, 2010. Laura Lindquist, "Utah Bill to Delist the Wolves Fails in Senate," *Times-News*, December 22, 2010.

68. Eric Baker, "Idaho Congressmen Co-sponsor Bills to Change Status of Wolves," *Lewiston Morning Tribune*, January 27, 2011.

69. "Rehberg Statement on Inclusion of Wolf Language in House Continuing Resolution," Congressional Documents, February 14, 2011. "Senate Includes Delisting Bill in Must Pass Funding Package," *States News Service*, March 4, 2011.

70. "House Denies Bid to Lift Wolf Protections in Wyo.," AP State & Local Wire, February 17, 2011. William N. Eskridge Jr., "The New Textualism," 37 *UCLA Law Review* 621, 638–39 (1990).

71. "Interior Announces Proposed Settlement of Gray Wolf Lawsuit," *Interior Press Release*, March 18, 2011. CBD Newsletter, March 24, 2011.

72. The ten favoring settlement were Cascadia Wildlands, CBD, DOW, Greater Yellowstone Coalition, Hells Canyon Preservation Council, Jackson Hole Conservation Alliance, NRDC, Oregon Wild, Sierra Club, and Wildlands Network. The four opposed to settlement were Alliance for the Wild Rockies, Western Watershed Project, Friends of the Clearwater, and the Humane Society.

73. "Deal Reached to Lift Protections in 2 States," AP Online, March 18, 2011.

74. *DOW v. Salazar*, CV 09-77-M-DWM, CV 09-82-M-DWM (April 9, 2011).

75. Eve Byron, "Budget Rider Will Delist Wolves," *Independent Record*, April 15, 2011. On April 15, 2011, President Obama signed the appropriation bill that delisted the NRM wolves. 76 *Federal Register* 25590 (May 5, 2011).

76. Phil Taylor, "Budget's Wolf Delisting Opens Pandora's Box," *New York Times*, April 13, 2011. "Wolf Delisting Excludes Wyoming," *Billings Gazette*, April 12, 2011. Richard Reeder, "Wolf Deal May Be a Negative for Wyoming," *Cody Enterprise*, April 6, 2011.

77. Becky Bohrer, "Who Will Pay for Wolf Costs Undecided," *Billings Gazette*, March 28, 2006. 74 *Federal REgister* 15151.

78. Wyoming Game and Fish Commission, *2008 Draft Wyoming Gray Wolf Management Plan*, 37. Jared Miller, "Feds Won't Kill Excess Wolves," *Wyoming Tribune*, January 18, 2007.

79. Idaho Department of Fish and Game, *Idaho Wolf Population Management Plan 2008-2012* (March 6, 2008), 38. The federal government provides $380,000 to the Nez Pearce Tribe for wolf management. "Fed Funds Crucial to Survival of Wolves in Idaho," *Idaho Statesman*, January 6, 2006.

80. Montana Fish, Wildlife & Parks, *Questions and Answers,* 2 (fwp.mt.gov/wildthings/wolf). Mike Stark, "Funding Questions Abound as Feds Change Wolf Status," *Billings Gazette*, February 21, 2008.

81. Wolf management in the Northern Rocky Mountains is costing the federal government $2.7 million per year for monitoring, public outreach, predator control. Becky Bohrer, "Who Will Pay for Wolf Costs Undecided," *Billings Gazette*, March 28, 2006.

82. Montana Fish, Wildlife & Parks, *Montana Gray Wolf Conservation and Management 2008 Annual Report,* 92. 70 *Federal Register* 1286 (January 6, 2005).

83. Scott McMillion, "Wolves and Money," *Bozeman Daily Chronicle*, April 7, 2006.

84. US FWS, *Rocky Mountain Wolves Recovery 2013 Interagency Report*, 1.

85. "Commission Questions Wash. Areas for Wolf Recovery," AP State & Local Wire, August 30, 2011. "Groups Seek to Delist Wolves in Eastern Washington," AP State & Local Wire (Oct. 5, 2011). Jeff Barnard, Oregon, "Washington Wants to Handle Wolves on Their Own," *Lewiston Morning Tribune*, August 28, 2012. "Groups Ask Obama to Protect Northwest Wolves," *States News Service*, August 14, 2012. Jim Camden, "Rule Allows Killing of Wolves," *Spokesman Review*, April 27, 2013.

86. U.S. FWS, *2013 Interagency Annual Report*, at 1.

87. *Oregon Wolf Conservation and Management Plan* (October 2010), 1–15.

88. 74 *Federal REgister* 15172–74.

89. Kirk Robinson, "Why Must Utah Be Kept Free of Wolves?" *Salt Lake Tribune*, February 4, 2010. Dan Weist, "Gray Wolf Bill Angers Advocates," *Standard-Examiner*, October 20, 2010. Brandon Loomis, "Panel Endorses Wolf Hunt," *Salt Lake Tribune*, November 18, 2011. "Utah Bill Would Reclassify Wolf as Game Animal," AP State & Local Wire, December 24, 2011.

90. "Utah Wants Wolves Kept Out," UPI, November 10, 2011. Juliet Eilperin, "Once Nearly Extinct, Wolves Now Fair Game," *Washington Post*, September 17, 2012. 77 *Federal Register* 61375 (Oct. 9, 2012)

91. 78 *Federal Register* 35719 (June 12, 2013).

92. Senator Cornyn (R. Tx) filed an amendment to the Economic Development Administration Act to stop the proposed endangered species listing of the dunes sagebrush lizard. "Attack

on Lizard Continues," *Alamogordo Daily News*, June 9, 2011. Zachary Bray, "The Hidden Rise of Efficient (De)Listing," 73 *Maryland Law Review* 201, 251–56 (2014).

Chapter Seven

Congress Behaving Badly

Alliance for the Wild Rockies v. Salazar

Section 1713 of the Department of Defense and Full-Year Continuing Appropriations Act of 2011 revived the Obama administration regulation delisting the wolf in the Northern Rocky Mountain Distinct Population Segment (NRM DPS), except Wyoming, and precluded judicial review of the regulation.[1] Environmental groups brought suit, alleging that section 1713 violated the separation of powers by dictating the outcome in the case. The U.S. District Court for the District of Montana and the Ninth Circuit in *Alliance for the Wild Rockies v. Salazar*[2] upheld the constitutionality of the appropriation rider. Congress can change the law to affect ongoing litigation and remove federal court jurisdiction over the issue. There were, however, novel alternative theories that could have been pursued, which would have established strong precedents for environmental protection and democratic governance. The courts could have invoked structural due process, enforced the rule that substantive legislation can't be attached to an appropriation bill, and remanded the issue to Congress. The courts could have found that congressional action violated federal public trust responsibilities and procedural due process. The courts could have subjected the unique treatment of the wolf to more exacting scrutiny because of the wolf's importance to the preservation of biodiversity and ecosystem maintenance. Congress could not have removed federal court jurisdiction over the constitutional questions. This chapter analyzes the litigation and explores the alternative theories of the case.

ALLIANCE FOR THE WILD ROCKIES V. SALAZAR

Environmental groups brought suit, challenging the delisting rider as a violation of separation of powers.[3] The Alliance for the Wild Rockies (AWR) declared, "Congress can change any law, but what they did here is not amend ESA, but reinstated the delisting and said it could not be challenged in court. They can't be both members of Congress and judges too; they can't decide what is legal." The Department of Justice (DOJ) countered. "Congress acted well within its constitutional authority. Congress's power to modify the law, which in turn affects judicial decisions based on an old law, is well established."[4]

The Montana federal district court determined that the rider undermined the ESA, but was constitutional. Judge Molloy noted that the rider represented "an undermining and disrespect for the fundamental idea of the rule of law." Nevertheless, he was bound to follow past Ninth Circuit precedent, which found similar language, "without regard to any other provision of statute or regulation that applies to the issuance of the regulation," constituted repeal by implication.[5] Environmental groups remained optimistic, declaring that Judge Molloy "did everything but buy us a ticket to San Francisco." Senator John Tester (D. Mt.) was also pleased, stating "returning Montana wolves to Montana management was the right thing to do, and we did it in a responsible way with utmost respect to existing law and to our constitution."[6]

While the case was being appealed, Montana and Idaho planned wolf hunts for the fall of 2011. Environmental groups went to court to stop the hunts. The AWR declared that "the states want to decimate the wolf population in the Northern Rockies. We want to stop this massive killing that is about to occur." The federal court denied the motion. The Wildlife Alliance stated that "we are discouraged we didn't win a stay of execution for wolves, but we are cautiously optimistic that we will win our lawsuit to protect wolves from further prosecution." Idaho governor Butch Otter pronounced that "wolves have had a robust recovery in Idaho, and the explosive growth of the population left unchecked continues to have an unacceptable impact."[7] During the winter of 2012 Montana hunters killed 166 of the 220 wolf quota. Yet, Montana's wolf population increased by 15 percent to 653 wolves. In Idaho, 255 wolves were shot and 124 wolves were trapped, leaving a wolf population of 746.[8]

The Ninth Circuit in 2012 affirmed the district court decision upholding the constitutionality of the appropriation rider.[9] Reactions to the decision varied. The Center for Biodiversity (CBD) declared, "Congress set a terrible precedent by passing this backdoor rider that took away protection from wolves. Scientists, not politicians, need to decide which species need protection." Representative Mike Simpson (R. Id.) stated, "this case has made it clear that those who persist in trying to manage wildlife through the courts, in spite of all scientific evidence that this species has recovered, no longer have a defensible position." Senator Tester explained that "this decision is right for Montana because Montana wolves are recovered, and they must be managed like other wildlife."[10]

ANALYSIS: *ALLIANCE FOR THE WILD ROCKIES V. SALAZAR*

The AWR litigation raised several major questions. Can Congress change the law to affect pending litigation? Can Congress by-pass the conventional lawmaking process and attach substantive statutory changes to an appropriation bill? Can Congress remove federal court jurisdiction over the issue? The answer to each of these questions reflects either the republican or public choice model of Congress.

Civic republicanism posits that Congress is a deliberative body in search of the public good. Congress is the "forum for identifying or defining [objectives], and acting towards those ends. The process is one of mutual search through joint deliberation. . . . Moral insight, sociological understanding, and goodwill are legislative virtues."[11]

The public choice model considers the legislature to be a marketplace in which public goods are distributed to private interests. Legislation is an economic transaction in which legislators, who are seeking reelection, enact policies that further private interests in return for votes, campaign contributions, and political influence. Legislation is not "reasonably related to some general social goal," but embodies deals that advance private preferences. There is no deliberative process striving toward the achievement of public interest. Instead, there are "too many laws that are 'rent seeking' (i.e., laws that distribute resources to a designated group without any contribution to society's overall efficiency)."[12]

Changing the Statutory Framework

Environmental groups, relying on *U.S. v. Klein*,[13] alleged that section 1713 violated the separation of powers. Section 1713 did not amend ESA, but was an attempt to affect the outcome of pending litigation regarding the subdivision of the NRM DPS. The Ninth Circuit held that the enactment of section 1713 did not violate the separation of powers. Congress did not interfere with pending litigation, but amended the ESA. Interior was instructed to restore the federal regulation "without regard to any other provision of statute or regulation that applies to issuance of the rule." Congress replaced preexisting standards with new standards, which the court must follow.[14]

The Ninth Circuit correctly determined that section 1713 did not violate the separation of powers. Klein is the only case in which the Court found congressional action affecting pending litigation unconstitutional. Klein has been implicitly overruled by *Robertson v. Seattle Audubon Society.*[15] Recent cases demonstrate that Congress has virtually unlimited power to affect pending litigation by amending or repealing any law; creating exceptions to existing law; or establishing new law that avoids compliance with existing legal requirements. Section 1713 repealed by implication other statutory requirements. Even if section 1713 did pose a problem with the separation of powers, the Ninth Circuit was required to adopt an interpretation that upheld its constitutionality. Judicial abandonment of Klein, however, reinforces interest group influence in Congress and supports public choice theory.

Separation of Powers

The U.S. Constitution separates power among the three branches of the federal government and provides each branch with authority to check and balance the exercise of power by other branches. Congress enacts the law. The executive implements the law. The judiciary interprets the law and decides cases. The constitutional separation of powers and checks and balances prevents the tyranny of one branch with respect to the others and over individuals.[16]

Congress can repeal or amend the law to affect the outcome of pending litigation. The court must utilize the new law in the litigation. For example, in *Pennsylvania v. Wheeling & Belmont Bridge*,[17] the Court initially determined that the bridge was a navigational obstruction. Congress responded by enacting a statute that changed the status of the bridge to a postal road and required navigation not to interfere with the bridge. Subsequently, the Court concluded that Congress had changed the law, and the bridge ceased to be a nuisance.

Congress can't, however, instruct the court on how to decide a particular case. The Supreme Court in *U.S. v. Klein* invalidated a congressional act for violating the separation of powers. The administrator of the deceased owner of property sold to the federal government during the Civil War brought suit pursuant to a federal statute allowing noncombatant Confederate landowners, who had demonstrated loyalty to the federal government, to recover the proceeds from such sales. In an earlier case, the Court held that a presidential pardon constituted sufficient proof of loyalty under this law.[18] Since the deceased owner had received a pardon, the Court of Claims awarded recovery. While the appeal was pending, Congress enacted a statute that declared a presidential pardon did not constitute proof of loyalty, but could be evidence of disloyalty. Federal courts were ordered to find that a claimant, who had accepted a presidential pardon without previously disclaiming disloyalty, was not entitled to land sale proceeds under the statute. Federal courts were instructed to dismiss any case in which the claimant had prevailed in the Court of Claims on an assertion of proof of loyalty by presidential pardon.

The Supreme Court held that the statute was not a valid exercise of the "exceptions and regulations" clause, but was simply an unconstitutional congressional instruction to the courts on how to rule in particular cases. Congress had exceeded "the limit which separates the legislative from the judicial power." The Court distinguished the earlier Wheeling Bridge decision on the grounds that "no arbitrary rule of law was prescribed in Wheeling Bridge, but the court was left to apply its ordinary rules to the new circumstances created by the Act."[19] No law had been changed in Klein.

The Supreme Court implicitly overruled Klein in *Robertson v. Seattle Audubon Society*. Several timber sales in the Pacific Northwest old-growth forests were challenged on the grounds they posed a risk to the threatened northern spotted owl. The Ninth Circuit temporarily halted the sales for alleged violations of the Migratory Bird Treaty Act (MBTA), National Environmental Policy Act (NEPA), Federal Land Policy and Management Act (FLMPA), and Oregon-California Railroad Land Grant Act (OCRLGA).[20] Congress responded by enacting section 318 of the Department of Interior (DOI) Appropriation Act 1990, popularly known as the Northwest Timber Compromise, which established the rules for temporary timber harvesting within designated geographical areas in "the 13 national forests in Oregon and Washington and Bureau of Land Management (BLM) district in western Oregon known to contain northern spotted owls." The rule expired on September 30, 1990, except that interim sales remained subject to section 318. The National Forest Service (NFS) and the BLM were required to offer specified quantities of lumber in the area during the year. Section (b)(3) identified areas in the national forests, and section (b)(5) identified areas on BLM lands where sales were prohibited. The litigation focused on section (b)(6), which states "the Congress hereby determines and directs that management of areas according to (b)(3) and (b)(5) of this section on the 13 national forests in Oregon and Washington and BLM lands in western Oregon known to contain northern spotted owls is adequate consideration for the purposes of meeting the statutory requirements that are the basis for the consolidated cases captioned *Seattle Audubon v. Robertson*, *Washington Contract Loggers Assoc. v. Robertson*, *Portland Audubon v. Lujan*."[21]

The federal district court dismissed the case on the grounds that section (b)(6) "can and must be read as temporary modification of the environmental laws" in the cases. The Ninth Circuit reversed and found section (b)(6) "does not, by its plain language, repeal or amend the environmental laws underlying this litigation," but rather "directs the court to reach a specific result and make certain factual findings under existing law in connection with two [pending] cases." This violated *U.S. v. Klein*, which prohibits Congress from "prescrib[ing] a rule for a decision of a cause in a certain way" when "no new circumstances have been created by legislation."[22]

The Supreme Court reversed and found section 318 did not command a result in pending litigation, but amended the underlying statutes to provide an alternative means for the timber sales to proceed. The Court found the tone of the language did not alter its view that section 318 changed the law. The specific reference to the cases being reversed was dismissed as a shorthand method of identifying the statutory provisions that were replaced. The enactment of section 318 through an appropriation rider did not pose any problem. The Court noted that repeals by implication were not favored, but were allowed if the language was explicit as in section 318. Even if section 318 posed a constitutional problem, the Court was required to adopt a statutory interpretation that upheld its constitutionality.[23]

Klein is based on several premises: First, Congress can't interfere with the president's pardon power. Second, Congress can't preclude suits against the federal government. Third, Congress can't force the courts to validate unconstitutional acts. Fourth, Congress can't dictate the outcome in a judicial proceeding.[24] Robertson undermined several of these rationales. Congress dictated the result in pending litigation. Sections 318 (b)(3) and (b)(5) excluded certain areas from leasing within threatened northern spotted owl habitat. Congress declared that timber sales in the remaining areas complied with statutory requirements without changing any of the provisions of the statutes allegedly being violated. Judicial review of sales in the remaining areas was explicitly precluded. Section 318 specifically identified the litigation that was being reversed and permitted timber sales that directly benefited the federal government.

Robertson indicates that federal courts must accord a high degree of respect for an act of Congress that is intended to affect litigation as long as it changes the underlying substantive law in any detectable way. The Ninth Circuit in *AWR v. Salazar*, noting its unsuccessful attempt to invoke Klein in the Robertson, acknowledged that the "Supreme Court showed us the error of our ways."[25] Section 1713, like section 318, amended preexisting law and directed Interior to restore the federal regulation. Since Congress changed the preexisting law, there was no violation of separation of powers.

Repeals by Implication

Section 1713 resurrected the April 2009 regulation "without regard to any other provision of statute or regulation that applies to issuance of such rule." Environmental groups argued that section 1713 did not repeal the ESA. Repeals by implication are not allowed, particularly in appropriation bills. The Ninth Circuit held that section 1713 amended the underlying law.[26] The court was correct that section 1713 repealed by implication any statute that interfered with federal delisting of the wolves.

Repeals by implication are not favored, particularly in appropriation bills. The Supreme Court held that the doctrine of disfavoring repeals by implication "applies with full vigor when . . . the subsequent legislation is an appropriations measure."[27] Repeals by implication, however, are not prohibited if congressional intent is explicit. Congress employed similar language, such as "notwithstanding" and "without regard to," in other statutes to exempt projects from the application of environmental laws. The Supreme Court held that the use of such language overrides other conflicting provisions in the law. The Court stated that "the use of . . . a notwithstanding clause clearly signals the drafter's intention that the provisions of the notwithstanding section override conflicting provisions of any other section."[28]

The Ninth Circuit in several cases found such language repealed by implication statutes that prevented the projects from going forward. The Ninth Circuit in *Stop H-3 v. Dole* determined that the "notwithstanding" language meant no other statute can interfere with the project going forward. The court stated that "by exempting the H-3 project from further 4(f) compliance, Congress clearly eliminates future delays in H-3 construction."[29] The Ninth Circuit made the same determination in *Consejode Desarrollo Economico v. U.S.*, stating "when Congress has directed immediate implementation 'notwithstanding any other provision of law,' we have construed the legislation to exempt the affected project from the reach of environmental statutes which would delay implementation."[30]

Even if there were problems regarding the separation of powers or repeal by implication, the Ninth Circuit was required to adopt an interpretation of section 1713 that upheld its constitutionality. The Supreme Court in Robertson held that "as between two possible interpretations of a statute, by one of which it would be unconstitutional and by the other valid, our plain duty is to adopt that which will save the act."[31]

Consequences

Judicial failure to invoke Klein allows Congress to enact exemptions to existing law, like section 1713. This reinforces public choice theory, which posits Congress is a legislative marketplace in which congresspersons parcel out public goods to private interests to enhance their opportunity for reelection. Organized economic interests utilize their influence to have Congress enact exceptions to environmental laws. This allows projects to go forward that benefit particular interest groups. Environmental laws that protect the public interest are sacrificed on the legislative altar to special interests.[32]

Judicial abandonment of Klein also poses problems for democratic theory. Klein requires the courts to ensure that Congress has not deceived the electorate by leaving the law in place, while directing an outcome that contradicts or undermines the law. In such cases, voters are deceived about the position of their elected representatives and denied the opportunity to hold their representatives accountable. This is why Klein mandates an explicit change in the underlying law.[33]

Section 1713 did not change the ESA. Congress was very clear about its motives for enacting section 1713. Sponsors of the bill explicitly stated that their intent was to reverse the district court decision in *DOW v. Salazar*, not to change the ESA. Senator Tester stated, "The Baucus-Tester bill would restore management practices as they were before the 2010 court ruling that resulted in the return of the gray wolf to federal management under the ESA." Representative Simpson announced that he was "spearheading an effort to undo the August 2010 ruling by Judge Molloy that put wolves back on the endangered species list."[34] Even the DOI Solicitor acknowledged that section 1713 did not change the ESA.[35] Yet, the Ninth Circuit held that 1713 directly amended the ESA and repealed by implication any legal impediments to the reenactment of the flawed 2009 federal regulation.[36] This permitted Congress to act in a duplicitous manner.

Policymaking through Appropriation Riders

Section 1713 was enacted through a rider on an appropriation bill. After a statute is enacted with authorized expenditures, funds must be allocated. Congress is required to enact thirteen appropriation bills that fund the federal government. House and Senate Appropriations Committees are primarily responsible for allocating annual funding. House and Senate rules prohibit the attachment of substantive legislation to appropriation bills,[37] but Congress often ignores this rule. If the relevant appropriation bill is not passed, funding can be sustained through a continuing resolution, which does not prohibit the attachment of unrelated legislation. Appropriation riders provide a legal means to enact statutory amendments. The Supreme Court has never invalidated a law because it was enacted by an appropriation bill.[38]

The enactment of legislation through appropriation riders, however, violates congressional rules that no substantive legislation can be attached to an appropriation bill. This rule recognizes that the appropriation process is dominated by well-organized interests and lacks visibility. Legislating through the appropriation process undermines the republic view that the political outcomes should be arrived at through open deliberative process. Political actors are not supposed to begin the process with pre-selected interests whose satisfaction is the goal of the process. Politics is not designed to satisfy private interests or achieve a balance among competing interest groups. The republican view advises politicians to subject interest group demands to examination through an open deliberative process. Republican theories "require public regarding justification offered after multiple points of view have been consulted and (to the extent possible) genuinely understood."[39]

Removal of Federal Court Jurisdiction

Section 1713 not only resurrected the flawed regulation delisting wolves in the NRM DPS, but also deprived the federal courts of jurisdiction to determine its validity. Congress controls federal court jurisdiction over statutory questions. The removal of federal court jurisdiction, however, undermines separation of powers; threatens the legitimacy of the administrative action; severs the partnership between courts and administrative agencies to further public interest; and weakens the foundation of the administrative state. Depriving the federal courts of jurisdiction patently endorses public choice theory.

Congressional Control of Federal Court Jurisdiction

Article III of the U.S. Constitution allows for, but does not mandate, the creation of the lower federal courts.[40] Debates at the constitutional convention demonstrate that the establishment of the lower federal courts was left to the discretion of Congress. Access to the federal courts was not a constitutional right, but was subject to political and legislative judgment. Since Congress created the lower federal courts, Congress can abolish them. The greater authority includes the lesser power, so Congress can adjust or withdraw lower federal court jurisdiction over issues.[41] The Supreme Court declared that the power to establish lower federal courts includes the power "of investing them of jurisdiction either limited, concurrent, or exclusive, and of withholding jurisdiction from them in the exact degrees and character which to Congress may seem in the public good."[42]

There is a long line of Supreme Court precedents that support congressional power to remove lower federal court jurisdiction over statutory questions.[43] Furthermore, the Administrative Procedures Act acknowledges that Congress can preclude the judicial review of agency action. There is a strong presumption against such removal, but this can be overcome by clear and convincing evidence.[44]

Problems Presented by Removal of Jurisdiction

Just because Congress has the power to limit federal court jurisdiction, this does not mean that it is wise policy.[45] Removing federal court jurisdiction frustrates the constitutional separation of powers, which is designed to avoid the concentration of power in any single branch. In the absence of judicial review, the legislative and executive branches can exercise their power without limit. Congress, acting in a judicial capacity, determines that executive action complies with the law.[46] This undermines judicial authority and frustrates the uniform application of federal law. The public is not able to question federal government action. This denigrates the value of citizen suit provisions in environmental laws, like the ESA, and the idea of the government being limited by law.[47]

Depriving the federal courts of jurisdiction threatens the legitimacy of administrative action. Judicial review promotes the legitimacy of administrative action, which can be defined as the "ensurance of legality, protection against arbitrariness and selectivity, promotion of procedural regularity, and ensurance against the twin evils of factional tyranny and self-interested representation."[48] The courts maintain the integrity of the process. Louis Jaffe stated that "the availability of judicial review is a necessary precondition, psychologically if not logically, of a system of administrative power which purports to be legitimate, or legally valid." The courts serve as "a constant reminder to the administrator and a constant source of assurance and security to the citizen."[49]

Precluding judicial review undermines the foundation of the modern administrative state. Congress delegates broad power to administrative agencies to implement the law with the assurance that the courts will keep federal agencies in check.[50] Courts review administrative action to ensure conformance with the law. Judge Leventhal observed that agencies and courts together constitute a "partnership in furtherance of the public interest" and the "court is in a real sense part of the total administrative process, and not a hostile stranger to the office of first instance."[51] Removing the court's jurisdiction terminates this partnership. It also frustrates the dialogue between Congress, the executive, and the judiciary over the formulation and implementation of public policy. Judicial review advances the republican ideal of honest, disinterested deliberation about the public interest.[52]

ALTERNATIVE THEORIES

There are other novel alternative theories that could have been pursued to question the legitimacy of the congressional delisting through an appropriation rider. The rider violated congressional rules that substantive legislation cannot be attached to an appropriation bill. The rider violated the public trust doctrine and procedural due process by infringing on the public's limited property rights through an invalid process, which precluded public participation. The rider violated the Equal Protection Clause by singling out the wolf for unique treatment. Congress could not remove the court's jurisdiction over the constitutional issues.

Violation of Congressional Rules

The enactment of section 1713 violated House and Senate rules prohibiting the attachment of substantive legislation to appropriation bills. The Supreme Court has invalidated legislative actions that violated congressional rules and recognized the unique nature and limitations of appropriation bills. Lawmaking through appropriations subverts the legislative process and results in the enactment of special interest legislation. Prominent scholars and jurists have urged the courts to remand to Congress legislation impinging on important values that was enacted through dubious legislative procedures. The Supreme Court has examined the legislative process and invalidated laws not supported by adequate fact-finding. Judicial enforcement of congressional rules, which is less intrusive, will move Congress toward "due process" lawmaking.

Supreme Court Precedent

The Constitution grants Congress the right to establish its own procedural rules.[53] The Supreme Court recognized that congressional rules are legally enforceable and invalidated congressional acts that violated congressional rules.[54] The Supreme Court has questioned the amendment of laws through the appropriation process. The Court has recognized important differences between authorizations and appropriations and limitations regarding the latter with respect to the former.[55]

The Supreme Court in *Andrus v. Sierra Club* determined that an Environmental Impact Statement was not required for appropriation bills because there was a clear distinction between authorizations and appropriations. House and Senate rules required a "previous choice of policy . . . before any item of appropriation might be included in a general appropriation bill." Appropriation bills "have the limited and specific purpose of providing funds for authorized programs." This division of labor allows the appropriation committees to focus on financial issues and precludes them from trespassing on the authority of the authorizing committees. The Court stressed that "appropriation bills are not proposals for legislation."[56]

The Supreme Court emphasized the difference between authorization and appropriations in *TVA v. Hill*. The Court noted that appropriation bills "have the limited and specific purpose of providing funds for authorized programs." If appropriation bills are used for substantive changes in legislation, it would "lead to the absurd result of requiring Congress to review exhaustively the background of every authorization before voting on an appropriation." Furthermore, the Court noted that repeals by implication are not favored, especially "with even greater force when the claimed repeal rests solely on an Appropriation Act."[57]

Flaws in Policy Making through Appropriation Riders

Policy making through appropriation riders not only violates congressional rules, but undermines deliberative lawmaking, which requires legislators to make explicit policy choices, employ procedures that limit arbitrary action, and produce a record that is subject to meaningful judicial review. This is particularly egregious when Congress enacts appropriations through continuing resolutions, which have to be enacted and are veto-proof.[58]

Theoretically, the normal legislative process encourages rational consideration of policy issues through discussion, participation, negotiation, and public scrutiny. The bill is introduced and moves to the committees with subject matter expertise. Hearings are held, which allow interest groups to voice their concerns. The bill can be amended in committee, which explains the details of the bill in the committee report. Often there are committees with overlapping jurisdiction, which provide for greater public access, discussion, and accountability. Congresspersons get the opportunity to change the bill through floor amendments. Legislation must be passed by both houses of Congress. Differences are generally negotiated in the conference committee with a subsequent report explaining the compromises. The president, who is generally an active participant in the process, must sign the bill or let it remain on his desk for ten days while Congress is in session before it becomes law. The president can veto the bill, but a two-thirds vote in both houses can override the veto.[59]

The enactment of legislation through appropriation riders undermines this process and poses many problems. First, substantive changes in legislation through appropriation riders don't receive adequate consideration. They are generally introduced late in the process, with little debate, often in the dark of night. Congresspersons and their staffs have little opportunity to examine the riders, which by-pass the legislative process and exclude the public from the debate.[60]

Second, policy making through the appropriation process alters the balance of power in Congress. Appropriation riders are not reviewed by the authorizing committees with subject matter expertise. Existing legislation is amended by the appropriation committee, which subverts the authority of the authorizing committee. Substantive legislation, which was often the product of long-term interest group bargains and legislative negotiation and compromise, is undermined. The Supreme Court noted that the congressional committees with authority and expertise "would be somewhat surprised to learn that their careful work on the substantive legislation had been undone by the simple-and brief-insertion of some inconsistent language in a [proposed appropriation measure]."[61] These amendments can create conflict between the authorizing and appropriating committees in both houses and between the Senate and the House.[62]

Third, appropriation riders enact legislation that cannot get through the front door of the conventional legislative process through the back door of the appropriation process. This encourages logrolling, which is "practice of jumbling together in one act inconsistent subjects in order to force passage by uniting minorities with different interests when the particular provisions could not pass on their own separate merits."[63] These amendments generally promote narrow local interests over broader national public interests. Interest groups pursue this path because there is little public scrutiny or accountability regarding such proposals. This is very typical of western public land policy.[64]

Fourth, appropriation riders interfere with the president's ability to veto bad legislation. Appropriation riders also frustrate the president's authority to properly implement the law. The Constitution does not distinguish between authorizations and appropriations.[65]

Section 1713 manifested most of these flaws. First, section 1713 was a stand-alone provision that was never debated. Second, section 1713 bypassed the Senate Environment and Public Works and House Resources Committees that have jurisdiction over the ESA. Third, section 1713 was attached to an unrelated appropriation bill that had to be enacted. The Obama administration, however, supported section 1713, so there was no interference with the executive's ability to veto the law.

Policy making through appropriation riders enhances interest group influence in Congress. Congress distributes public benefits to special interest groups at the expense of the general public. Congresspersons seeking reelection defer to other congresspersons on local issues with the expectation of a corresponding quid pro quo.[66] Congresspersons are not required to take controversial stands and are able to avoid resolving conflicts over public values. There is little accountability for such action, which deceives the public. Laws enacted to further the public interest, such as the ESA, are undermined through an appropriation rider like section 1713.

Policy making through appropriation riders not only contradicts the republican view of a deliberative representative process, but poses a dilemma for public choice theory. In the congressional marketplace interest groups are willing to pay more for deals that are long lasting. The enactment of special-interest legislation through an appropriation rider helps congresspersons get reelected, but diminishes the value of the interest group deals negotiated during enactment and makes future deals more difficult.[67] Judge Easterbrooke noted that "if courts become instruments by which packages are undone, laws will be harder to pass. Bargains must be kept to be believed."[68]

Judge Molloy in *AWR v. Salazar* recognized problems with the enactment of legislation through appropriation riders like section 1713. Judge Molloy declared that inserting "environmental policy changes into appropriation bills may be politically expedient, but it transgresses the process envisioned by the

Constitution by avoiding the very debate on issues that provides legitimacy." Policy changes that cannot be enacted through the normal legislative process "can be forced using insider tactics without debate by attaching riders to legislation that must be passed."[69]

Due Process Lawmaking/Structural Review

The Supreme Court expressed concern with circumstances that "curtail the operation of . . . political processes."[70] Prominent scholars have argued that federal courts should review legislative procedures when the laws enacted impinge on important public values. If the process was defective, federal courts should remand the legislation back to Congress. The courts would not be telling Congress that its goals could not be achieved, but that the process followed was defective.[71]

Judge Linde proposed the "due process" model of lawmaking, which views policy making as a rational process of establishing the means to achieve articulated ends. This is accomplished through a transparent process that enables the public to hold legislators accountable. The entire process is governed by rules. The court's role is not to question the substance of the legislation, but to ensure that Congress followed the proper procedures when enacting the law.[72]

Professor Tribe argued that federal courts can provide structural justice. Professor Tribe pointed out that "the process and rules that constitute the enterprise and define the roles of its participants matter quite apart from any identified 'end state' that is ultimately produced."[73] Federal courts should examine the "structures through which policies are both formed and applied, and formed in the very process of being applied" to ensure consistency with due process of law.[74] Professor Tribe stated that judicial review of due process lawmaking focuses on "who promulgated the provision, to what ends, and in what manner."[75]

Professor Ely stressed that the Constitution is concerned "with procedural fairness in the resolution of individual disputes" and "with ensuring broad participation in the processes and distributions of government." When the political system malfunctions, the court's role is to "police the mechanisms by which the system seeks to ensure that our elected representatives will actually represent." This representation–reinforcing focuses on political processes rather than legislative outcomes. Judges are "conspicuously well suited to fill" this role because they are experts on "the processes by which issues of public policy are fairly determined." Professor Ely supports the "second look" approach that underlies due process lawmaking and structural review.[76]

Professors Frickey and Farber urge the courts to examine the legislative "structure and process." Courts should pay attention to when laws "were passed, by whom, or how." Courts should "require legislatures to adhere to established procedures." This will check interest group influence and promote "democratic deliberation without imposing judicial value judgment on the public."[77]

Henry Hart and Albert Sacks stress the "vitally important relationship between procedure and substance. A procedure which is soundly adapted to the type of power to be exercised is conducive to well-informed and wise decision. An unsound procedure invites ill-informed and unwise ones." Hart and Sacks assert that "the best criterion of sound legislation is . . . whether it is the product of a sound process of enactment," namely, a process that is informed, deliberative, and efficient.[78]

Judicial Review of Congressional Procedures

The Supreme Court has promoted due process lawmaking. The Court in several cases examined the internal workings of Congress and found there was not a sufficient factual basis to justify the enactment of legislation.[79] Justice Stevens held that when Congress impinges on important public values, the Court should examine the legislative procedures involved in the enactment of the statute.[80] Since the Court is willing to examine congressional procedures and question congressional fact finding,[81] less intrusive judicial enforcement of congressional rules should not pose any difficulty.

Supporters of structural review argue that Congress should be required to produce a record of evidence or "clear statement" that demonstrates that it acted reasonably in concluding that federal legislation is necessary and proper to exercise its enumerated powers. Federal courts should police "Congress's deliberative process and its reasons for regulating" to ensure that Congress seriously considered federal concerns and adequately justified federal government action. Supporters suggest that federal courts should conduct a "hard look review" of congressional action. This will promote procedural regularity, provide equal protection, protect due process, generate institutional dialogue, encourage deliberation, and ensure that the political process is open and fair.[82]

Professor Sunstein urges the courts to strictly scrutinize legislation enacted through appropriation riders. This will improve the performance of governmental institutions and counteract defects in their procedures. It will also discourage special interest legislation and "promote the primacy of ordinary lawmaking, in which the constellation of interests is quite different and the likelihood of deliberation higher."[83] Professor Rose-Ackerman goes further and argues that "courts should prohibit Congress from waiving its own rules governing appropriations." Congress should not be allowed to include "substantive provisions in spending bills."[84]

Other scholars raise objections to judicial review of congressional procedures. First, critics argue that courts can't treat Congress like an administrative agency. The uncertain constitutional position of administrative agencies and their tendency to be captured require rigorous judicial review. Congress, which is a co-equal branch of government, is not plagued by the same problems.[85] Public choice theory, however, suggests a different conclusion.

Second, critics assert that judicial interference with congressional procedures violates the separation of powers. Federal courts should not get involved with the internal workings of Congress. The Constitution grants each house of Congress the authority to develop its own rules of procedure. Judicial review of congressional procedures presents a non-justiciable political question, which lacks judicially manageable standards.

Third, critics point out that Congress has a unique way of doing business. Requiring Congress to follow its own rules, engage in an open deliberative process, and justify its positions undermines the efficacy of the institutional process. Congress receives information from various sources. The legislative process consists of bargains and compromises among members, interest groups, and the general public. Ambiguity and deception are part of the process.[86] Professor Tushnet asserts that judicial review of the legislative process might "destroy the legislative process as we know it."[87]

Fourth, critics argue that imposing new procedural requirements is post-hoc. Congress did not know it was required to develop an adequate record or sufficient evidence to support legislation.[88]

None of these fears would have been realized if section 1713 had been remanded to Congress for violating congressional rules. The court would not have developed rules for Congress, interfered with the legislative process, or established post-hoc requirements. The court would simply have enforced long-standing congressional rules that prohibit the attachment of a substantive rider to an appropriation bill. This would help "to limit 'rent seeking' in the budgetary process."[89]

Public Trust Doctrine

Section 1713 violated the public trust doctrine, which posits that certain natural resources are common property held in trust by the government for the benefit of its citizens.[90] The federal government holds public lands and resources in trust for citizens.[91] The Supreme Court recognized federal public trust responsibilities.[92] The classic public trust doctrine, which prohibits the disposition of the trust resources, is not applicable to federal lands. The public trust doctrine has, however, evolved with changes in the philosophy of public land management. From 1888 through 1970 in the era of federal retention and management, the public trust doctrine was invoked to justify federal protection of public lands from private interests. In the environmental protection era beginning in 1970, the public trust doctrine has been utilized to constrain federal management of public lands.[93]

The public trust doctrine is an implied right. Environmental statutes in total "set a tone, a context, a milieu. When read together they require a trustee's care."[94] The public trust doctrine constrains congressional action and protects "public expectations against destabilizing changes."[95] The U.S. District Court for the District of East Virginia stated that "under the public trust doctrine, . . . the United States have the right and the duty to protect and preserve the public's interest in natural wildlife resources. Such a right does not derive from ownership of the resources but from a duty owing to the people."[96]

Several commentators envision the public trust doctrine as a vehicle for the protection of ecosystems. Professor Rieser argues that the public trust doctrine should protect functioning ecosystems, which are "public goods." Ecosystems containing endangered species "are irreproducible products of nature that must remain intact in order to provide benefits." Conserving natural resources is a collective or public good, which will not be accomplished by the market and individuals.[97] Professor Bader asserts that "the public trust doctrine must be used to maintain the general health of natural systems." The role of the court is to "determine whether a particular activity would be likely to impair substantially the health of a local ecological system." This inquiry requires the court to assess "the impact of the activity on the diversity and stability of the biotic community."[98]

The public trust doctrine, like structural review, focuses on process. Judicial involvement occurs when organized interest groups use their power in the legislative arena to adversely affect public resources. Such resources are important to a free society and "have a peculiar public nature." The court examines government decisions that are "calculated either to relocate that resource to more restricted uses or to subject public uses to the self interest of private parties." Judicial skepticism should be particularly acute when a decision regarding public resources has been made in a closed political process dominated by particular interest groups, which questions "the usual presumptions that all relevant issues have been adequately considered and resolved by routine statutory and administrative processes."[99]

The court subjects the trustee's decision to a hard look, which requires detailed explanations of decisions, rationales for departures from past practice, effective participation in process, and consideration alternatives. The court focuses on "process fairness and reasoned decision-making, . . . rather than particular substantive rights."[100] The hard look ensures "diligence, fairness, and faithfulness" regarding the protection of the public resource. If problems are discovered, the court remands the issue back to the legislature to be resolved in open deliberate political process. The legislature, not the court, makes policy, but through the proper means. The public trust doctrine has no intrinsic content, but is "a technique by which courts may mend perceived imperfections in the legislative and administrative process . . . a medium for democratization."[101]

The Constitution grants Congress plenary power over public property,[102] but the disposition and use of such property must serve a public purpose. The public trust doctrine is based on the common law, so can be trumped by statute.[103] Congress controls public resources, but must exercise that authority through an open deliberative political process,[104] not by backroom deals attached to an appropriation bill like section 1713, which violate congressional rules.

Due Process Violation

Section 1713 also violated the Due Process Clause of the Fifth Amendment by infringing on the public's limited property rights in species preservation and management of public lands. Property rights are legal protected interests with respect to a thing, tangible or intangible.[105] The public's limited property rights include the protection of environmentally critical resources. Federal decisions regarding public resources should not be made exclusively on the basis of development, but should recognize their ecological values. The public has a right to the ecological integrity of the resources on which its survival depends. Preserving nature "is an obligation to our cultural tradition." Citizens have a right "to their history, to the signs and symbols of their culture, and therefore to some means of protecting and using their surroundings in a way consistent with their values."[106]

The federal government can create property rights, which constitute an entitlement. Such rights cannot be taken be taken away without procedural due process.[107] The federal statutory scheme regarding environmental protection and public land management in total establishes a limited public property right that complements the public trust doctrine. Environmental statutes are "trustee statutes," which seek to stop the destruction of natural resources and provide for "the restoration of natural resources."[108] For example, the National Environmental Policy Act states that "it is the continuing policy of Federal Government . . . to use all practicable means and measures . . . to create and maintain conditions under which man and nature can coexist in productive harmony [for] present and future generations of Americans."[109] The ESA declares that endangered and threatened "species of fish, wildlife, and plants are of esthetic, ecological, educational, historical, recreational, and scientific value to the Nation and to its people."[110] The Federal Land Policy and Management Act mandates that public lands "be managed in a manner that will protect the quality of scientific, scenic, historical, ecological, environmental, air and atmospheric, waters resource, and archeological values; that, where appropriate, will preserve and protect certain public lands in their natural condition; that will provide food and habitat for fish and wildlife and domestic animals; and that will provide for outdoor recreation and human occupancy and use."[111] Citizen suit provisions in these and other environmental and public land management statutes recognize the public's interest in proper public land management.[112] Section 1713 infringed on the public's limited property right by interfering with the proper management of public lands. Few statutory goals regarding public lands can be accomplished in the absence of proper management.

Generally, due process protections are not afforded when the government impinges on a public right. Individuals, who are part of a large class adversely affected by government action, are expected to seek redress in the legislative arena. Due process protections are afforded by the courts when individuals suffer unique personal injuries that make it impractical to seek legislative redress. Since the public must rely on the political process to protect its interests, the courts should examine the political process to ensure that the public rights are only curtailed through an open and deliberative political process.[113]

Section 1713 was not enacted through an open deliberate political process, but was attached to an appropriation bill in violation of congressional rules. Environmental groups were not afforded "environmental due process," which guarantees the right to participate in the political decision and entails "a minimum requirement that government action give adequate consideration to environmental values."[114] Section 1713 should have been remanded to Congress for reconsideration in an open deliberative legislative process.

Equal Protection Violation

Section 1713 should have been subject to heightened judicial scrutiny for violating the "equal protection" component of the Due Process Clause of the Fifth Amendment.[115] The rationales that support less rigorous review and the non-recognition of due process rights are not applicable. Section 1713 is special interest legislation that undermined important public values. The federal government should have been required to articulate the substantial government interests being served by section 1713.

Section 1713 violated the "equal protection" component of the Fifth Amendment by providing unique treatment for wolves in the NRM. Generally, distinctions in environmental statutes, like economic and social legislation, are reviewed by the courts under the deferential rational basis standard. The plaintiff must show that distinctions in the law are not rationally related to the public interest. Courts are generally deferential to distinctions made by Congress. Judicial deference is accorded because environmental values are less important than the protection of individual rights, which are essential to the proper functioning of the political process. Legislatures are more competent than courts to deal with these policy matters.[116]

These rationales do not support the deferential review of section 1713, which provided unique treatment for the NRM wolves. The Ninth Circuit recognizes that environmental protection is an important public value.[117] Endangered species, like the wolf, are important components in a balanced ecosystem, which is one of the central purposes of the ESA. Disruptions in the ecosystem cause environmental instabilities that diminish nature's ability to establish food chains, cycle nutrients, sustain atmospheric quality, control the climate, regulate the fresh water supply, maintain the soil, dispose of wastes, pollinate crops, and control pests and disease. Robert Costanza estimated the value of services derived from ecosystems to be in the range of sixteen to fifty-four trillion dollars per year. With an estimated value of thirty-three trillion dollars per year, ecosystems provide services that cost almost twice the gross domestic product of all the nations in the world combined.[118] Section 1713 was not enacted through an open deliberative political process, but was attached to an appropriation bill. This specifically violated congressional rules that prohibit the enactment of substantive legislation in appropriation bills.

Section 1713 was special interest legislation with concentrated benefits and dispersed costs.[119] Section 1713 specifically advanced the interest of the farmers, livestock producers, hunters, and certain state governments. Section 1713 undermined the ESA, which declares the protection of endangered and threatened species to be in the national interest. It also deprived the public of ecologically balanced public land management.[120]

Lawmaking is a dialogue in which laws, unlike naked commands, must be explained to those they touch. Individuals are entitled to know why the law is being applied. Such an explanation entails reasons that rationally fit the rule being defended.[121] Congress should not respond to the naked preferences of politically powerful interest groups, but should select public values through a process of deliberation and debate. Federal courts should ensure that government actions promote public values by subjecting special interest legislation to heightened scrutiny.[122] Federal courts "should invalidate spending provisions in appropriations acts that clearly benefit a narrower range of interests than those contemplated in the original substantive act."[123]

Justice Stevens supported heightened judicial scrutiny of statutes that contain discriminatory classifications or impinge on liberty or due process. Such statutes must be enacted by a rational purposive legislative process. Justice Stevens held that when a statute contains a "questionable" classification, "due process requires that there be a legitimate basis for presuming that the rule was actually intended to serve [the] interest put forward by the government as its justification."[124] The court must examine the legislative process to discover which government interests were considered as part of the legislative purpose.[125]

Given the important interests at stake and the procedure utilized, section 1713 should have received heightened scrutiny.[126] Section 1713 should have been subjected to intermediate scrutiny, which requires the federal government to show that the legislative distinction furthers a substantial government interest and the means chosen are rationally related to achieving the substantial government interest. Alternatively, section 1713 should have been subject to rigorous rational basis scrutiny, which shifts the burden of proof to the government to demonstrate the reason for the legislative distinction.[127]

The federal government should have been required to explain how section 1713 was consistent with public purposes of the ESA or why the NRM wolf delisting was being exempted from legal requirements of the ESA. This was particularly warranted because the federal regulation delisting the NRM wolves had been adjudicated as violating the ESA. In the absence of such an explanation, there was no way to justify the unique treatment of the NRM wolves. Such a requirement would have increased the interest groups' transactional costs; encouraged greater deliberation and explanation on the part of Congress; made the public aware of the congressional action; facilitated judicial review; and enhanced "due process" lawmaking.[128]

Removal of Federal Court Jurisdiction

Congress would not have been able to remove federal court jurisdiction over the equal protection and due process violations. There is a debate among scholars regarding congressional power to remove federal court jurisdiction over constitutional questions. Justice Story asserted that Article III mandated Congress to create the federal courts and grant them authority over all cases in which the Supreme Court lacks original jurisdiction. Lower federal courts are essential to establish national judicial power.[129] Professor Hart argued that Congress can't remove jurisdiction that interferes with the court's essential functions.[130] Professor Sager asserted that some federal judicial forum is necessary to protect federal constitutional rights. Professor Gunther pointed out that Congress cannot "require a court to decide cases in disregard of the Constitution." Professors Redish and Woods acknowledged that Congress "has the power to prevent the adjudication of claims based upon statutorily created rights," but the Fifth Amendment grants a litigant the "right to an independent judicial hearing, state or federal, of a constitutional claim."[131]

Professor Eisenberg expressed the point most clearly. Professor Eisenberg argued that "because of changed circumstances, the framers' aspirations for the national judiciary cannot be fulfilled today without the lower federal courts." Federal courts are essential to check other branches, provide uniformity, and counteract local bias. The Supreme Court cannot do the job alone.

Lower federal courts are necessary to protect constitutional rights and implement Supreme Court decisions. Federal courts "must be invested with jurisdiction to hear federal issues." Professor Eisenberg noted that "it is clear that jurisdictional statutes are subject to constitutional limitations. . . . When their effect is to abrogate constitutional rights, they are no more valid than any other statute violating the Constitution." Congress has the authority to "withdraw jurisdiction from all cases except those in which a particular outcome is mandated by the Constitution." Jurisdictional statutes "which have substantive impact must be subject to constitutional scrutiny. The conclusion is also inescapable that Congress cannot withdraw jurisdiction to hear cases in which constitutional rights are at stake."[132]

CONCLUSION

The Ninth Circuit in AWR correctly held that Congress can exempt the project from existing law through an appropriation rider. The appropriation rider delisting the wolf in the NRM DPS did not violate the constitutional separation of powers. Congress can deprive the federal courts of jurisdiction over this statutory issue. The exercise of each of these legislative prerogatives undermines civic republicanism and supports public choice theory. Section 1713 was special interest legislation that advanced the interests of farmers, hunters, livestock owners, and state governments at the expense of ecologically managed public lands and the protection of an endangered species. Section 1713 undermined the ESA and deceived the public.

Other novel alternative legal theories could have been employed to question the legality of section 1713. The enactment of section 1713 as a rider on an unrelated appropriation bill violated congressional rules that no substantive legislation can be attached to an appropriation bill; the public trust doctrine, which requires Congress to manage public resources in the long-term public interest; the Due Process Clause of the Fifth Amendment by impinging on the public's limited property right in species protection and balanced public land management through a flawed legislative process that precluded public participation; and the "equal protection" component of the Due Process Clause of the Fifth Amendment by providing unique treatment for the NRM wolves. Section 1713 should have been subject to more rigorous judicial review. Judicial action under each of these theories would have decreased interest group influence and forced Congress to operate through conventional procedures subject to public scrutiny. Congress could not have removed federal court jurisdiction over the constitutional issues.

The premature delisting of the NRM wolves by Congress undermined the ESA, which mandates that decisions be based on science, not politics. The wolves in the NRM DPS should not have been considered for delisting until Wyoming's management plan was approved.

NOTES

A version of this chapter originally appeared as an article: "*Alliance for the Wild Rockies v. Salazar*: Congress Behaving Badly," 25 *Villanova Environmental Law Journal* 351 (2014).

1. Section 1713 states: "Before the end of the 60-day period beginning on the date of enactment of this Act, The Secretary of Interior shall reissue the final rule published on April 2, 2009 (74 Fed. Reg. 15123 et seq.) without regard to any other provision of statute or regulation that applies to issuance of such rule. Such reissuance (including this section) shall not be subject to judicial review and shall not abrogate or otherwise have any effect on the order and judgment issued by the United State District Court for the District of Wyoming in Case Numbers 09-CV-118J and 09-CV-138J on November 18, 2010 [involving Wyoming's management plan for gray wolves]." President Obama signed the act into law on April 15, 2011. Pub. L. 112-10, 125 Stat. 38 (2011). See also, Eve Byron, "Budget Rider Will Delist Wolves," *Independent Record*, April 15, 2011. On May 5, 2011, FWS complied with Section 1713 by reissuing the 2009 rule. 50 C.F.R. Part 17, 76 *Federal Register* 25590.

2. 800 F. Supp. 2d 1123, 1127 (D. Mont. 2011). 672 F.3d 1170 (9th Cir. 2012).

3. The plaintiffs were AWR, CBD, Wildlife Guardians, and Friends of Clearwater.

4. "Lawsuits Challenge New Wolf Rules in Northern Rockies," AP Online (May 5, 2011). "Lawsuit Challenges Constitutionality of Anti-wolf Rider," CBD, May 5, 2011. "Wolf delisting slated again for Montana," *Independent Record*, May 5, 2011. "Wolf Law Challenged as Hunting Dates Draw Near," *Lewiston Morning News*, July 27, 2011.

5. 800 F. Supp. 2d, 1127.

6. "Montana Judge Upholds Congress' Change to Wolf Status," *Great Falls Tribune* (August 4, 2011).

7. Becky Kramer, "Rules on Idaho Wolf Hunt Include No Statewide Quota," *Spokesman Review*, July 9, 2011. "Wolf Cull Outrages Wildlife Groups," *Gazette*, August 10, 2011. "Groups Ask Court to Halt Idaho Wolf Hunts," *Lewiston Morning Tribune*, August 14, 2011. "Motion to Bar Idaho and Montana Hunts Denied," AP, August 26, 2011.

8. Matt Volz, "Montana Gives Initial OK to Plans for Wolf Hunt," *Lewiston Morning Tribune*, May 11, 2012. "Idaho Wolf Hunt Continues on Private Lands," AP State & Local Wire, July 5, 2012.

9. 672 F.3d 1170 (9th Cir. 2012).

10. "Appeals Court Denies Challenge to Congressional Rider," *Targeted News Service*, March 14, 2012. "Simpson Statement on Wolf Delisting Decision," *Coeur d'Alene Press*, March 14, 2012. "Tester: Court Ruling on Wolves Right for Montana," U.S. Senate Documents, March 14, 2012.

11. Frank I. Michelman, "Political Markets and Community Self-Determination: Competing Models of Judicial Legitimacy," 53 *Indiana Law Journal* 145 (1977–78).

12. William N. Eskridge, "Dynamic Statutory Interpretation," 135 *University of Pennsylvania Law Review* 1479, 1511–21 (1987). William N. Eskridge, "Politics Without Romance: Implications for Public Choice Theory for Statutory Interpretation," 74 *Virginia Law Review* 275, 285 (1988).

13. 80 U.S. 128 (1871).

14. 672 F.3d, 1174.

15. 503 U.S. 429 (1992).

16. *Misretta v. U.S.*, 488 U.S. 361, 380 (1989). 800 F. Supp. 2d., 1127.

17. 59 U.S. 421 (1855).

18. *U.S. v. Padelford*, 76 U.S. (9 Wall.) 531 (1870).

19. 80 U.S. 146–47.

20. 914 F.2d 1311 (9th Cir. 1990).

21. *Department of Interior and Related Agencies Appropriations Act for Fiscal Year 1990*, Pub. L. No. 101–121, 103 Stat. 701, 745–50 (1989).
22. 914 F. 2d, 1315–16.
23. 503 U.S. 438–42.
24. Amy D. Ronner, "Judicial Self-Demise: The Test When Congress Impermissibly Intrudes on Judicial Powers After *Robertson v. Seattle Audubon Society*," 35 *Arizona Law Review* 1037, 1045–48 (1993).
25. 672 F. 3d, 1174.
26. 672 F. 3d, 1131.
27. 437 U.S. 153, 190 (1978).
28. *Cisnerous v. Alpine Ridge Group*, 508 U.S. 10, 18 (1993).
29. 870 F. 2d 1417, 1432 (9th Cir. 1989).
30. 482 F. 3d 1157, 1168–69 (9th Cir. 2007).
31. 503 U.S. 441. *Communications Workers v. Beck*, 487 U.S. 735, 762 (1988).
32. Eskridge, "Romance," 286. Michael A. Fitts, "The Vices of Virtue: A Political Party Perspective on Civic Virtue Reforms of the Legislative Process," 136 *University of Pennsylvania Law Review* 1567, 1579–84 (1988).
33. Martin H. Redish and Christopher R. Pudelski, "Legislative Deception, Separation of Powers, and the Democratic Process: Harnessing the Political Theory of *United States v. Klein*," 110 *Northwestern University Law Review* 437, 439–40 (2006).
34. *Complaint for Declaratory and Injunctive Relief*, U.S. District Court for District of Montana, *AWR v. Salazar*, 11–17.
35. Memorandum from Hilary Tompkins, Solicitor, to Secretary of Interior M-37024 (March 16, 2007), n.4.
36. 672 F.3d, 1174–75.
37. Senate Rule 16.2 (2012) states: "The Committee on Appropriations shall not report an Appropriation bill containing amendments to such bill proposing new or general legislation." House Rule XXI (2)(b) (2012) states: "A provision changing existing law may not be reported in a general appropriation bill."
38. Chrisopher J. Deering and Steven S. Smith, *Committees in Congress*, 3d ed. (Congressional Quarterly, 1997), 198–202. *U.S. v. Dickerson*, 310 U.S. 554, 555 (1940).
39. Cass R. Sunstein, "Beyond the Republican Revival," 97 *Yale Law Quarterly* 1539, 1548–50, 1582 (1988).
40. Article III, section 1, of the Constitution states: "The judicial power of the United States shall be vested in one Supreme Court, and in such inferior Courts as the Congress may from time to time ordain and establish."
41. Gerald Gunther, "Congressional Power to Curtail Federal Court Jurisdiction: An Opinionated Guide to the Ongoing Debate," 36 *Stanford Law Review* 895, 912–14(1984). Martin H. Redish and Curtis E. Woods, "Congressional Power to Control the Jurisdiction of Lower Federal Courts: A Critical Review and a New Synthesis," 124 *University of Pennsylvania Law Review* 45, 46–47 (1975).
42. *Lockerty v. Phillips*, 319 U.S. 182, 187 (1943). *Kline v. Burke Construction Co.*, 460 U.S. 226, 234 (1922).
43. *Palmore v. U.S.*, 411 U.S. 389, 400–1 (1973); *Glidden v. Zdanok*, 370 U.S. 530, 551 (1962); *Yakus v. U.S.*, 321 U.S. 414 (1944); *Borsv v. Preston*, 111 U.S. 252 (1884); *U.S. v. Union Pac. R.R.*, 98 U.S. 569 (1878); *Sewing Machine Co. Case*, 85 U.S. 553 (1873); *U.S. v. Klein*, 80 U.S. (13 Wall.) 128 (1872); *Sheldon v. Sill*, 49 U.S. (8 How.) 441 (1850); *U.S. v. Hudson*, 11 U.S. (7 Cranch) 32 (1812).
44. 5 U.S.C. 701. *Bowen v. Michigan Academy of Family Physicians*, 476 U.S. 667, 670 (1986).
45. Gunther, 898.
46. *Springer v. Philippine Islands*, 277 U.S. 189, 202 (1927). *Buckley v. Valeo*, 424 U.S. 1, 38–41 (1976). *INS v. Chadha*, 462 U.S. 919, 964–66 (1983).
47. 16 U.S.C. 1540(g). Gordon G. Young, "Congressional Regulation of Federal Courts' Jurisdiction and Processes: *U.S. v. Klein* Revisited," 1981 *Wisconsin Law Review* 1189, 1248. Victor M. Sher and Carole Sue Hunting, "Eroding the Landscape, Eroding the Law: Congres-

sional Exemptions from Judicial Review of Environmental Laws," 15 *Harvard Environmental Law Review* 435, 482 (1991).

48. Cass R. Sunstein, "On the Costs and Benefits of Aggressive Review of Judicial Action," 1989 *Duke Law Journal* 1169 (2001).

49. Louis Jaffe, *Judicial Control of Administrative Action* (Little Brown, 1965), 320–25.

50. Cynthia R. Farina, "Statutory Interpretation and the Balance of Power in the Administrative State," 89 *Columbia Law Review* 452. Linda M. Bolduan, "The Hatfield Riders: Eliminating the Role of Courts in Environmental Decision Making," 20 *Environmental Law* 322, 372–75 (1990).

51. *Greater Boston Television v. FCC*, 444 F. 2d 841, 850–51.

52. Cass R. Sunstein, "Forward: Leaving Things Undecided," 110 *Harvard Law Review* 4, 101 (1996). Cass R. Sunstein, "Interest Groups in American Public Law," 38 *Stanford Law Review* 29 (1985).

53. Article I, section 5, cl. 2, of the Constitution provides: "Each House may determine the Rules of its Proceedings."

54. *U.S. v. Ballin*, 144 U.S. 1 (1892); *Cristoffel v. U.S.* 338 U.S. 84 (1949); *Yellin v. U.S.*, 374 U.S. 109 (1963); *Gojack v. U.S.*, 384 U.S. 302 (1966).

55. Kathleen M. Vanderziel, "The Hatfield Riders & Environmental Preservation: What Process Is Due?" 19 *Boston College Environmental Affairs Law Review* 431, 436-45 (1991). Sher and Hunting, 469–70.

56. 442 U.S. 347, 361–65 (1979).

57. 437 U.S. 153, 190 (1978).

58. Hans A. Linde, "Due Process of Lawmaking," 55 *Nebraska Law Review* 197, 223–24 (1976). Sandra Beth Zellmer, "Sacrificing Legislative Integrity at the Altar of Appropriations Riders: A Constitutional Crisis," 21 *Harvard Environmental Law Review* 457, 510–13 (1997).

59. Zellmer, 500–504. Other scholars argue that this textbook version has been supplanted by "unorthodox lawmaking." Institutional changes, including the reduction of committee power, the expansion of the leadership's authority, and the use of omnibus legislation and the budget process to enact policy have caused this transformation. Barbara Sinclair, *Unorthodox Lawmaking, New Legislative Processes in the U.S. Congress* (CQ Press, 2012) .

60. Neil E. Devins, "Regulation of Government Agencies Through Limitation Riders," 1987 *Duke Law Journal* 456, 464–65. Jacques B. LeBoeuf, "Limitations on the Use of Appropriation Riders by Congress to Effectuate Substantive Policy Changes," 19 *Hastings Constitutional Law Quarterly* 457, 474 (1992). Sher and Huntington, 478–79. Zellmer, 500–510.

61. 437 U.S. 19.

62. Deering and Smith, 199–202.

63. William N. Eskridge and Philip P. Frickey, *Cases and Material on Legislation: Statutes and the Creation of Public Policy*, 2d ed. (West Publishing, 1994), 250.

64. Alyson C. Flournoy, "Beyond the 'Spotted Owl': Learning from the Old-Growth Controversy," 17 *Harvard Environmental Law Review* 261, 304–05 (1993). Zellmer, 486. Michael C. Blumm, "Ancient Forests and the Supreme Court: Issuing a Blank Check for Appropriation Riders," 43 *Journal Urban and Contemporary Law* 35, 51–57 (1993).

65. Devins, 471–74. Zellmer, 526–28. LeBoeuf, 472–78.

66. Einer R. Elhauge, "Does Interest Group Theory Justify More Intrusive Judicial Review?" 101 *Yale Law Review* 31, 41 (1991).

67. William M. Landes and Richard A. Posner, "The Independent Judiciary in an Interest-Group Perspective," 18 *Journal Law and Economics* 875, 877–79, 894 (1975).

68. Richard Easterbrooke, "Foreword: The Supreme Court and the Economic System," 98 *Harvard Law Review* 4, 9 (1984).

69. 800 F. Supp. 2d, 1125.

70. *U.S. v. Carolene Products*, 304 U.S. 144, 152–53n4 (1938).

71. Laurence Sagar, "Insular Minorities," 91 *Harvard Law Review* 1373, 1412 (1978). Dan T. Coenen, "The Rehnquist Court, Structural Due Process, and Semi-substantive Constitutional Review," 75 *Southern California Law Review* 1281 (2002). Dan T. Coenen, "A Constitution of Collaboration: Protecting Fundamental Values with Second-Look Rules of Interbranch Di-

alogue," 42 *William & Mary Law Review* 1575 (2001). Mark Tushnet, "Alternative Forms of Judicial Reasoning," 101 *Michigan Law Review* 2781, 2794 (2003).

72. Linde, 222–24, 238–54.

73. Laurence H. Tribe, "Policy Science: Analysis of Ideology," 2 *Philosophy & Public Affairs* 66, 83 (1972).

74. Laurence H. Tribe, "Structural Due Process," 10 *Harvard Civil Rights–Civil Liberties Law Review* 269 (1975).

75. Laurence Tribe, *American Constitutional Law*, 2d ed. (Foundation Press, 1988), 1682. Mark V. Tushnet, "Legal Realism, Structural Review, and Prophecy," 8 *University Dayton Law Review* 809, 816 (1983).

76. Jonathan Hart Ely, *Democracy and Distrust: A Theory of Judicial Review* (Harvard University, 1980), 87, 102–3, 169.

77. Daniel A. Farber and Philip P. Frickey, *Law and Public Choice* (University of Chicago, 1991), 9. Farber and Frickey, 920–25.

78. Henry M. Hart and Albert M. Sacks, *The Legal Process: Basic Problems in the Making and Application of Law* (Fountain Press, 1994), 694–95.

79. *U.S. v. Lopez*, 514 U.S. 549 (1995), *Seminole Tribe v. Florida*, 517 U.S. 44 (1996), *Boerne v. Flores*, 521 U.S. 507 (1997), *Kimel v. Florida Board of Regents*, 528 U.S. 62 (2000), *Board of Trustees of Univ. of Alabama v. Garrett*, 531 U.S. 356 (2001). For a complete list, see Ruth Colker and James J. Brudnoy, "Dissing Congress," 100 *Michigan Law Review* 80, 81 ns. 3–5 (2001).

80. *Fullilove v. Klutznick*, 448 U.S. 448, 549–52 (1980).

81. Philip P. Frickey, "The Fool on the Hill: Congressional Findings, Constitutional Adjudication, and *U.S. v. Lopez*," 46 *Case Western Reserve Law Review* 695, 728–29 (1996). Coenen, 1688–89.

82. Stephen Gardbaum, "Rethinking Constitutional Federalism," 74 *Texas Law Review* 795, 799–800, 825–26 (1996). William W. Buzbee and Robert A. Shapiro, "Legislative Record Review," 54 *Stanford Law Review* 87, 119–31 (2001). Vicki L. Jackson, "Federalism and the Uses and Limits of Law: Printz and Principle," 111 *Harvard Law Review* 2180, 2240 (1998). Harold J. Krent, "Turning Congress Into an Agency: The Propriety of Requiring Legislative Findings," 46 *Case Western Reserve Law Review* 731, 743–46 (1966).

83. Cass R. Sunstein, "Interpreting Statutes in the Regulatory State," 103 *Harvard Law Review* 405, 476–78 (1989).

84. Susan Rose-Ackerman, "Judicial Review and the Power of the Purse," 12 *International Review of Law and Economics* 194, 192–98 (1992).

85. Coenen, 1845–51. A. Christopher Bryant and Timothy J. Simeone, "Remanding to Congress: The Supreme Court's New 'on the Record' Constitutional Review of Federal Statutes," 86 *Cornell Law Review* 328, 370–73 (2001). Neil Devins, "Congressional Fact Finding and Scope of Judicial Review," 50 *Duke Law Journa*l 1169, 1182–83 (2001).

86. Bryant and Simeone, 376–89. Devins, "Fact Finding," 1180.

87. Tushnet, "Legal Realism," 826.

88. Philip P. Frickey and Steven S. Smith, "Judicial Review, the Congressional Process, and Federalism Cases: An Interdisciplinary Critique," 111 *Yale Law Journal* 1707, 1723 (2002).

89. Rose-Ackerman, 197.

90. Jan S. Stevens, "The Public Trust: A Sovereign's Ancient Prerogative Becomes the People's Environmental Right," 14 *University California Davis Law Review* 195. David Takas, "The Pubic Trust Doctrine, Environmental Human Rights, the Future of Private Property," 16 *N.Y.U. Environmental Law Journal* 711 (2008). Anna R. C. Caspersen, "The Public Trust Doctrine and the Impossibility of 'Takings' by Wildlife," 23 *Boston College Environmental Affairs Law Review* 357, 358–62 (1996).

91. For a contrary view, Richard J. Lazarus, "Changing Conceptions of Property and Sovereignty in Natural Resources: Questioning the Public Trust Doctrine," 71 *Iowa Law Review* 631 (1986). Eric Pearson, "The Public Trust Doctrine in Federal Law," 24 *Journal Law, Resources & Environmental Law* 173 (2004). James L. Huffman, "A Fish Out of Water: The Public Trust in a Constitutional Democracy," 19 *Environmental Law* 527 (1989).

92. *Light v. U.S.,* 220 U.S. 523 (1911), *Ruddy v. Rossi,* 248 U.S. 104 (1918), *U.S. v. City & County of San Francisco,* 310 U.S. 36 (1940).

93. Charles F. Wilkinson, "The Public Trust Doctrine in Public Land Law," 14 *University California Davis Law Review* 269, 273–74, 280–84 (1980).

94. Wilkinson, 299.

95. Joseph L. Sax, "Liberating the Public Trust Doctrine from Its Historical Shackles," 14 *University California Davis Law Review* 185, 188 (1980).

96. *In re Steuart Transp. Co.*, 495 F. Supp. 38, 20 (E.D. Va. 1980).

97. Alison Rieser, "Ecological Preservation as a Public Property Right: An Emerging Doctrine In Search of a Theory," 15 *Harvard Environmental Law Review* 393, 422–26 (1991).

98. Harry R. Bader, "Antaeus and the Public Trust Doctrine: A New Approach to Substantive Environmental Protection in the Common Law," 19 *Environmental Affairs Law Review* 749, 756–57 (1992).

99. Joseph Sax, "The Public Trust Doctrine in Natural Resources Law: Effective Judicial Intervention," 68 *Michigan Law Review* 471, 484–90, 556–62 (1970).

100. Michael C. Blumm, "Public Property and the Democratization of Western Water Law: A Modern View of the Public Trust Doctrine," 19 *Environmental Law* 573, 589–95 (1989). Gary D. Meyers, "Variation on a Theme: Expanding the Public Trust Doctrine to Include Protection of Wildlife," 19 *Environmental Law* 723, 735 (1989).

101. William H. Rodgers, *Environmental Law*, 1st ed. (West, 1986), 177, 509, 559–60. Ronald E. Klipsch, "Aspects of a Constitutional Right to a Habitable Environment: Towards an Environmental Due Process," 49 *Indiana Law Journal* 203, 216–19 (1970).

102. U.S. Constitution, Art IV sect. 3.

103. Notes, "Proprietary Duties of the Federal Government Under the Public Trust Doctrine," 75 *Michigan Law Review* 586, 592–96 (1977).

104. Klipsch, 218–19. Sax, 559–61. Rodgers, 170–80.

105. Charles Reich, "The New Property," 73 *Yale Law Journal* 733, 739 (1964).

106. David B. Hunter, "An Ecological Perspective on Property," 12 *Harvard Environmental Law Review* 311, 312–13 (1988). Mark Sagoff, "On Preserving the Natural Environment," 84 *Yale Law Journal* 205, 265–67 (1974).

107. Vanderziel, 453–61. The Supreme Court established a balancing test, which defines the requirements of procedural due process. Courts must weigh the individual interest at stake, risk to individual interest under current procedures, and burden of providing alternative procedures. *Matthews v. Eldridge*, 424 U.S. 319, 334–35 (1976).

108. Thomas A. Cambell, "The Public Trust, What's It Worth," 34 *Natural Resources Journal* 73, 74–75 (1994).

109. 42 U.S.C. 4331.

110. 16 U.S.C. 1531.

111. 43 U.S.C. 1701.

112. Vanderziel, 453–61. *U.S. v. SCRAP,* 412 U.S. 669 (1973).

113. William D. Azaria, "The Trouble with Robertson," 48 *Catholic University Law Review* 1055, 1089–1107 (1999). Sunstein, 103 *Harvard Law Review*, 471.

114. Klipsch, 222–30. Comments, 17 *UCLA Law Review* 1070, 1079–81 (1970). Philip Soper, "The Constitutional Framework of Environmental Law," in Erica L. Dolgin and Thomas G. P. Gilbert (eds.), *Federal Environmental Law* (West, 1974), 119.

115. The Fifth Amendment includes an equal protection guarantee. *Bolling v. Sharpe*, 347 U.S. 497, 499 (1954).

116. Soper, 110–13.

117. 870 F. 2d, 1430. Sher and Hunting, 482–85. Vanderziel, 461–65. William H. Rogers Jr., *Environmental Law* 2d ed. (West, 1994), 62–67.

118. Robert Costanza et al., "The Value of World's Ecosystem Service and National Capital," 387 *Nature* 253, 259 (1987).

119. Eskridge and Frickey, *Cases*, 55.

120. 16 U.S.C. 1531(a). Robert B. Keiter, *Keeping Faith with Nature: Ecosystems, Democracy, and America's Public Lands* (Yale University, 2003).

121. Laurence H. Tribe, "From Environmental Foundations to Constitutional Structures: Learning from Nature's Future," 84 *Yale Law Quarterly* 545, 554 (1975).

122. Cass R. Sunstein, "Naked Preferences and the Constitution," 84 *Columbia Law Review* 1689, 1699–1700 (1984). Eskridge, "Romance," 279, 298–99, 303–9, 324–25.

123. Rose-Ackerman, 191–92, 197.

124. *Hampton v. Mow Sun Wong*, 426 U.S. 88, 103 (1976).

125. Jonathan C. Carlson and Alan D. Smith, "The Emerging Constitutional Jurisprudence of Justice Stevens," 46 *University of Chicago Law Review* 157, 218–19, 225–26 (1978).

126. Azaria, 1089–1101.

127. *Plyler v. Doe,* 457 U.S. 202, 210–14(1982). *Romer v. Evans*, 517 U.S. 629, 631–36 (1996). Jerald W. Rogers, "Romer v. Evans: Heightened Scrutiny Has Found a Rational Basis," 45 *Kansas Law Review* 953 (1997). Cass R. Sunstein, "Interest Groups," 69. Brenda Swierenga, "Still Newer Equal Protection: Impermissible Purpose Review in the 1984 Term," 53 *University Chicago Law Review* 1454, 1461–68 (1986).

128. Tribe, *American Constitutional Law*, 2d ed. (1988), 657, 1440. Jonathan R. Macey, "Promoting Public-Regarding Legislation Through Statutory Interpretation: An Interest-Group Model," 86 *Columbia Law Review* 223 (1986). Eskridge, "Romance," 310. Sunstein, "Interest Groups," 78.

129. *Martin v. Hunters Lessee*, 14 U.S. (1Wheat.) 304, 328–31 (1816).

130. Redish and Woods, 66.

131. Henry Hart, "The Power of Congress to Limit the Jurisdiction of Federal Courts: An Exercise in Dialectic," 66 *Harvard Law Review* 1362, 1365 (1953). Lawrence Sager, "Forward: Constitutional Limitations on Congress' Authority to Regulate the Jurisdiction of the Federal Courts," 95 *Harvard Law Review* 17, 61–68 (1981). Gerald Gunther, "Congressional Power to Curtail Federal Court Jurisdiction: An Opinionated Guide to the Ongoing Debate," 36 *Stanford Law Review* 895, 910 (984). Redish and Woods, 76 n.142.

132. Theodore Eisenberg, "Congressional Authority to Restrict Lower Federal Court Jurisdiction," 83 *Yale Law Journal* 498, 504–6, 511–14, 527–33 (1974). Redish and Woods, 68–75.

Conclusion

The reintroduction and recovery of the gray wolf to the Northern Rocky Mountains (NRM) demonstrates the interaction of law and politics. NRM wolf reintroduction and recovery under the Endangered Species Act (ESA) involved the interplay between three branches of the federal government, state and local governments, and interest groups. The conflict generated public law litigation. The livestock and hunting industries, western states, and environmental groups challenged Interior's implementation of the ESA. Federal courts were called upon to determine the meaning of the statutory mandates and decide whether Interior complied with the law.

There are different positions regarding public law litigation. Judicial proponents argue that judicial review of federal agency action is necessary to ensure compliance with statutory mandates. Agencies, seeking to satisfy the demands of interest groups, Congress, and the president, often do not properly implement statutory mandates. Judicial review is essential to ensure that the public values acknowledged in the halls of Congress are not lost in the administrative process.

Judicial skeptics counter that public law litigation interferes with executive policy implementation. Interest groups, which have been unsuccessful in the congressional or executive branches, use the courts to advance their political aims. Courts lack the capacity and expertise to deal with complex policy disputes. The courts' anecdotal involvement fails to recognize that the policy implementation involves tradeoffs, resource constraints, and political realities. Federal judges, who are not democratically accountable, use the law to impose their own views on the agencies. Judicial involvement frustrates and fragments the implementation of national policy.

The public law litigation surrounding the reintroduction and delisting of the NRM wolves provided opportunity to examine these positions. The assessment criteria were 1) did the federal courts properly interpret the statutory mandates, and 2) did the outcome realize the statutory purposes. The study concludes that wolf recovery in the NRM was successful in large part because of public law litigation. Federal courts properly interpreted the mandates of the ESA and National Environmental Protection Act (NEPA), both upholding and reversing relevant executive action. Judicial decisions advanced the overarching goals of the ESA to restore a balanced ecosystem and preserve biodiversity in the NRM.

During the Clinton administration, wolves were reintroduced as a non-essential experimental population into central Idaho and Yellowstone National Park. Wolves were naturally returning to northwest Montana. The Wyoming Farm Bureau Federation, representing tradition resource users, utilized public law litigation to stop wolf reintroduction. Standing would not pose a problem for judicial skeptics in this public law litigation because the plaintiffs were asserting an injury to their common law interests, grazing and hunting. The Tenth Circuit in *Wyoming Farm Bureau Federation v. Babbitt*, employing the traditional tools of statutory interpretation—text, intent, and purposes—properly upheld Interior's action. The court found the reintroduced non-essential population was wholly geographically separate from and outside the range of known wolf packs. The occasional appearance of dispersers in the area did not constitute a natural population. Congressional inaction, continued appropriations, and failure to enact contrary statutory amendments indicated approval of the court's decision. The Tenth Circuit decision was consistent with the earlier Ninth Circuit decision in *U.S. v. McKittrick*, so there was no policy fragmentation. The Tenth Circuit also found that Interior complied with the NEPA, adequately considering the potential environmental impacts of NRM wolf reintroduction. Neither judicial proponents nor skeptics would criticize the decision. Skeptics would question the court's examination of legislative history, but the court did defer to Interior's expertise. Wolf reintroduction was allowed to proceed. Wolf recovery was so successful that the Clinton administration proposed the creation of four distinct population segments (DPSs) covering most of the continental United States and downlisting the wolves where warranted.

Wolves in the NRM region exceeded recovery goals by 2002. The Bush administration modified the Clinton proposal and created three DPSs and downlisted wolves in the Eastern and Western DPSs, which included the NRM. Environmental groups brought suit challenging the action. The U.S. District Court for the District of Oregon in *Defenders of Wildlife v. Interior* properly invalidated the action. The court employing the traditional tools of statutory interpretation determined that Interior misinterpreted the legal meaning of significant portion of the range. Interior could not delist the wolves, which were absent from 96 percent of their historic range. The court did not impose its own policy view, but followed congressional directions evidenced in the text, intent, and purposes of the ESA and prior precedent. There were other significant areas in the wolf's historic range that could support wolves. The court also scrutinized the Interior's DPS policy change to ensure the change was based on statutory, not political, factors. The court found Interior inverted its DPS policy, which could be used to isolate discrete significant populations, not to delist large areas inhabited by phantom wolves. Both of these errors precluded the accurate downlisting analysis required under the ESA.

The U.S. District Court for the District of Vermont in *National Wildlife Federation v. Interior* arrived at similar conclusions regarding Interior's abandonment of the Eastern DPS. The court held that Interior did not follow the proper procedures. Interior's alteration of the proposed rule establishing four DPSs undermined public involvement, which is one of the benefits of administrative decision making through the notice and comment process. Interior violated the best available science mandate of the ESA by ignoring scientific comment. Experts pointed out that the Eastern DPS contained two distinct subspecies of wolves, the recovered Western Great Lakes wolves and the non-existent eastern wolves. Alternatively, wolves were missing from the Northeast, which represented a significant gap in the taxon. Either of these factors precluded downlisting. Judicial skeptics worry about the fragmentation of national policy with different courts rendering different decisions on the same issue, but this did not occur.

Judicial skeptics would disagree with both decisions. Skeptics argue that environmental groups, which are not asserting an injury to their common law interests, should not be granted standing to challenge federal government actions. Skeptics assert that the court should adopt a strong reading of Chevron and defer to the administrative decision, unless there is express congressional direction to the contrary. Skeptics are also wary of the hard-look doctrine, which federal judges allegedly use to substitute their policy preferences for those of expert executive agencies. Judicial involvement ossifies agency action. Interior needed flexibility to change policy in the face of new circumstances and political dynamics. Judicial skeptics also criticize the courts for being too concerned with process.

Following the decision, Interior approved Montana and Idaho's wolf management plans, and the states assumed regulatory authority. Wyoming's plan had earlier been rejected, so wolves in Wyoming remained under federal supervision. There were unsuccessful attempts to amend the ESA, but none of the relevant provisions regarding the significant portion of the range or distinct population segments were proposed for change. This indicated congressional approval of the court's decision.

Interior created a smaller NRM DPS that included Montana, Idaho, Wyoming, eastern Washington, eastern Oregon, and north-central Utah. The U.S. Fish and Wildlife Service (FWS), fulfilling Secretary Kempthorne's confirmation promise, abandoned its insistence that Wyoming establish a statewide trophy game designation for the wolf. Instead, Interior approved Wyoming's wolf management plan that only protected wolves in northwest Wyoming. Judicial skeptics argue that judicial review paralyzes agency action, but this was not the case. Environmental groups brought suit. The U.S. District Court for the District of Montana in *Defenders of Wildlife v. Hall* scrutinized and properly invalidated the action. The court found Interior violated the best available science mandate in ESA. There was no connectivity between the three wolf populations in the NRM DPS, which the FWS stressed was a necessary condition for delisting. Further, the court determined that Interior should not have approved Wyoming's management plan, which contained the same defects identified by Interior for its rejection of the 2004 Wyoming plan.

Judicial skeptics would criticize the court for substituting its views for that of the expert agency, the FWS. The Montana federal court did not implement its own views, but simply enforced existing agency policy. The FWS declared a functioning metapopulation was necessary before delisting and admitted that no functioning metapopulation existed. Scientific studies supported this conclusion. Furthermore, Interior should not have approved the Wyoming management plan because there was no substantial change from the earlier plan rejected in 2004. Interior later admitted its approval was premature and returned to its former position that a statewide trophy designation was necessary.

The Obama administration, resurrecting a Bush administrative proposal, subdivided the NRM DPS, delisting the wolf in Montana and Idaho, eastern Washington, eastern Oregon, and north-central Utah, while retaining federal protection for the wolf in Wyoming. Judicial skeptics argue that agencies are reluctant to act in the face of potential judicial challenge, but this was not manifested. Both the Bush and Obama administrations relied on the 2007 memo by the Interior solicitor that focused on the current range of the wolves. Since the wolf had recovered in significant portions of its current range in the NRM, wolves in these areas could be delisted. The U.S. District Court for the District of Montana federal court in *Defenders of Wildlife v. Salazar* correctly decided that the DPS could not be subdivided.

Skeptics would argue that the court substituted its views for those of Interior, but this was not the case. The Montana federal district court followed the text of ESA, which defines the DPS as the lowest unit for ESA consideration; Interior's earlier policy statements that the DPS can't be subdivided; and existing case law. Interior essentially attempted to create a new DPS within the NRM DPS. In addition, since Wyoming constituted a significant portion of the NRM DPS, the NRM DPS could not be delisted until Wyoming's wolf management plan was approved.

Subsequent developments did manifest one of the principal concerns of judicial skeptics: policy fragmentation. Skeptics point out that different federal courts can render different decisions on the same question of law, which makes the implementation of national policy difficult. The U.S. District Court for the District of Wyoming, in *Wyoming v. United States*, found Interior's rejection of Wyoming's 2008 wolf management plan in 2009 arbitrary and capricious. The court relied on Interior's approval of Wyoming's program in 2007, which had been invalidated by the Montana federal district court in 2008. Skeptics would be critical of this decision because the court substituted its view for that of Interior. The court focused on Interior's plan approval in 2007 but ignored Interior's earlier rejection of a similar plan, Interior's subsequent statement and earlier court decisions, which determined a statewide trophy game designation for wolves in Wyoming was necessary. The Obama administration did not appeal, but negotiated a deal with Wyoming.

The federal court decisions generated a congressional response. Western congresspersons dissatisfied with the judicial decisions that threatened livestock and hunting interests enacted the Obama regulation delisting the wolves in the NRM DPS, except Wyoming, through an appropriation rider and prevented judicial review of the regulation. This was the first time Congress delisted a species. The Ninth Circuit, in *Alliance for the Wild Rockies v. Salazar*, correctly upheld the congressional action. Congress can change the law to affect pending litigation and remove federal court jurisdiction over an issue. Nevertheless, the premature congressional delisting of the NRM wolves undermined the ESA, which mandates that decisions be based on science, not politics. The removal of federal court jurisdiction violated the separation of powers; threatened the legitimacy of the administrative action; severed the partnership between courts and administrative agencies to further the public interest; and weakened the foundation of the modern administrative state. Judicial skeptics would applaud this decision, which removed judicial obstacles to executive policy implementation.

There were, however, alternative legal theories that could have been employed to invalidate the congressional delisting. The court could have invoked structural review and examined the process by which the law was enacted because important interests were at stake. Congress delisted wolves and removed federal court jurisdiction through a rider on an appropriation bill. This violated House and Senate rules that prohibit the attachment of substantive legislation to an appropriation bill. Congress violated its public trust obligation and Due Process Clause of the Fifth Amendment by impinging on the public's limited property rights in public lands and resources through an invalid process, the appropriation rider, which precluded public participation. Congress violated the Equal Protection Clause, which is subsumed in the Fifth Amendment's Due Process Clause, by singling out the

NRM wolves for unique treatment. Generally, such legislation is only subject to deferential rational basis review. However, given the importance of the wolf for ecosystem maintenance and the preservation of biodiversity, the appropriation rider should have been subjected to intermediate scrutiny or rigorous rational-basis review. Judicial reversal and remand would have decreased interest group influence and forced Congress to operate through conventional procedures that are subject to public scrutiny. Congress could not have removed federal court jurisdiction over the constitutional issues.

Despite the premature delisting, the wolf has prospered in the NRM DPS. At the end of 2013, the NRM DPS contained 1,691 wolves in 320 packs with 78 breeding pairs. There are currently 627 wolves in Montana in 152 packs with 28 breeding pairs; 659 wolves in Idaho in 107 packs with 20 breeding pairs; 306 wolves in 43 packs with 23 breeding pairs in Wyoming; 38 wolves in 10 packs and 3 breeding pairs in Washington; and 61 wolves in 8 packs and 4 breeding pairs in Oregon. No wolves are present in Utah.[1]

Public hunting in 2013 removed 25 percent of the absolute minimum NRM DPS estimated wolf population.[2] Lethal control, legal harvest, and other causes of mortality removed 34 percent of the absolute minimum NRM DPS estimated wolf population.[3] Wolf depredation of livestock in 2013 included 143 cattle and 476 sheep, which cost private and state agencies $273,548 in compensation. The federal government through the Wolf-Livestock Project Grant Program provided the NRM states with $542,597, $321,347 to prevent depredation and $221,250 to compensate livestock owners for their losses. The federal government provided federal, state, and tribal agencies approximately $2,552,128 in funding for NRM wolf monitoring, management, control, and research.[4]

Wolves have been very beneficial to the ecosystem in the NRM. Wolf depredation provides for the removal of diseased animals, the culling of deformed or genetically inferior animals before reproduction, the acceleration of reproductive rates among prey through higher twining and fertility, and the maintenance of prey populations at levels that can be supported by the habitat. Reduction in the bison and elk, the principal prey of the wolves, has allowed willows and aspen trees to regain their place in the area, which had been overgrazed. The increase in plant life stabilizes the soil, prevents erosion, and improves water quality. It also expands carbon sequestration, which helps to address climate change. Beaver colonies have increased, which has improved riparian hydrology and resulted in an increase in waterfowl.[5]

Wolf reintroduction has improved biodiversity in the NRM. The wolves kill an elk every few days. The carcasses provide food for other animals. Grizzly bears benefit from wolf kills, which provide nourishment before and after hibernation. Wolves also terminate coyotes. This has led to an increase in rodents and hares, which are the prey of other species, including foxes, owls, hawks, eagles, badgers, and pine martens. The increase in hares has been particularly beneficial for the recovery of the lynx. A recent Oregon State University study concluded that "predation and predation risk associated with large predators appear to represent powerful ecological forces capable of affecting the interactions of numerous animals and plants, as well as the structure and function of ecosystems."[6]

FUTURE CONCERNS

There are several outstanding issues that will affect the future of the wolf in the NRM: the litigation regarding the Wyoming delisting, President Obama's proposed delisting of the wolf across much of the United States, and proposed amendments to the ESA.

Wyoming Settlement and Litigation

After the Obama administration decided not to appeal the U.S. District Court for the District of Wyoming's decision that found Interior's 2009 rejection of the Wyoming management arbitrary and capricious, a deal was negotiated. Wolves in Yellowstone and Grand Teton National Parks and the National Elk Refuge remain under federal protection. A trophy game area is established outside the parks in northwest Wyoming, which expands from October 15 to the end of February. Wyoming commits to manage one hundred wolves and ten breeding pairs outside of Yellowstone with a promised buffer above this number. Wolves are considered predators in the remaining 90 percent of the state where they can be shot on sight. Wyoming will allow the killing of fifty-two wolves in the trophy area, 22 percent of the state's wolf population, reducing wolves in the area to ten packs.[7]

Environmental groups criticized the deal. The Defenders of Wildlife (DOW) stated, "Wyoming has settled on indiscriminate shooting of wolves as the primary management tool in the state, which is a huge step backwards. Instead, the state should be working with all stakeholders to promote tolerance and prevent conflict by implementing nonlethal, proactive management tools." The Center for Biodiversity (CBD) stated, "This is going to make it incredibly difficult for wolves to get extensive habitat in Colorado and make a comeback there as well." Interior and Wyoming officials praised the outcome. Secretary Salazar stated, "The agreement we reached with Wyoming recognizes the success of this iconic species and will ensure the long-term conservation of gray wolves." Senator Enzi (R. Wy.) announced that "wolf populations have exceeded all recovery goals. . . . It is time to remove ESA protection from these predators in Wyoming in the same way that protection was removed from wolves in Idaho and Montana." Senator Barrasso (R. Wy) declared that "after more fits than starts, the Obama administration has finally recognized that Wyoming should be in control of managing the wolf, not Washington."[8]

Representative Lummis (R. Wy.) attached a provision to the House Interior 2012–2013 appropriation bill that prohibited judicial review of the Wyoming management plan. The provision was dropped in the conference report. Representative Dicks (D. Wash.) stated, "I have reminded my Republican colleagues that nothing has done more to obstruct the process than loading down appropriation bills with partisan or ideological baggage in the form of legislative provisions that are unrelated to the mission of this Committee."[9]

The scientific peer review of Wyoming's management plan was divided. Three of the five scientists determined that the plan "followed the scientific literature and appropriate standards." The two dissenters found the state's promise of a population buffer above the minimum protected population "problematic because that buffer was vague and undefined."[10] One of the dissenters, Dr. Vucetich, asserted that the plan overestimated the annual sustainable wolf mortality rate, and was designed to increase the elk population for hunters. He also questioned the long-term commitment of state officials to retain a sustainable wolf population.[11]

The Wyoming legislature amended the state wolf plan to achieve federal approval in March 2012. Wolves outside of public lands in Wyoming were delisted in August 2012.[12] At the end of 2012, there were 277 wolves in 43 packs with 21 breeding pairs in Wyoming. Public hunting removed 66 wolves (6 percent of the absolute minimum Wyoming estimated population) in 2012. Human-caused mortality in 2012 was responsible for the death of 120 wolves in Wyoming (29 percent of the absolute minimum Wyoming estimated population). This jeopardized wolf recovery, so Wyoming halved its hunting quota for 2013.[13]

Environmental groups criticized the Wyoming delisting, which "fails to rely on the best science and represents the worst kind of political intrusion by Secretary Salazar into the management of endangered species." Two environmental coalitions filed suit challenging the delisting of the Wyoming wolves. Earthjustice represented one coalition consisting of DOW, CBD, Natural Resource Defense Council, and Sierra Club, which filed suit in the U.S. District Court for the District of Columbia. The second coalition, which includes Wildlife Guardians, AWR, Biodiversity Conservation Alliance, Conservation Congress, Friends of Animals, Friends of Clearwater, National Wolf Watcher Coalition, and Western Watersheds Project, filed suit, which ended up in the U.S. District Court for the District of Wyoming. The Wyoming suit was dropped at the plaintiff's request, much to the consternation of Wyoming and the resource industries.[14]

The filing of two different suits presented the problem of the proper venue, which deals with where a case can be brought. Traditionally, venue is based on the location most convenient for parties and participants and least onerous on the judicial system. Federal rules regarding administrative challenges allow the case to be brought where the plaintiff resides, the defendant resides, or where cause of action arose.[15] The Wildlife Guardian suit began in the U.S. District Court for the District of Colorado, where the plaintiffs are located. The case was moved to the Wyoming federal district court before Judge Johnson, who had already determined that Interior's rejection of the Wyoming plan was arbitrary and capricious. The suit brought by Earthjustice was brought in the U.S. District Court for the District of Columbia. The issue in the case was a regulatory matter, which would be decided primarily on the administrative record. The plaintiffs and defendants reside in and the action arose in Washington D.C., which is the most convenient forum.

The U.S. District Court for the District of Columbia in September 2014 found Interior's acceptance of the Wyoming plan to be "arbitrary and capricious." The court upheld the FWS findings that there was adequate genetic exchange between the wolf populations in the NRM DPS and that Wyoming did not have treat the wolf as trophy game throughout the entire state. The court, however, determined "that the FWS could not reasonably rely on [Wyoming's] unenforceable representations . . . to maintain a particular number of wolves when the availability of that specific numerical buffer [that] was such a critical aspect of the delisting decision" remained undefined.[16] The federal district court correctly held that Interior could not rely on Wyoming's unenforceable promise to establish a buffer population above the minimum population requirement that would ensure Wyoming met its recovery goals. Interior had insisted that such a popultion buffer was necessary. The genetic connectivity between the three wolf populations in the NRM DPS had been achieved under federal regulation. The federal district court, however, was mistaken in upholding Interior's contention that Wyoming did not have to grant the wolf statewide trophy-game status because the remainder of Wyoming did not constitute a significant portion of its range. Interior had rejected Wyoming's wolf management plan in 2004 and 2009 and insisted that Wyoming treat the wolf as trophy game statewide. Nevertheless, as the NRDC observed, "the decision makes clear that 'shoot on sight' is not an acceptable management plan for wolves across the majority of states. It's time for Wyoming to step back and develop a more science-based approach to managing wolves."[17]

Obama's Proposed Delisting

The Obama administration proposed delisting the wolf across much of the United States in June 2013. Interior relied on a recent FWS in-house study by Chambers, et al. that reviewed the existing scientific literature defining wolf taxonomy. The study concluded that there are three distinct species of wolves in North America: *Canis lupus*, *Canis rufus*, and *Canis lycaon*. The gray wolf, *Canis lupus*, is subdivided into three subspecies. *Canis nubilus* exists in the Western Great Lakes region, Washington, Oregon, northeast British Columbia, northwest Alberta, the Northwest Territories, Manitoba, Ontario, and Quebec. Other likely locations include the Pacific Northwest, central United States, the southern Rockies, and Colorado. *Canis occidentalis* resides in eastern Oregon and eastern Washington, Alaska, the northern Rockies, the Yukon, the Northwest Territories, British Columbia, Alberta, Saskatchewan, and western and southern Manitoba. *Canis baileyi*, the Mexican wolf, lives in the Southwest. No specific geographic boundaries exist between subspecies, just intermediate zones of variable width.[18] Interior admits that wolf taxonomy remains open for debate and further study. Scientific consensus may shift in the future, but this study served as the basis for the proposed regulation.

Each subspecies, including the Canadian populations, was evaluated under the five ESA delisting criteria. Interior determined that *Canis nubilus* and *Canis occidentalis* are not at risk for extinction and should be delisted. *Canis bailyei*, however, remains threatened because of its small population size and numerous illegal killings. Interior is investigating the creation of a Southwest DPS across central and southern Arizona and New Mexico where the Mexican wolf will be treated as an endangered species.[19]

The Obama proposal is premature. The taxonomic changes are based on uncertain science. Interior continues to limit its analysis of the significant portion of the range to the wolf's current range. The status of the eastern wolf is being debated. The FWS decision-making process was flawed.

Taxonomy

The proposal rests on a change in the taxonomy of the wolf. Taxonomy is an art, not a science. Federal agencies often use taxonomy to mask the discretionary components and political ramifications of their decisions. Taxonomic classifications are influenced by "the staff's own ideologies and goals" and "include political considerations."[20] Prominent scientists criticized Interior's reliance on the in-house Chambers study, which was not published in a scientific journal for peer review. Instead, the study was published in North America Fauna, an internal FWS publication that had been dormant for twenty years.[21]

Critics argue that Interior should not rely on a single study whose conclusions are not shared by the majority of scientists in the field. For example, a study by vonHoldt found genetic differences among North American wolves corresponding to their different habitats in northern Quebec (eastern forests), northern Canada (tundra/taiga), Yellowstone National Park (rocky mountain forest), Alaska-Canada (boreal forests), British Columbia (western coastal forest), southwest U.S. and Mexico (arid lands). It also discovered distinct genetic differences among wolf/coyote mixes that include the Red, Algonquin, and Western Great Lake wolves. The study indicates that different subspecies of wolves in different habitats should be the focus of delisting decisions.[22]

Interior's delisting proposal concludes that even if wolves recolonize the Pacific Northwest they will not be ecologically or genetically distinct, even though wolves that formerly occupied the area were once considered a distinct subspecies. Critics point out that recent research, including the vonHoldt study, determined that wolves just north of the Pacific Northwest are ecologically and genetically different than those in the NRM region. It follows that wolves occupying the Pacific Northwest will also be ecologically and genetically unique.[23]

Significant Portion of Its Range

The major problem with the delisting proposal is Interior's continual adherence to a mistaken view of the "significant portion of its range" language in the ESA. Interior asserts that "the significant portion of its range" is that part of the range that is essential for the continued existence of the species. Without that portion of the range, the species will be at risk for extinction. Interior focuses on the current range of the species. The historic range is only important if it affects the continued existence of the species.[24]

Interior's definition of "the significant portion of its range" is inconsistent with the text, intent, and purposes of the ESA. The ESA seeks to prevent species extinction, but is also concerned with restoring the species as a vital component of the ecosystems within its historic range to preserve biodiversity.

Interior's definition of "significant portion of its range" is contrary to case law. Federal courts have principally adopted a geographic or quantitative definition and secondarily a functional definition for the significant portion of the range. Interior's definition that the key factor determining the significant portion of the range is the relevance to the survival of the taxon as a whole has been rejected by most federal courts.

The FWS applauded the effort by environmental groups to restore endangered species to significant portions of their historic range as an "admirable goal," but argues it "would have decidedly negative consequences." These would include the diversion of "scarce resources needed to help species at high risk . . . to species no longer facing extinction's peril." Furthermore, it would undermine the criteria of "success measured by species recovered and taken off the endangered species list," which "is critical to sustaining public and political support for this vital law."[25]

There are other significant areas within the historical range of the gray wolf that can support gray wolves in the Pacific Northwest, southern Rockies, and the Southwest. A recent study indicates that 44 percent of the western U.S. is suitable for wolf breeding. Possible wolf occupation of this habitat is 49 percent under current conditions (human population as of 2000 with restoration on public lands), 32 percent under future conditions (human population as of 2025 with increased road development on both private and public), 61 percent under current conditions with the closure of roads, 45 percent under future conditions with road removal on public lands. Under current conditions, Montana, Colorado, and Wyoming will have the greatest potential wolf populations, followed by Arizona, Utah, and New Mexico. The largest wolf populations will likely inhabit Greater Yellowstone Ecosystem and central Idaho. Other potential population centers in the order of their importance include western Montana and western Colorado, the Blue Range in Arizona and New Mexico, Utah's high plateau region, and the Oregon Cascades.[26]

Scientists assert that the wolf still remains in danger in a significant portion of its range. The NRM recovery area occupied by wolves represents only 26 percent of the historic range of the non-Mexican wolf population west of ninety-seventh parallel (excluding Arizona and New Mexico). The removal of ESA protections will preclude the reestablishment of wolf populations in suitable habitat in significant areas across the mountainous West and frustrate ecosystem restoration in these areas.[27]

Critics point out that the wolf is still in danger from human-caused mortality. In 2012 and 2013, 34 percent of the absolute minimum NRM DPS estimated population was removed by humans. If this continues or increases, the wolf's long-term survival will be jeopardized. A breeding population outside, but connected to the NRM, such as in Washington and Oregon, is necessary to ameliorate adverse impacts.[28]

Critics argue that the population goals are too conservative. The NRM region has only met recovery goals for the past five years. Scientists contend that "both the initial recovery goals and the goals of state management plans are unrealistically low for full recovery." Small wolf populations in small areas present the risk of inbreeding. A larger population throughout the historic range will increase the possibility of genetic variability. Furthermore, the historic range contains different types of habitat that produce subspecies variations through adaptation. Both factors will increase the wolf's chance of survival from catastrophic events.[29]

Critics agree with Interior's decision to establish a Southwest DPS and accord the Mexican wolf endangered species status therein. Critics, however, argue that the Mexican wolf needs more space to roam, possibly in Colorado and Utah, where there is suitable habitat. The Mexican wolf should not be confined to Arizona and New Mexico.[30]

Canis Lycaon: The Eastern Wolf

Interior, employing molecular analysis, determined that the gray wolf is not present in the Northeast. The eastern wolf is not a subspecies, but a separate wolf species, *Canis lycaon*. Its range extends westward to Minnesota, where it can reproduce with gray wolves, *Canis nubilus*, in eastern Canada and the Western Great Lakes region. Genetic data show a close relationship between the eastern and red wolf, but they are not the same species. They more likely evolved separately from different lineages of a common coyote ancestor.[31]

Scientists assert that currently there is not sufficient scientific evidence to support the recognition of *Canis lycaon* as a separate species. Molecular evidence suggests a contrary conclusion. *Canis lycaon* mates with *Canis lupus* and *Canis latern*, which complicates its recognition as a separate species. Authoritative taxonomic organizations, such as the American Society of Mammologists and International Commission on Zoological Nomenclature, do not acknowledge *Canis lycaon* as a separate species. Furthermore, scientific evidence indicates that *Canis lupus* did occupy the eastern United States.[32]

Scientists assert that since the status of the eastern wolf is under investigation, it should not be listed as a separate species until scientific consensus is established. The eastern wolf may be a gray wolf subspecies. This uncertainty warrants protection for any wolf that may colonize suitable habitat in the region, whether it is *Canis lupus* or *Canis lycaon*.[33]

FWS Decision-Making Process

The FWS decision-making process demonstrates that the delisting proposal was based on politics, not science. The Public Employees for Environmental Responsibility made a Freedom of Information Act request and obtained the minutes of the August 2010 meeting in which the delisting decision was made. The meeting included representatives from fourteen state wildlife agencies, in seven FWS regions. Five state wildlife agencies, one tribal commission, and one tribe declined to participate. Documents show that the wolf delisting proposal was designed to meet political and social concerns. The FWS asked, "Where should wolves exist? What does the public want? What can the public tolerate?" The FWS was worried about the legal defensibility of its action. The FWS was also concerned with addressing state objections, particularly those of Colorado and Utah officials, who oppose wolves in their states where there is suitable wolf habitat.[34] Scientists, who were responsible for much of the research cited in the draft proposal, stated that "we do not believe the rule reflects the conclusions of our work or the best available science concerning the recovery of wolves, or is in accordance with the fundamental purposes of the ESA to conserve endangered species and the ecosystems on which they depend." FWS director Ashe defended the decision stating "an exhaustive review of the latest scientific and taxonomic info shows that we have accomplished that goal with the gray wolf, allowing us to focus our work under the ESA on recovery of the Mexican wolf subspecies in the Southwest."[35]

The FWS handling of the peer review process raises additional questions regarding the legitimacy of the delisting proposal. FWS regulations require independent peer review of its proposals to ensure that decisions are based on scientifically sound data, assumptions, and analyses.[36] The FWS is not supposed to know the identity of the experts, but the contractor, AMEC, provided the FWS with the names of potential reviewers. Three prominent scientists, John Vucetich, Robert Wayne, Roland Kays, who signed a letter criticizing the delisting as premature, were excluded. After the violation was exposed, the FWS cancelled the AMEC contract and reinstituted peer review. FWS director Ashe stated, "We looked at the criticism and we actually agreed with it. The Service was too close in the selection of panelists." The FWS promised to pursue further inquiry.[37]

The National Center for Ecological Analysis and Synthesis conducted an independent review of the regulation, sponsored by the FWS. The review determined that the Chambers study did not make "appropriate use of the literature on species level taxonomy" and was "not universally accepted." The review concluded that the proposal "does not currently represent 'the best available science.'"[38] Environmental groups applauded the review. The CBD stated, "This peer review is a major blow to the Obama Administration's highly political effort to prematurely remove protections for wolves." Representative Peter DeFazio, the ranking Democrat on the House Natural Resources Committee, declared that the "peer review today leaves no option but for the FWS to rescind the proposed rule. . . . Continued protection is the only way that the gray wolf will ever return to significant portions of their range and reclaim their place as a keystone species of the American landscape."[39]

ESA Amendments

Wolf reintroduction is part of a larger battle over the ESA. President Obama promised to support the ESA. In May 2009, he stated "for more than 3 decades, the ESA has successfully protected our nation's most threatened wildlife, and we should be looking for ways to improve it—not weaken it." During his first two years in office, President Obama did little to fulfill his promise, much to the consternation of environmental groups. Facing litigation, the administration changed direction in 2011. The FWS agreed to speed up ESA protections for 757 imperiled species. The administration followed this initiative by requesting twenty-five million dollars for listings, an 11 percent increase from 2011.[40]

The settlement agreement generated public law litigation. Industry groups brought several suits, alleging that the agreement violated the procedural requirements of the ESA. Federal courts determined that the settlement agreement did not compel any action, but only established a timetable for such decisions. Since the industry groups did not suffer any injury, they lacked standing to challenge the agreement.[41] The CBD declared that there is ample opportunity for industry groups to participate in the ESA decision-making process, but "what they can't do is trample democracy by insisting that the government make no decision at all."[42]

The settlement agreement regarding 757 potential ESA listings generated a congressional response. Over two dozen bills were introduced in the 112th Congress attacking the ESA, but none were enacted.[43] Representative Hastings (R-Wash.), the chair of the House Resources Committee, led the charge for overhauling the ESA. Representative Hastings stated that "the ESA unfortunately is now used as a tool in costly lawsuits where politics trumps science and jobs and economic prosperity are put in jeopardy."[44]

Republican opposition to the ESA continued in the next session. In November 2013, Senators Rand Paul (R. Ky.), Mike Lee (R. Utah), and Dean Heller (R. Nev.) and Representative Mark Amodei (R. Nev.) introduced the Endangered Species Management Self-Determination Act of 2012, which would eviscerate the ESA. The bill requires that all protected species be removed from the endangered and threatened species list every five years. Congress must pass a joint resolution to renew their protections for another five years. All critical habitat protection is eliminated. State governments can veto any conservation measures designed to protect designated species within their state. Federal wildlife agencies must complete onerous accounting reports estimating the costs of protecting endangered species, rather than undertaking conservation activities to protect species. The CBD stated, "This bill would devastate species protections and open the door to log, mine, and pave some of the last places on earth where these animals survive. It's a boon for profiteers like the Koch brothers but will rob every American who values wildlife and wild places."[45]

Thirteen Republican representatives, known as the ESA Working Group, released a report in February 2014 proposing specific reforms for the ESA, which were designed to decrease litigation by environmental groups and expand state authority over endangered species within their borders. The report was particularly critical of the earlier settlement agreement.[46]

The House Natural Resources Committee reported out four bills amending the ESA in April 2014. Chairman Hastings bill, H.R. 4315, the Twenty-First Century Endangered Species Transparency Act, requires the federal government to publish all information regarding listing decisions on-line. Senator John Cornyn (R. Tex.) has introduced companion legislation in the Senate. Representative Lummis's bill, H.R. 4316, the Endangered Species

Recovery Transparency Act, requires the federal government to report to Congress annually, and make records available online of federal taxpayer funds used to respond to ESA litigation and the attorney fees awarded in the course of ESA litigation and settlement agreements. Senator Lee (R. Utah) has introduced companion legislation in the Senate. Representative Randy Neugebauer (R. Tex.) bill, H.R. 4317, the State, Tribal and Local Species Transparency and Recovery Act, requires the federal government to divulge to the states all of the data used to justify listing decisions. It mandates that the "best available scientific and commercial data" used by the federal government include data from states, tribes, and local governments. Senators Enzi and Barrasso have introduced similar legislation. Representative Bill Huizenga (R. Mich.) bill, H.R. 4318, the Endangered Species Litigation Reasonableness Act, limits the amount of attorney fees awarded to prevailing parties in ESA citizen suits to "reasonable" fees, $125 per hour. Representative DeFazio, the ranking Democrat on the Committee, declared that the four bills produced by the partisan ESA Working Group were "not serious attempts to reform" the ESA. The CBD stated that these bills "are part of a long-running strategy to hobble the law that, over the past 40 years, has put whales, wolves, grizzly bears, bald eagles and hundreds of other iconic species on the path toward recovery."[47]

Environmental groups raised several objections to the bills: First, the public disclosure of information used in ESA listing decisions in HR 4315 will undermine scientific work by requiring the release of data before peer review and publication. Scientists will be reluctant to participate in species status evaluations. Public disclosure will jeopardize species by encouraging poaching and collection. Second, the limitation on citizen suits in HR 4316 is contrary to existing evidence. FWS director Ashe stated, "On the scale of challenges that we face implementing the ESA, litigation does not even show up on the radar screen." In fact, citizen suits have been praised as "very important in selecting species worthy of protection. In many cases, outside groups could serve as the only impetus for protection of biologically threatened taxas that would otherwise be ignored because they conflict with development projects and related political pressures or because they are low level subspecies." Third, the requirement in HR 4317 that the federal government consult with state, tribal, and local governments is unnecessary. Section four of the ESA requires the federal government to provide notice regarding listing decisions. Section six of the ESA mandates federal-state cooperation. Furthermore, requiring the federal government to accept state, tribal, and local data, regardless of its scientific validity, undermines the ESA's mandate that decisions be based on the best available science. Finally, limiting the awarding of attorney fees in HR 4318 will discourage lawyers from taking cases, undermine judicial oversight of ESA implementation, and deny federal courts the authority to award reasonable attorney fees. Environmental critics stress that the real goal of the bills is to delay and dismantle the ESA.[48]

Despite criticism, the House passed the Endangered Species Transparency and Reasonableness Act, which aggregates the four bills, by bipartisan vote of 233–190 on July 29, 2014. Action on corresponding legislation moves over to Senate. The future of the ESA may be bleak as a result of the Republican take-over of Congress in 2015. The Obama administration, however, opposes the bill and promises a presidential veto if it reaches his desk.[49]

NOTES

1. In 2012, the NRM DPS contained 1,674 wolves in 321 packs including 103 breeding pairs. Montana recorded 625 wolves in 147 packs including 37 breeding pairs. Idaho recorded 683 wolves in 117 packs including 35 breeding pairs. Wyoming recorded 277 wolves in 43 packs including 21 breeding pairs. Washington recorded 43 wolves in 7 packs including 7 breeding pairs. Oregon recovered 46 wolves in 7 packs including 6 breeding pairs. U.S FWS, *Annual Report 2012*, 1.

2. Legal harvest removed 231 wolves in Montana (24 percent decrease in the absolute minimum Montana estimated wolf population), 356 wolves in Idaho (31 percent decrease in the absolute minimum Idaho estimated population), 62 wolves in Wyoming (15 percent decrease in the absolute minimum Wyoming estimated wolf population), and 1 wolf in Washington (3 percent decrease in absolute minimum Washington estimated wolf population). No wolves were harvested in Oregon. U.S. FWS, *Annual Report 2013*, 1.

3. A total of 335 wolves were removed from Montana; 473 wolves in Idaho; 109 wolves from Wyoming; 2 wolves from Washington; and 3 wolves in Oregon (Ibid. at 1–2). In 2012, 231 wolves were killed in livestock control actions in NRM DPS (Montana 108, Idaho 73, Wyoming 43, Washington 7). U.S. FWS, *Annual Report 2012*, 1.

4. US FWS, *Annual Report 2013*, at 3–4. In 2012, confirmed depredations included 194 cattle and 470 sheep. Federal funding for state, federal, and tribal agencies was $3,345,618. State and private compensation programs spent $564,558 to compensate livestock owners for their losses. U.S. FWS, *Annual Report 2012*, 3.

5. William J. Ripple et al., "Status and Ecological Effects of the World's Largest Carnivores," 343 *Science* 151 (Jan. 10, 2014). David Todd, "Wolf-Predator Control and Endangered Species Protection: Thoughts on Politics and Law," 33 *South Texas Law Review* 459, 478 (1992).

6. "Yellowstone Wolves in Diversity," *New York Times*, January 4, 1998. "Wolf Recovery Might Aid Other Species," *Spokesman Review*, September 11, 2011. "Yellowstone Transformed 15 Years After Return of the Wolves," *Targeted News Service*, December 21, 2011.

7. 76 *Federal Register* 61782, 61785–89 (Oct. 5, 2011).

8. "DOI Releases Details of Wyoming Shoot on Sight Wolf Plan," *States News Service*, August 3, 2011. "Feds Release Wyo. Delist Plan," AP State & Local Wire, October 4, 2011. "Wyoming, Feds Announce Plan for Delisting Wolves," *Bismarck Tribune*, August 4, 2011. "Enzi Encouraged by Wolf Management Agreement," Capitol Hill Press Release, August 3, 2011. "Delegation Statement on Proposed Wolf Delisting," Congressional Documents, October 4, 2011. "Wyoming, Feds Announce Plan for Delisting Wolves," AP, August 4, 2011.

9. "Norman Dick's Statement and Summary of Conference Report," Congressional Documents, December 15, 2011. "Administration Playing Both Sides When It Comes to Wolves, Sen. Enzi News Release," Congressional Documents, December 22, 2011.

10. *Defenders of Wildlife v. Jewell*, Case 1:12-cv-o1833-ABJ (September 23, 2014), 10

11. U.S. FWS, *Final Peer Review of Four Documents Amending and Clarifying the Wyoming Gray Wolf Management Plan* (May 2012), 1–5. "1 of 5 Scientists Takes Issue with Wyo. Wolf Plan," AP State & Local Wire, January 6, 2012.

12. "Wyoming Approves Flawed Wolf Plan, Gov. Mead Signs Bill to Treat Wolves as Vermin Across Majority of State," *States News Service*, March 7, 2012. "Federal Government Issued a Proposed Regulation That Will Delist the Wyoming Wolves," 77 *Federal Register* 25664 (May 1, 2012). "Service Declares Wyoming Gray Wolf Recovered Under the ESA and Returns Management to the State," *States News Service*, August 31, 2012.

13. U.S. FWS, *Annual Report 2012*, 1–2. Matt Brown, "Northern Rockies Wolf Numbers Drop 7 Percent," AP State & Local Wire, April 12, 2013.

14. "Conservation Groups Challenge Kill-at-Will Policy for Wyoming Wolves," *States News Service*, September 10, 2012. Ben Neary, "Groups Intend to Sue Feds over Wyoming Delisting," *Lewiston Morning Tribune*, September 11, 2012.

15. Cass R. Sunstein, "Participation, Public Law, and Venue Reform," 49 *University of Chicago Law Review* 976, 978–85 (1982).

16. *Defenders of Wildlife v. Jewell*, 2.

17. "Victory for Wolves in Wyoming," CBD Press Release, September 23, 2014.

18. Steven M. Chambers, Steven R. Fain, Bud Fazio, and Michael Amaral, "An Account of the Taxonomy of North American Wolves From Morphological Genetic Analysis," *North America Fauna* (October 2012).

19. 78 *Federal Register* 35664 (June 13, 2013). 78 *Federal Register* 35719 (June 13, 2013).

20. Holly Doremus, "Listing Decisions Under the Endangered Species Act: Why Better Science Isn't Always Better Policy," 75 *Washington University Law Quarterly* 1029, 1087, 1123–29 (1997). Steven Lewis Yaffee, *Prohibitive Policy, Implementing the ESA* (MIT Press, 1982), 75–86.

21. Letter from Rep. Peter DeFazio, to Secretary Jewell (September 4, 2013).

22. Letter from the American Society of Mammologists to Secretary Jewell (May 22, 2013). Bridgett M. von Holdt, et al., "A Genome-wide Perspective on the Evolutionary History of Enigmatic Wolf-like Canids," 21 *Genome Research* 1294 (2011). Carlos Carroll, John Vucetich, Michael Nelson, Daniel Rohlf, Michael Phillips, "Geography and Recovery under the U.S. ESA," 24 *Conservation Biology* 395 (2010).

23. NCEAS, "Conclusions of Sylvia Fallon, Robert Wayne, Paul Wilson," *Review of the Proposed Rule Regarding Status of the Wolf Under the ESA* (January 2014).

24. 76 *Federal Register* 76987 (Dec. 9, 2011). 78 *Federal Register* 35714–7.

25. Dan Ashe and Eileen Sobeck, "Letter to Editor," *New York Times*, September 5, 2014.

26. Carlos Carroll, et al., "Defining Recovery Goals and Strategies for Endangered Species: The Wolf as a Case Study," 56 *BioScience* 25, 32–33 (Jan. 2006).

27. Letter from the American Society of Mammologists to Secretary Jewell (May 22, 2013), citing B. J. Bergstrom, S. Vignieri, S. R. Shefield, W. Sechrest, and A. A. Carlson, "The Northern Rocky Mountain Gray Wolf Is Not Yet Recovered," 59 *BioScience* 991(2009). Letter from Bradley Bergstrom, et al. (16 scientists) to Secretary Jewell (May 21, 2013).

28. Letter from American Society of Mammologists, citing Scott Creel and Jay Rotella, "Meta-Analysis of Relationships Between Human Offtake, Total Mortality and Population Dynamics of Gray Wolves," *PLoS One* (Sept. 29, 2010). U.S. FWS, *2013 Annual Report 2013*, 2.

29. Letter from American Society of Mammologists, citing Bergstrom, Vignieri, Shefield, Sechrest, and Carlson. John B. Theberge, "An Ecologist's Perspective on Wolf Recovery in the Northeastern United States," in John Elder (ed.), *The Return of the Wolf: Reflections on the Future of the Wolf in the Northeast* (Middlebury College Press, 2000) 29–38.

30. Letter from the American Society of Mammologists to Secretary Jewell (May 22, 2013). Letter from Bradley Bergstrom, et al. (16 scientists) to Secretary Jewell (May 21, 2013).

31. 78 *Federal Register* 35670, 35717–18 (June 13, 2013).

32. NCEAS, "Conclusions Sylvia Fallon, Robert Wayne, Paul Wilson."

33. Letter from the American Society of Mammologists to Secretary Jewell (May 22, 2013). Letter from Bradley Bergstrom, et al. (16 scientists) to Secretary Jewell (May 21, 2013). Richard Thiel and Adrian Wydeven, *Eastern Wolf (Canis Lycaon) Status Assessment Report* (November 2011).

34. "Public Employees Sue Over 'Political Deals' Behind Wolf Delisting," Eens-newswire.com, May 22, 2013. "Politics Dominated Wolf Delisting Meeting," *Targeted News*, June

27, 2013. U.S. FWS, Wolf Structured Decision Making Workshop, "Summary for Deputy Director," August 23–27, 2010.

35. Letter from Bradley Bergstrom, et al. (16 scientists) to Secretary Jewell (May 21, 2013). "Washington: FWS Wolves No Longer Need ESA Protection," *Plus Media Solutions*, June 4, 2013.

36. 59 *Federal Register* 34270 (July 1, 1994).

37. "Agency Backtracks on Attempt to Exclude Wolf Experts," *Times News Service*, August 12, 2013. "Wolves Under Review," *New York Times*, August 16, 2013. "Feds Seek New Review of Dangerous Nationwide Wolf Plan," *CBD Newsletter*, October 3, 2013. John Flesher, "Feds Defend Plan to Drop Gray Wolf Protection," AP, September 30, 2013.

38. NCEAS, "Summary of Discussions at Meeting at NCEAS."

39. "Top Wolf Scientists Unanimous: Science Does Not Support Plan to Strip Protections," *CBD Newletter*, February 7, 2014. Raju Chebium, "Administration Backs Away from Plan to Remove Protections for Gray Wolves," *Gannett News Service*, February 7, 2014.

40. Jamie Rapport Clark, "An Interior Decision Imperils More Than Wolves," *Washington Post*, January 1, 2010. Paul Rogers, "Obama Decisions on Wildlife Raising Environmentalists Ire," *San Jose Mercury News* (Feb. 21, 2010). "Court Approves Historic Agreement to Speed ESA Protections for 757 Imperiled Species," *CBD Press Release*, September 9, 2011. Matthew Brown, "Hundreds of Plants, Animals up for New Protections," AP, September 29, 2011.

41. *National Assoc. of Home Builders v. FWS,* CV No. 12-2013 (March 31, 2014). *In re ESA Deadline Litigation,* 277 F.R.D. 1 (D.D.C. 2011), aff'd 704 F.3d 972 (D.C. Cir. 2013); *In re ESA Section 4 Deadline Litigation,* 270 F.R.D. 1 (D.D.C. 2010).

42. "Federal Court Rejects Industry Lawsuit to Stop Landmark Endangered Species Agreement," CBD Press Release, April 1, 2014.

43. Melissa Clark, "The Living Dead: Why One Species' Interference with Development May Undermine the Entire ESA," 18 *Roger Williams University Law Review* 79, 102–7 (2013).

44. "Hundreds of Plants, Animals up for New Protections," AP, September 29, 2011.

45. "Tea Party Bill Would Eviscerate ESA," *CBD Press Release* (Nov. 22, 2013).

46. Matt Brown, "Lawmakers Seek ESA Overhaul," AP, February 4, 2014.

47. "Rep. Gosar Supports Efforts to Modernize and Bring Increased Transparency to the ESA," Congressional Documents, April 28, 2014. "DeFazio Reacts to Committee Passage of Misguided Republican ESA Legislation," *States New Service*, April 30, 2014. "House Republicans Approve Bills to Weaken the ESA," *CBD Newsletter*, April 30, 2014. "House GOP Launches Another Attack on the ESA," *CBD Newsletter*, May 1, 2014. "Enzi: Let States See the Data before Endangered Species Listings," *Plus Media*, July 19, 2014.

48. "Congress Launches New Attacks On Endangered Species," *Defenders of Wildlife Press Release*, citing Laura Peterson, "Lawsuits Not Hurting ESA—FWS Director," *Greenwire*, July 5, 2012, and Berry Bosi and Eric Biber, "Citizen Involvement in ESA," 337 *Science* 802, August 2012.

49. "U.S. House Amendments to ESA Would Burden Agencies," *Plus Media Solutions*, August 11, 2014.

Bibliography

Adams, L. G., et al., "Population Dynamics and Harvest Characteristics of Wolves in the Central Brooks Range, Alaska," 170 *Wildlife Monograph* 1 (2008).

Alienikoff, T. Alexander, "Updating Statutory Interpretation," 87 *Michigan Law Review* 20 (1988).

Allen, Durwood L., *Our Wildlife Legacy* (Funk and Wagnalls, 1962).

Aman, Alfred C., "Administrative Law in a Global Era," 73 *Cornell Law Review* 1101(1988).

Aman, Alfred C., and William T. Mayton, *Administrative Law* (West, 1992).

Arabas, Karen, and Joe Bowersox (eds.), *Forest Futures: Science, Politics, and Policy for the Next Century,* (Rowman and Littlefield, 2004).

Aubert, Victor, "Competition and Dissensus: Two Forms of Conflict Resolution," *Journal of Conflict Resolution* 7 (1963).

Ausness, Richard C., "Federal Preemption of State Products Liability Doctrines," 44 *South Carolina Law Review* 187 (1993).

Azaria, William D., "The Trouble with Robertson," 48 *Catholic University Law Review* 1055 (1999).

Babbitt, Bruce, "Federalism and the Environment: An Intergovernmental Perspective of the Sagebrush Rebellion," 12 *Environmental Law* 847 (1982).

Bader, Harry R., "Antaeus and the Public Trust Doctrine: A New Approach to Substantive Environmental Protection in the Common Law," 19 *Environmental Affairs Law Review* 749 (1992).

Bader, Harry R., "Wolf Conservation: The Importance of Following Endangered Species Recovery Plans," 13 *Harvard Environmental Law Review* 517 (1989).

Baum, Robert A., *Public Interest Law: Where Law Meets Social Action* (Oceana, 1987).

Bean, Michael J., and Melanie J. Rowland, *The Evolution of Natural Wildlife Law,* 3d ed. (Praeger, 1997).

Beisher, Brian N., "Comments: Are Ranchers Legitimately Trying to Save Their Hides or Are They Just Crying Wolf," 29 *Land and Water Law Review* 417 (1994).

Bergoffen, Marty, *ESA Reauthorization: A Biocentric Approach* (American Bar Association, 1995).

Bergstrom, B. J., S. Vignieri, S. R. Shefield, W. Sechrest, and A. Carlson, "The Northern Rocky Mountain Gray Wolf Is Not Yet Recovered," 59 *BioScience* 991 (2009).

Blumm Michael C., "Ancient Forests and the Supreme Court: Issuing a Blank Check for Appropriation Riders," 43 *Journal Urban and Contemporary Law* 35 (1993).

Blumm, Michael C., "Public Property and the Democratization of Western Water Law: A Modern View of the Public Trust Doctrine," 19 *Environmental Law* 573 (1989).

Bolduan, Linda M., "The Hatfield Riders: Eliminating the Role of Courts in Environmental Decision Making," 20 *Environmental Law* 322 (1990).

Boyd, William S., "Federal Protection of Endangered Wildlife Species," 22 *Stanford Law Review* 1289 (1970).

Bray, Zachary, "The Hidden Rise of Efficient (De)Listing," 73 *Maryland Law Review* 201 (2014).

Breyer, Stephen, "Judicial Review of Questions of Law and Policy," 38 *Administrative Law Review* 363 (1986).

———. "On the Uses of Legislative History in Interpreting Statutes," 65 *Southern California Law Review* 845 (1992).

Brick, Philip D., and R. McGreggor Cawley (eds.), *A Wolf in the Garden: The Land Rights Movement and the New Environmental Debate* (Rowman & Littlefield, 1996).

Brown, David E., *The Wolf in the Southwest* (University of Arizona, 1984), 48.

Brown, Elizabeth C., "The 'Wholly Separate' Truth: Did Yellowstone Wolf Reintroduction Violate Section 10(J) of the ESA?" 27 *Boston College Environmental Affairs Law Review* 425 (2000).

Brown, Jacqueline L., "Preserving Species: The Endangered Species Act versus Ecosystem Management Regime," 12 *Journal Environmental Law & Litigation* 151 (1997).

Bruff, Harold H., "Legislative Formality, Administrative Rationality," 63 *Texas Law Review* 207 (1984).

Bryant, A. Christopher, and Timothy J. Simeone, "Remanding to Congress: The Supreme Court's New 'on the Record' Constitutional Review of Federal Statutes," 86 *Cornell Law Review* 328 (2001).

Buzbee, William W., and Robert A. Shapiro, "Legislative Record Review," 54 *Stanford Law Review* 87 (2001).

Byse, Clark, "Judicial Review of Administrative Interpretation of Statutes: An Analysis of Chevron's Two Step," 2 *Administrative Law Journa*l 255 (1988).

Callahan, Maureen B., "Must Federal Courts Defer to Agency Interpretations of Statutes?" 1991 *Wisconsin Law Review* 1275.

Cambell, Thomas A., "The Public Trust, What's It Worth," 34 *Natural Resources Journa*l 73 (1994).

Cameron, Jenks, *The Bureau of Biological Survey: Its History, Activities and Organization* (John Hopkins University, 1929).

Canon, Bradley, and Charles Johnson, *Judicial Policies: Implementation and Impact,* 2d ed. (Congressional Quarterly, 1998).

Carlson, Jonathan C., and Alan D. Smith, "The Emerging Constitutional Jurisprudence of Justice Stevens," 46 *University Chicago Law Review* 157 (1978).

Carroll, Carlos, Michael K. Phillips, Carlos A. Lopez-Gonzalez, and Nathan Schumaker, "Defining Recovery Goals and Strategies for Endangered Species: The Wolf as a Case Study," 56 *BioScience* 25 (2006).

Carroll, Carlos, John Vucetich, Michael Nelson, Daniel Rohlf, and Michael Phillips, "Geography and Recovery under the U.S. ESA," 24 *Conservation Biology* 395 (2010).

Carp, Robert, and Ronald Stidham, *The Federal Courts*, 3d ed. (Congressional Quarterly, 1998).

Caspersen, Anna R. C., "The Public Trust Doctrine and the Impossibility of 'Takings' by Wildlife," 23 *Boston College Environmental Affairs Law Review* 357(1996).

Causey, Inga H., "The Reintroduction of the Wolf into Yellowstone," 11 *Tulane Environmental Law Journal* 461 (1998).

Cawley, R. McGreggor, *Federal Land, Western Anger: The Sagebrush Rebellion and Environmental Politics* (University of Kansas, 1993).

Chambers, Steven M., Steven R. Fain, Bud Fazio, and Michael Amaral, "An Account of the Taxonomy of North American Wolves From Morphological Genetic Analysis," *North America Fauna* (October 2012).

Chase, Alston, *Playing God in Yellowstone* (Harcourt Brace Jankovich, 1987).

Chayes, Abram, "The Role of the Judge in Public Law Litigation," 89 *Harvard Law Review* 1281 (1976).

———. "The Supreme Court 1981 Term, Forward: Public Law Litigation and the Burger Court," 96 *Harvard Law Review* 4 (1982).

Cheever, Frederico, "The Rhetoric of Delisting Species Under the ESA," 31 *Environmental Law Reporter* 11302 (2001).

Christensen, Eric, "Genetic Ark: A Proposal to Preserve Genetic Diversity for Future Generations," 40 *Stanford Law Review* 279 (1987).

Clark, Melissa, "The Living Dead: Why One Species' Interference with Development May Undermine the Entire ESA," 18 *Roger Williams University Law Review* 79 (2013).

Cleere, Scott R., "Wolf Reintroduction as an Experimental Population Under the ESA," 36 *Idaho Law Review* 83 (1999).

Coenen, Dan T., "A Constitution of Collaboration: Protecting Fundamental Values with Second-Look Rules of Interbranch Dialogue," 42 *William & Mary Law Review* 1575 (2001).

———, "The Rehnquist Court, Structural Due Process, and Semi-substantive Constitutional Review," *75 Southern California Law Review* 1281 (2002).

Coggins, George Cameron, "Federal Wildlife Management," 60 *Oregon Law Review* 59 (1981).

———, "Of Succotash Syndromes and Vacuous Platitudes: The Meaning of Multiple Use and Sustained Yield for Public Land Management," 53 *University of Colorado Law Review* 229 (1982).

Coggins, George Cameron, and Parthenia B. Evans, "Predators' Rights and American Wildlife Law," 24 *Arizona Law Review* 821 (1982).

Coggins, George Cameron, and Anne Fleishel Harris, "The Greening of American Law?" 27 *Natural Resources Journa*l 247 (1987).

Coggins, George Cameron, and Doris K. Nagel, "'Nothing Besides Remains': The Legal Legacy of James G. Watts Tenure as Secretary of Interior on Federal Land Law and Policy," 17 *Boston College Environmental Affairs Law Review* 473 (1990).

Colker, Ruth, and James J. Brudnoy, "Dissing Congress," 100 *Michigan Law Review* 80 (2001).

Corry, J. A., "The Use of Legislative History in the Interpretation of Statutes," 32 *Canadian Bar Review* 624 (1954).

Corwin, Wick, "Predator Control and the Federal Government," 51 *North Dakota Law Review* 787 (175).

Costanza Robert et al., "The Value of the World's Ecosystem Services and Natural Capital," 387 *Nature* 253 (1987).

Creel, Scott, and Jay Rotella, "Meta-Analysis of Relationships between Human Offtake, Total Mortality and Population Dynamics of Gray Wolves," *PLoS ONE* (September 2010).

Cross, Frank B., "Pragmatic Pathologies of Judicial Review of Administrative Rulemaking," 78 *North Carolina Law Review* 1013 (2000).

———, "Shattering the Fragile Case for Judicial Review of Rulemaking," 85 *Virginia Law Review* 1243 (1999).

Curtis, Charles, *It's Your Law* (Harvard University, 1954).

Czarnezi, Jason J., "An Empirical Investigation of Judicial Decisionmaking, Statutory Interpretations, and the Chevron Doctrine in Environmental Law," 79 *University of Colorado Law Review* 767 (2008).

Davis, Charles (ed.), *Western Public Lands and Environmental Policy*, 2d ed. (Westview, 2001).

Davis, Kenneth Culp, *Administrative Law Treatise* (West, 1978).

Davis, Sue, and Donald R. Songer, "The Changing Role of the U.S. Court of Appeals: The Flow of Litigation Revisited," 13 *Justice System Journal* 323 (1988–1989).

Deering, Chrisopher J., and Steven S. Smith, *Committees in Congress,* 3d ed. (Congressional Quarterly 1997).

Denvir, John, "Towards a Political Theory of Public Interest Litigation," 54 *North Carolina Law Review* 1133 (1976).

Devins, Neil E., "Appropriations Redux: A Critical Look at Fiscal Year 1988 Continuing Resolution," 1988 *Duke Law Journal* 389.

———, "Congressional Fact Finding and Scope of Judicial Review," 50 *Duke Law Journal* 1169 (2001).

———, "Regulation of Government Agencies Through Limitation Riders," 1987 *Duke Law Journal* 456.

Dickerson, Reed, *The Interpretation and Application of Statutes* (Little Brown, 1975).

Dinger, Daniel R., "Throwing Canis Lupus to the Wolves: *United States v. McKittrick* and the Existence of the Yellowstone and Central Idaho Experimental Wolf Populations under a Flawed Provision of the ESA," 2000 *Brigham Young Law Review* 377.

Diver, Colin S., "Statutory Interpretation in the Administrative State," 133 *University of Pennsylvania Law Review* 549 (1985).

Dolgin, Erica L., and Thomas G. P. Gilbert (eds.), *Federal Environmental Law* (West, 1974).

Doremus, Holly, "Delisting Endangered Species: An Aspirational Goal, Not a Realistic Expectation," 30 *Environmental Law Reporter* 10435 (2000).

———, "Listing Decisions Under the Endangered Species Act: Why Better Science Isn't Always Better Policy," 75 *Washington University Law Quarterly* 1029 (1997).

———, "The ESA's Best Available Science Mandate," 34 *Environmental Law* 397 (2004).

———, "The Purposes, Effects, and Future of ESA's Best Available Science Mandate," 34 *Environmental Law* 397 (2004).

Dunlap, Thomas R., *Saving America's Wildlife* (Princeton University, 1988).

———, "Values for Varmints: Predator Control and Environmental Ideas, 1920-1939," 53 *Pacific Historical Review* 141 (1983).

Easterbrooke, Richard, "Foreword: The Supreme Court and the Economic System," 98 *Harvard Law Review* 4 (1984).

Edley, Christopher F., *Administrative Law, Rethinking Judicial Control of Bureaucracy* (Yale University, 1990).

Edvenson, June C., "Predator Control and Regulated Killing: A Biodiversity Analysis," 13 *Journal of Environmental Law* 31 (1995).

Edwards, Lee (ed.)., *Bringing Justice to the People: A Story of the Freedom Based Public Law Movement* (Heritage, 2004).

Ehrlich, Paul, and Anne Ehrlich, *Extinction: The Causes and Consequences of the Disappearance of Species* (Random House, 1981).

Eisenberg, Theodore, "Congressional Authority to Restrict Lower Federal Court Jurisdiction," 83 *Yale Law Journal* 498 (1974).

Elder, John (ed.), *The Return of the Wolf: Reflections on the Future of the Wolf in the Northeast* (Middlebury College Press, 2000) .

Elhauge, Einer R., "Does Interest Group Theory Justify More Intrusive Judicial Review?" 101 *Yale Law Review* 31 (1991).

Ely, Jonathan Hart, *Democracy and Distrust: A Theory of Judicial Review* (Harvard University, 1980).

Enochs, Craig R., "Gone Today, Here Tomorrow: Policies and Issues Surrounding Wildlife Reintroduction," 4 *West-Northwest Journal of Environmental Law & Policy* 91 (1997).

Eskridge Jr., William N., "Dynamic Statutory Interpretation," 135 *University of Pennsylvania Law Review* 1479 (1987).

———, "Interpreting Legislative Inaction," 87 *Michigan Law Review* 67 (1988).

———, "Overriding Supreme Court Statutory Interpretation Decisions," 101 *Yale Law Journal* 331 (1991).

———, "Politics Without Romance: Implications for Public Choice Theory for Statutory Interpretation," 74 *Virginia Law Review* 275(1988).

———, "Post-Enactment Legislative Signals," 57 *Law and Contemporary Problems* 75 (1994).

———, "The New Textualism," 37 *UCLA Law Review* 621 (1990).

Eskridge Jr., William N., and Philip P. Frickey, *Cases and Material on Legislation: Statutes and the Creation of Public Policy*, 2d ed. (West Publishing, 1994).

———, "Legislation Scholarship and Pedagogy in the Post-Legal Process Era," 48 *University of Pittsburgh Law Review* 691 (1987).

———, "Statutory Interpretation as Practical Reasoning," 42 *Stanford Law Review* 321 (1990).

Farber, Daniel A., "Politics and Procedure in Environmental Law," 8 *Journal Law Economics & Organization* 59 (1992).

Farber, Daniel A., and Philip P. Frickey, "Forward: Positive Political Theory in the Nineties," 80 *Georgetown Law Journal* 457 (1992).

———, *Law and Public Choice: A Critical Introduction* (University of Chicago, 1991).

Farina, Cynthia R., "Statutory Interpretation and the Balance of Power in the Administrative State," 89 *Columbia Law Review* 452 (1989).

Fascione, Nina, Aimee Delach, and Martin E. Smith (eds.), *People and Predators: From Conflict to Coexistence* (Island Press, 2005).

Fischer, Louis, "The Authorization-Appropriation Process in Congress: Formal Rules and Informal Practices," 29 *Catholic University Law Review* 51 (1979).

Fishman, Steven B., "A Preliminary Assessment of the NEPA of 1969," 1973 *Urban Law Annual* 209.

Fiss Owen, "The Forms of Justice," 93 *Harvard Law Review* 1 (1979).

Fitts, Michael A., "The Vices of Virtue: A Political Party Perspective on Civic Virtue Reforms of the Legislative Process," 136 *University of Pennsylvania Law Review* 1567 (1988).

Fitzgerald, Edward A., "*Alliance for the Wild Rockies v. Salazar*: Congress Behaving Badly," 25 *Villanova Environmental Law Journal* 351 (2014).

———, "*Defenders of Wildlife v. Secretary of Interior*: Dysfunctional Downlisting Defeated," 34 *Boston College Environmental Affairs Law Review* 37 (2007).

———, "*Defenders of Wildlife v. Salazar*: Delisting the Children of the Night in the Northern Rocky Mountains, 31 *Public Land & Resources Law Review* 1 (2010).

———, "Delisting Wolves in the Northern Rocky Mountains: Congress Cries Wolf," 41 *Environmental Law Reporte*r 10840 (2011).

———, "*Gibbs v. Babbitt*: Seeing Red," 13 *Villanova Environmental Law Journal* 1 (2002).

———, "*New Mexico Cattlegrowers Association v. U.S. Fish and Wildlife Service*: Lobo Returns from Limbo," 46 *Natural Resources Journal* 9 (2006).

———, "The Alaskan Wolf War: The Public Trust Doctrine Goes Missing in Action," 15 *Animal Law Review* 193 (2009).

———, "Wolf Delisting: Old Wine in New Bottles," 44 *Environmental Law Reporter* 10413 (May 2014).

———, "*Wyoming Farm Bureau Federation v. Babbitt*: The Children of the Night Return to the Northern Rocky Mountains," 16 *Journal of Natural Resources and Environmental Law* 79 (2001–2).

Flournoy, Alyson C., "Beyond the 'Spotted Owl': Learning from the Old-Growth Controversy," 17 *Harvard Environmental Law Review* 261 (1993).

Frickey, Philip P., "The Fool on the Hill: Congressional Findings, Constitutional Adjudication, and *United States v. Lopez*," 46 *Case Western Reserve Law Review* 695 (1996).

Frickey, Philip P., and Steven S. Smith, "Judicial Review, the Congressional Process, and Federalism Cases: An Interdisciplinary Critique," 111 *Yale Law Journal* 1707 (2002).

Fuller, Lon, "The Forms and Limits of Adjudication," 92 *Harvard Law Review* 92 (1978).

Gambitta, Richard A. L., Marlynn L. May, and James C. Foster, *Governing Through Courts* (Sage, 1981).

Gardbaum, Stephen, "Rethinking Constitutional Federalism," 74 *Texas Law Review* 795 (1996).

Garland, Merrick, "Deregulation and Judicial Review," 98 *Harvard Law Review* 505 (1985).

Gebbia-Pinetti, Karen M., "Statutory Interpretation: Democratic Legitimacy and Legal System Values," 21 *Seton Hall Legislation Journal* 233 (1997).

Gleaves, Karl, Michele Kuruc, and Patricia Montanio, "The Meaning of 'Species' Under the ESA," 13 *Public Law Review* 25 (1992).

Goble, Dale D., "Of Wolves and Welfare Ranching," 16 *Harvard Environmental Law Review* 101 (1992).

Goble, Dale D., J. Michael Scott, and Frank W. Davis (eds.), *The Endangered Species Act at Thirty* (Island, 2006).

Goldman-Carter, Janice, "Federal Conservation of Threatened Species: By Administrative Discretion or By Legislative Standard?" 11 *Boston College Environmental Affairs Law Review* 63 (1983).

Grabow, John C., "Congressional Silence and the Search for Legislative Intent: A Venture into 'Speculative Unrealities,'" 64 *Boston University Law Review* 737 (1985).

Greve, Michael S., *The Demise of Environmentalism in American Law* (American Enterprise Institute, 1996).

Grooms, Steve, *The Return of the Wolf* (NorWord, 1993).

Gunther, Gerald, "Congressional Power to Curtail Federal Court Jurisdiction: An Opinionated Guide to the Ongoing Debate," 36 *Stanford Law Review* 895 (984).

Hampton, Bruce, *The Great American Wolf* (H. Holt & Co., 1997).

Hart, Henry M., "The Power of Congress to Limit the Jurisdiction of Federal Courts: An Exercise in Dialectic," 66 *Harvard Law Review* 1362.

Hart, Henry M., and Albert M. Sacks, *The Legal Process: Basic Problems in the Making and Application of Law* (Foundation Press, 1994).

Hausrath, Katherin M., "The Designation of 'Distinct Population Segments' Under the ESA In Light of *National Association of Homebuilders v. Norton*," 80 *Chicago Kent Law Review* 449 (2005).

Hebblewhite, Mark, et al., "Human Activity Mediates a Trophic Cascade Caused By Wolves," 86 *Ecology* 2135 (2005).

Hebblewhite, Mark, Marco Musiani, and L. Scott Mills, "Restoration of Genetic Connectivity among Northern Rockies Wolf Populations, "19 *Molecular Biology* 4383 (2010).

Heiken, Douglas O., "The Pacific Yew and Taxol," 7 *Journal Environmental Law & Litigation* 175 (1992).

Henshen, Beth M., "Statutory Interpretations of the Supreme Court: Congressional Response," 11 *American Political Quarterly* 441 (1983).

Henschen, Beth M., and Edward I. Sidlow, "The Supreme Court and the Congressional Agenda Setting Process," 5 *Journal of Law and Politics* 685 (1989).

Horowitz, Donald, *The Courts and Social Policy* (Brookings Institution, 1977).

Houck, Oliver A., "Why Do We Protect Endangered Species," 80 *Iowa Law Review* 297 (1995).

Huffman, James L., "A Fish Out of Water: The Public Trust in a Constitutional Democracy," 19 *Environmental Law* 527 (1989).

Hunter, David B., "An Ecological Perspective on Property," 12 *Harvard Environmental Law Review* 311 (1988).

Jackson, Vicki L., "Federalism and the Uses and Limits of Law: Printz and Principle," 111 *Harvard Law Review* 2180 (1998).

Jaffe, Louis, *Judicial Control of Administrative Action* (Little Brown, 1965).

Jennes, Ryan, "*Defenders of Wildlife v. Norton*: 'Extinction' Under the ESA Construed Favorably to Conservation Efforts," 15 *Tulane Environmental Law Journal* 143 (2001).

Kagan, Robert A., "Adversarial Legalism and American Government," 10 *Journal of Policy Analysis and Management* 369 (1991).

Keiter, Robert B., *Keeping Faith with Nature: Ecosystems, Democracy, and America's Public Lands* (Yale University, 2003).

Keiter, Robert, and Patrick Holshea, "Wolf Recovery Under the ESA: A Study in Contemporary Federalism," 11 *Public Land Law Review* 19 (1990).

Kingdon, John W., *Agendas, Alternative, and Public Policy*, 2d ed. (Harper Collins, 1995).

Kirwan, Christopher J., "Wolves and Recovery Plans: The Difficult Road to Wolf Preservation in the Greater Yellowstone Ecosystem," 60 *University of Missouri Kansas City Law Review* 517 (1992).

Klipsch, Ronald E., "Aspects of a Constitutional Right to a Habitable Environment: Towards an Environmental Due Process," 49 *Indiana Law Journal* 203 (1970).

Klyza, Christopher McGrory, *Who Controls Public Lands?* (MIT, 1996).

Kovacic, William E., "The Reagan Judiciary and Environmental Policy," 18 *Boston College Environmental Affairs Law Review* 669 (1994).

Krent, Harold J., "Turning Congress Into an Agency: The Propriety of Requiring Legislative Findings," 46 *Case Western Reserve Law Review* 731 (1966).

Kubasek, Nancy, "Proposed Changes to ESA in the Spotlight Again," 34 *Real Estate Law Journal* 235 (2005).

Lamm, Richard D., and Michael McCarthy, *The Angry West* (Houghton Mifflin, 1982).

Landes, William M., and Richard A. Posner, "The Independent Judiciary in an Interest-Group Perspective," 18 *Journal of Law and Economics* 875 (1975).

Lazarus, Richard J., "Changing Conceptions of Property and Sovereignty in Natural Resources: Questioning the Public Trust Doctrine," 71 *Iowa Law Review* 631 (1986).

LeBoeuf, Jacques B., "Limitations on the Use of Appropriation Riders by Congress to Effectuate Substantive Policy Changes," 19 *Hastings Constitutional Law Quarterly* 457 (1992).

Leopold, Aldo, *A Sand County Almanac* (New Press, 1968).

Leshy, John D., "Unraveling the Sagebrush Rebellion: Law, Politics and Federal Lands," 14 *University of California Davis Law Review* 317 (1980).

Lester, James P., and Joseph Stewart, *Public Policy: An Evolutionary Approach* (Wadsworth, 1996).

Leventhal, Harold, "Environmental Decisionmaking and the Role of the Courts," 122 *University of Pennsylvania Law Review* 509 (1974).

Li, Jennifer, "The Wolves May Have Won the Battle, But Not the War: How the West Was Won Under the Northern Rocky Mountain Wolf Recovery Plan," 30 *Environmental Law* 677 (2000).

Linde, Hans A., "Due Process of Lawmaking," 55 *Nebraska Law Review* 197 (1976).

Lipset, Seymour, *The Third Century: America as a Post Industrial Society* (Hoover Institute, 1979).

Liroff, Richard Allen, "Administrative, Judicial, and Natural Systems: Agency Response to the NEPA of 1969," 3 *Loyola University of Chicago Law Journal* 19 (1972).

Lowi, Theodore, *The End of Liberalism,* 2d ed, (Norton, 1979).

Macey, Jonathan R., "Promoting Public-Regarding Legislation Through Statutory Interpretation: An Interest-Group Model," 86 *Columbia Law Review* 223 (1986).

———, "Separated Powers and Positive Political Theory: Tug of War Over Administrative Agencies," 80 *Georgetown Law Journa*l 671 (1992).

Maranzana, Linda C., "*Defenders of the Wildlife v. Norton*: A Closer Look at the 'Significant Portion of Its Range' Concept," 29 *Ecology Law Quarterly* 263 (2002).

Marcel, Kathleen W., "The Role of the Courts in a Legislative and Administrative Legal System: The Use of Hard Look Review in Federal Environmental Litigation," 62 *Oregon Law Review* 403 (1983).

Marion, Nancy E., *Making Environmental Law: The Politics of Protecting the Earth*, (Praeger, 2011).

Marshall, Thomas R., "Policymaking and the Modern Court: When Do Supreme Court Rulings Prevail?" 42 *Western Political Quarterly* 493 (1989).

Mashaw, Jerry L., "Why Administrators Should Make Political Decisions," 1 *Journal Law, Economics, and Organization* 95 (1985).

Mashaw, Jerry L., and David L. Harst, "Regulation and Legal Culture: The Case of Motor Vehicle Safety," 4 *Yale Journal of Regulation* 257 (1987).

McFarland, Andrew S., *Public Interest Lobbies: Decision Making on Energy* (American Enterprise Institute, 1976).

McIntyre, Rick, *War Against the Wolf* (Voyager Press, 1995).

McGarity, Thomas O., "The Courts and Ossification of Rulemaking: A Response to Professor Seidenfeld," 75 *Texas Law Review* 525 (1997).

McNollgast, "Positive Canons: The Role of Legislative Bargains in Statutory Interpretation," 80 *Georgetown Law Journa*l 705 (1992).

McNulty, Faith, *Must They Die?* (Doubleday, 1971).

Mech, L. David, "Managing Minnesota's Recovered Wolves," 72 *Journal Wildlife Management* 89 (2001).

Melnick, R. Shep, *Administrative Law and Bureaucratic Reality,* 44 *Administrative Law Review* 245 (1992).

———, *Regulation Through the Courts* (Brookings Institution, 1983).
Merrill, Thomas W., "Judicial Deference to Executive Precedent," 101 *Yale Law Journal* 969 (1992).
———, "Textualism and the Future of the Chevron Doctrine," 72 *Washington University Law Quarterly* 351 (1994).
Meyers, Gary D., "Variation on a Theme: Expanding the Public Trust Doctrine to Include Protection of Wildlife," 19 *Environmental Law* 723 (1989).
Michelman, Frank I., "Political Markets and Community Self-Determination: Competing Models of Judicial Legitimacy," 53 *Indiana Law Journal* 145 (1977–1978).
Mikva, Abner J., "How Should the Courts Treat Administrative Agencies?" 36 *American University Law Review* 1 (1986).
Mikva, Abner, and Eric Lane, *An Introduction to Statutory Interpretation and the Legislative Process* (Aspen Law, 1997).
———, "The Muzak of Justice Scalia's Revolutionary Call to Read Unclear Statutes Narrowly," 53 *Southern Methodist University Law Review* 11, 123 (2000).
Mollison, Richard M., and Richard W. Eddy, "Sagebrush Rebellion: A Simplistic Response to Complex Problems of Federal Land Management" 19 *Harvard Journal on Legislation* 97 (1982).
Monaghan, Henry P., "Marbury and the Administrative State," 83 *Columbia Law Review* 1 (1983).
Moore, Robert, "The Pack is Back," 12 *Thomas M. Cooley Law Review* 647 (1995).
Mortensen, Robert K., *In the Cause of Progress: History of New Mexico Cattlegrowers Assoc.* (New Mexico Cattlegrowers Assoc., 1983).
Murray, Dennis L., et al., "Death from Anthropogenic Causes Is Partially Compensatory in Recovering Wolf Populations," 143 *Biological Conservation* 2514 (2010).
Nagle, John C., "Playing Noah," 82 *Minnesota Law Review* 1171 (1998).
Nichol Jr., Gene R., "Justice Scalia, Standing, and Public Law Litigation," 42 *Duke Law Journal* 1141 (1993).
Nie, Martin, *Beyond Wolves* (University of Minnesota Press, 2003).
Note, "Congressional Reversals of Supreme Court Decisions: 1945–1957," 71 *Harvard Law Review* 1324 (1958).
Notes, "Judicial Intervention and Organizational Theory: Changing Bureaucratic Behavior and Policy," 89 *Yale Law Journal* 513 (1980).
Notes, "Proprietary Duties of the Federal Government Under the Public Trust Doctrine," 75 *Michigan Law Review* 586 (1977).
Oakleaf, John K., Dennis L. Murray, James R. Oakleaf, Edward E. Bangs, Curt M. Mack, Douglas W. Smith, Joseph A. Fontaine, Michael D. Jimenez, Thomas J. Meier, Carter C. Niemeyer, "Habitat Selection by Recolonizing Wolves in the Northern Rocky Mountains of the United States," 70 *Journal Wildlife Management* 554 (2006).
O'Brien, David M., "Marbury, the APA, and Science-Policy Disputes: The Alluring and Elusive Judicial/Administrative Partnership," 7 *Harvard Journal of Legislation and Public Policy* 443 (1984).
O'Connor, Karen, and Lee Epstein, "Rebalancing the Scales of Justice: An Assessment of Public Interest Law," 7 *Harvard Journal Law and Public Policy* 483 (1984).
O'Leary, Rosemary, "The Impacts of Federal Court Decisions on the Policies and Administration of the U.S. EPA," 41 *Administrative Law Review* 549 (1989).
Olsen, Mancur, *The Logic of Collective Action* (Harvard University, 1965).
Parenteau, Patrick, "Rearranging the Deck Chairs: Endangered Species Act Reforms in the Era of Mass Extinctions," 22 *William & Mary Environmental Law & Policy Review* 227 (1998).
Paschal, Richard A., "Continuing Colloquy," 8 *Journal of Law and Politics* 143, 196–204 (1991).
Pearson, Eric, "The Public Trust Doctrine in Federal Law," 24 *Journal Law, Resources & Environmental Law* 173 (2004).
Pedersen Jr., William F., "Formal Records and Informal Rulemaking," 85 *Yale Law Journa*l 38 (1975).

Pierce, Richard C., "Issues Raised by Laidlaw: Access to the Courts," 11 *Duke Environmental Law & Policy Forum* 207 (2001).

———, "*Lujan v. Defenders of Wildlife*: Standing as a Judicially Imposed Limit on Legislative Power," 42 *Duke Law Journal* 1170, 1171–88 (1993).

———, "Reconciling Chevron and Stare Decisis," 85 *Georgetown Law Journal* 2225, 2237–48 (1997).

———, "The Role of the Judiciary in Implementing an Agency Theory of Government," 64 *New York University Law Review* 1239 (1989).

———, "Seven Ways to Deossify Agency Rulemaking," 47 *Administrative Law Review* 59 (1995).

———, "Two Problems in Administrative Law," 1988 *Duke Law Journal* 300.

Poisner, Jonathan, "Environmental Values and Judicial Review after Lujan: Two Critiques of Separation of Powers Theory of Standing," 18 *Ecology Law Quarterly* 335 (1991).

Posner, Richard A., "The Jurisprudence of Skepticism," 86 *Michigan Law Review* 827 (1988).

———, "Statutory Interpretation—in the Classroom and in the Courtroom," 50 *University of Chicago Law Review* 800 (1983).

Public Land Law Review Commission, *One Third of the Nation's Land* (1970).

Rabin, Robert L., "Lawyers for Social Change: Perspectives on Public Interest Law," 28 *Stanford Law Review* 207 (1976).

Rabkin, Jeremy A., *Judicial Compulsions: How Public Law Distorts Public Policy* (Basic Books, 1989).

Radin, Max, "Statutory Interpretation," 43 *Harvard Law Review* 863 (1929–30).

Ray, Justina C., Kent H. Redford, Robert S. Stenneck, Joel Berger (eds.), *Large Carnivores and the Conservation of Biodiversity* (Island Press, 2005).

Redish, Martin H., and Theodore T. Chung, "Democratic Theory and the Legislative Process: Mourning the Death of Originalism in Statutory Interpretation," 68 *Tulane Law Review* 803 (1994).

Redish, Martin H., and Christopher R. Pudelski, "Legislative Deception, Separation of Powers, and the Democratic Process: Harnessing the Political Theory of *United States v. Klein*," 110 *Northwestern University Law Review* 437 (2006).

Redish, Martin H., and Curtis E. Woods, "Congressional Power to Control the Jurisdiction of Lower Federal Courts: A Critical Review and a New Synthesis," 124 *University of Pennsylvania Law Review* 45 (1975).

Reich, Charles, "The New Property," 73 *Yale Law Journal* 733 (1964).

Rieser, Alison, "Ecological Preservation as a Public Property Right: An Emerging Doctrine In Search of a Theory," 15 *Harvard Environmental Law Review* 393 (1991).

Ripple. William J., "Status and Ecological Effects of the World's Largest Carnivores," 343 *Science* 151 (2014).

Robinson, Michael J., *Predatory Bureaucracy: The Extermination of Wolves and the Transformation of the West* (University of Colorado, 2005).

Robinson, Michael, Dave Parsons, and Rob Edward, "South From Yellowstone, What Remains to Be Done," *International Wolf* (Spring 2006).

Rodgers, William H., *Environmental Law,* 1st and 2d ed. (West, 1997).

———, "A Hard-Look at Vermont Yankee: Environmental Law Under Close Scrutiny," 67 *Georgetown Law Journal* 699, 704–6 (1979).

———, "Judicial Review of Risk Assessments," 11 *Environmental Law* 301 (1981).

Rodriquez, Daniel B., "The Substance of the New Legal Process," 77 *California Law Review* 919 (1989).

Rogers, Jerald W., "Romer v. Evans: Heightened Scrutiny Has Found a Rational Basis," 45 *Kansas Law Review* 953 (1997).

Rohlf, Daniel J., *ESA: A Guide to Its Protections and Implementation* (Stanford Environmental Law Society, 1989).

———, "Six Biological Reasons Why the ESA Doesn't Work—And What to Do About It," 5 *Conservation Biology* 273 (1991).

Ronner, Amy D., "Judicial Self-Demise: The Test When Congress Impermissibly Intrudes on Judicial Powers After *Robertson v. Seattle Audubon Society*," 35 *Arizona Law Review* 1037 (1993).

Rose-Ackerman, Susan, "Judicial Review and the Power of the Purse," 12 *International Review of Law and Economics* 191 (1992).

Rosenbaum, Walter A., *Environmental Policy and Politics,* 3d ed. (Congressional Quarterly, 1995).

Rosenberg, Gerald N., *The Hollow Hope: Can Courts Bring About Social Change?* (University of Chicago, 1991).

Ruhl, John, "Congress?—An Agenda for Administrative Reform," 6 *New York University Environmental Law Journal* 368 (1998).

Sager, Lawrence, "Forward: Constitutional Limitations on Congress' Authority to Regulate the Jurisdiction of the Federal Courts," 95 *Harvard Law Review* 17 (1981).

———, Insular Minorities, 91 *Harvard Law Review* 1373 (1978).

Sagoff, Mark, "On Preserving the Natural Environment," 84 *Yale Law Journal* 205 (1974).

Sargentich, Thomas O., "The Critique of Active Judicial Review of Administrative Agencies: A Reevaluation," 49 *Administrative Law Review* 599 (1997).

Satterfield, James E., "A Funny Thing Happened on the Way to the Revolution: The Environmental Record of the 104th Congress," 27 *Environmental Law Reporter* 10019 (1997).

Sax, Joseph L., "Liberating the Public Trust Doctrine from Its Historical Shackles," 14 *University California Davis Law Review* 185 (1980).

———, "The Public Trust Doctrine in Natural Resources Law: Effective Judicial Intervention," 68 *Michigan Law Review* 471 (1970).

———, "The (Unhappy) Truth About NEPA," 26 *Oklahoma Law Review* 239 (1973).

Saxe, Keith, "Regulated Taking of Threatened Species Under the Endangered Species Act," 39 *Hastings Law Journal* 399 (1988).

Scalia, Antonin, "The Doctrine of Standing as an Essential Element of the Separation of Powers," 17 *Suffolk Law Review* 881 (1983).

———, "The Judicialization of Standardless Rulemaking: Two Wrongs Make a Right," *Regulation* (July–August 1977).

———, *A Matter of Interpretation, Federal Courts and the Law* (Princeton University, 1997).

Schuck Peter H., and E. Donald Elliot, "To the Chevron Station," 1990 *Duke Law Journal* 984.

Schmidhauser, John, Larry Berg, Albert Melone, "The Impact of Judicial Decisions: New Dimensions in Supreme Court-Congressional Relations," 1971 *Washington University Law Quarterly* 209.

Schullery, Paul (ed.), *The Yellowstone Wolf: A Guide and Source Book* (High Plains, 1996).

Schwartz, Bernard, "Shooting the Piano Player? Justice Scalia and Administrative Law," 47 *Administrative Law Review* 1 (1995).

Seidenfeld, Mark, "Demystifying Deossification: Rethinking Recent Proposals to Modify Judicial Review of Notice and Comment Rulemaking," 75 *Texas Law Review* 483 (1997).

Shapiro, Martin, "APA: Past, Present, Future," 72 *Virginia Law Review* 447 (1986).

Shapiro, Michael E., "Sagebrush and Seaweed Robbery: State Revenue Losses for Onshore and Offshore Federal Lands," 12 *Ecology Law Quarterly* 481 (1985).

———, *Who Guards the Guardians? Judicial Control of Administration* (University of Georgia, 1988).

Sheingold, Stuart, *The Politics of Rights: Lawyers, Public Policy and Political Change* (Yale University, 1974).

Sher, Victor M., and Carole Sue Hunting, "Eroding the Landscape, Eroding the Law: Congressional Exemptions from Judicial Review of Environmental Laws," 15 *Harvard Environmental Law Review* 435 (1991).

Sinclair, Barbara, *Unorthodox Lawmaking, New Legislative Processes in the U.S. Congress* (CQ Press, 2012).

Smith, Christopher, *Courts, Politics, and the Judicial Process,* 2d ed. (Nelson Hall, 1997).

Soden, Dennis L., *The Environmental Presidency* (SUNY Press, 1999).

Soule, Michael, and Reed Noss, "Rewilding and Biodiversity, Complementary Goals for Continental Conservation," 8 *Wild Earth* 18 (Fall 1998).

Soule, Michael E., and John Terborgh (eds.), *Continental Conservation, Scientific Foundations of Regional Reserve Networks* (Island Press, 1999).

Southworth, Ann, "Conservative Lawyers and the Contest Over the Meaning of Public Interest Law," 52 *UCLA Law Review* 1223 (2005).

Starr, Kenneth W., "Judicial Review in the Post-Chevron Era," 3 *Yale Journal on Regulation* 283 (1986).

Starr, Kenneth W., Cass R. Sunstein, Richard K. Willard, Alan B. Morrison, "Judicial Review of Administrative Action in a Conservative Era," 39 *Administrative Law Review* 353.

Stevens, Jan S., "The Public Trust: A Sovereign's Ancient Prerogative Becomes the People's Environmental Right," 14 *University California Davis Law Review* 195.

Stewart, Richard, "The Reformation of American Administrative Law," 88 *Harvard Law Review* 1667 (1975).

Strauch, Timothy B., "Holding the Wolf By the Ears: The Conservation of the Northern Rocky Mountain Wolf in Yellowstone National Park," 27 *Land and Water Law Review* 33 (1992).

Strauss, Peter L., "One Hundred and Fifty Cases per Year: Some Implications of the Supreme Court's Limited Resources for Judicial Review of Agency Action," 87 *Columbia Law Review* 1093 (1987).

———, "Considering Political Alternatives to 'Hard Look' Review," 1989 *Duke Law Journal* 538.

Stumpf, Harry P., "Congressional Response to Supreme Court Rulings," 14 *Journal of Public Law* 377 (1965).

Sunstein, Cass R., "Beyond the Republican Revival," 97 *Yale Law Quarterly* 1539 (1988).

———, "Constitutionalism After the New Deal," 101 *Harvard Law Review* 421 (1987).

———, "Deregulation and the Hard-Look Doctrine," 1983 *Supreme Court Review* 177.

———, "Factions, Self-Interest, and the APA: Four Lessons since 1946," 72 *Virginia Law Review* 271 (1986).

———, "Forward: Leaving Things Undecided," 110 *Harvard Law Review* 4 (1996).

———, "Interest Groups in American Public Law," 38 *Stanford Law Review* 29 (1985).

———, "Interpreting Statutes in the Regulatory State," 103 *Harvard Law Review* 405 (1989).

———, "Law and Administration After Chevron," 90 *Columbia Law Review* 2071 (1990).

———, "Naked Preferences and the Constitution," 84 *Columbia Law Review* 1689 (1984).

———, "On the Costs and Benefits of Aggressive Review of Judicial Action," 1989 *Duke Law Journal* 1169 (2001).

———, "Participation, Public Law, and Venue Reform," 49 *University Chicago Law Review* 976 (1982).

———, "What's Standing After Lujan? Of Citizen Suits, Injuries, and Article III," 91 *Michigan Law Review* 1 (1993).

Swierenga, Brenda, "Still Newer Equal Protection: Impermissible Purpose Review in the 1984 Term," 53 *University Chicago Law Review* 1454 (1986).

Takas, David, "The Pubic Trust Doctrine, Environmental Human Rights, the Future of Private Property," 16 *New York University Environmental Law Journal* 711 (2008).

Thrower, Julie S., "Ranching with Wolves: Reducing Conflicts Between Livestock and Wolves Through Integrated Grazing and Wolf Management Plans," 29 *Journal Land, Resources, and Environmental Law* 319 (2009).

Tiefer, Charles, "The Reconceptualization of Legislative History in the Supreme Court," 2000 *Wisconsin Law Review* 205.

Titus, A. Constandina, "The Nevada 'Sagebrush Rebellion' Act: A Question of Constitutionality," 23 *Arizona Law Review* 264 (1981).

Todd, David, "Wolf-Predator Control and Endangered Species Protection: Thoughts on Politics and Law," 33 *South Texas Law Review* 459 (1992).

Trefethen, James B., *An American Crusade for Wildlife* (Wincesters, 1975).

Tribe, Laurence H., *American Constitutional Law*, 2d ed. (Foundation Press 1988) .

———, "From Environmental Foundations to Constitutional Structures: Learning from Nature's Future," 84 *Yale Law Quarterly* 545 (1975).

——— "Policy Science: Analysis of Ideology," 2 *Philosophy & Public Affairs* 66 (1972).

——— "Structural Due Process," 10 *Harvard Civil Rights–Civil Liberties Law Review* 269 (1975).

———, "Toward a Syntax of the Unsaid," 57 *Indiana Law Journal* 515 (1982).

Tushnet, Mark V. "Alternative Forms of Judicial Reasoning," 101 *Michigan Law Review* 2781 (2003).

———, "Legal Realism, Structural Review, and Prophecy," 8 *University Dayton Law Review* 809 (1983).

Udall, Stewart L. *The Quiet Crisis and the Next Generation* (Gibbs-Smith, 1988).

Urbanski, Mark A., "Chemical Prospecting, Biodiversity Conservation, and the Importance of International Protection of Intellectual Property Rights in Biological Materials," 2 *Buffalo Journal International Law* 131 (1995).

Vanderziel, Kathleen M., "The Hatfield Riders & Environmental Preservation: What Process Is Due?" 19 *Boston College Environmental. Affairs Law Review* 431(1991).

Vig, Norman J., and Michael E. Kraft (eds.), *Environmental Policy in the 1990s* (Congressional Quarterly, 1997).

vonHoldt, Bridgett M., et al., "A Novel Assessment of Population Structure and Gene Flow in the Grey Wolf Populations of the Northern Rocky Mountains of the United States," 19 *Molecular Biology* 4412 (2010).

vonHoldt, Bridgett, Daniel Stahler, Douglas Smith, Dent Earl, Johan Pollinger, and Robert Wayne, "The Genealogy and Genetic Variability of Reintroduced Yellowstone Wolves," 17 *Molecular Ecology* 252 (2007).

Wald, Patricia, "The Contribution of the D.C. Circuit to Administrative Law," 40 *Administrative Law Review* 507 (1988).

————, "The D.C. Circuit: Here and Now," 55 *George Washington Law Review* 718 (1987).

————, "The Sizzling Sleeper: The Use of Legislative History in Construing Statutes in the 1988–89 Term of the US Supreme Court," 39 *American University Law Review* 277 (1990).

Walker, James L., and Michael E. Solomine, "The Next Word: Congressional Response to Supreme Court Statutory Decisions," 65 *Temple Law Review* 425 (1992).

Weisberg, Robert, "The Calabresian Judicial Artist: Statutes and the New Legal Process," 35 *Stanford Law Review* 213 (1983).

Weisbrod, Burton A., Joel F. Handler, and Neil K. Komesar., *Public Interest Law* (University of California, 1978).

Wellman, Vincent, "Dworkin and the Legal Process Tradition," 29 *Arizona Law Review* 413.

Weydeven, Adrian, Timothy R. VandEelen, *Recovery of the Gray Wolf in the Great Lakes Region of the U.S.: An Endangered Species Success Story* (University of Wisconsin, 2009).

Wilkerson, Charles F., "The Public Trust Doctrine in Public Land Law," 14 *University of California Davis Law Review* 269 (1980).

Wilson, Matthew H., "The Wolf in Yellowstone: Science, Symbol, or Politics?" 10 *Society and Natural Resources* 453 (1997).

Wilson, Patrick Impero, "Wolves, Politics, and the Nez Perce: Wolf Recovery in Central Idaho and the Role of Native Tribes," 39 *Natural Resources Journa*l 543 (1999).

Wolf Management Committee, *Wolves in Yellowstone National Park and the Central Idaho Wilderness Area* (1991).

Yaffee, Steven, *Prohibitive Policy: Implementing the Federal ESA* (MIT, 1982).

Young, Gordon G., "Congressional Regulation of Federal Courts' Jurisdiction and Processes: *U.S. v. Klein Revisited*," 1981 *Wisconsin Law Review* 1189.

Young, Stanley P., and Edward A. Goldman, *Wolves of North America* (Dover, 1944).

Youngblood, Scott, "Wildlife Restoration Projects: Hope for Life or a Death Sentence: A Look at Reintroduction of Wolves to the Northern Rocky Mountains," 40 *South Texas Law Review* 1045 (1999).

Zellmer, Sandra Beth, "Sacrificing Legislative Integrity at the Altar of Appropriations Riders: A Constitutional Crisis," 21 *Harvard Environmental Law Review* 457 (1997).

Zeppos, Nicholas S., "Legislative History and the Interpretation of Statutes: Toward a Fact-Finding Model of Statutory Interpretation," 72 *Virginia Law Review* 1295 (1990).

Zuccotti, John Andrew, "A Native Returns: The Endangered Species Act and Wolf Reintroduction to the Northern Rocky Mountains," 20 *Columbia Journal Environmental Law* 329 (1995).

Cases

Alliance for the Wild Rockies v. Salazar, 800 F. Supp. 2d 1123 (2011); 672 F.3d 1170 (9th Cir. 2012).
Alsea Valley Alliance v. Evans, 161 F. Supp.2d 1154, (D. Or. 2001).
Arizona Cattlegrowers v. FWS, 273 F.3d 1229 (9th Cir. 2001).
Arlington Texas v. FCC, 133 S. Ct. 1863 (2013).
Associated Data Processing Service Organizations v. Camp, 397 U.S. 150 (1970).
Bennett v. Spear, 520 U.S. 154 (1997).
Board of Trustees of Univ. of Alabama v. Garrett, 531 U.S. 356 (2001).
Bob Jones University v. U.S., 451 U.S. 574 (1983).
Boerne v. Flores, 521 U.S. 507 (1997).
Borsv v. Preston, 111 U.S. 252 (1884).
Bowen v. Michigan Academy of Family Physicians, 476 U.S. 667 (1986).
Buckley v. Valeo, 424 U.S. 1, 38–41 (1976).
Calvert's Cliffs Coordinating Committee v. U.S. Atomic Energy Commission, 449 F.2d 1109 (D.C. Cir. 1971).
Chemical Manufacturers Assoc. v. NRDC, 470 U.S. 116 (1985).
Chevron v. NRDC, 467 U.S. 837 (1984).
Cisnerous v. Alpine Ridge Group, 508 U.S. 10 (1993).
Citizens to Preserve Overton Park v. Volpe, 401 U.S. 402 (1971).
Communications Workers v. Beck, 487 U.S. 735 (1988).
Consejo Desarrollo Economico v. U.S., 482 F. 3d 1157 (9th Cir. 2007).
Cristoffel v. U.S. 338 U.S. 84 (1949).
Defenders of Wildlife v. Hall, 565 F. Supp.2d 1160 (D. Mont. 2008).
Defenders of Wildlife v. Jewell, Case No. 1: 12-cv-01833-ABJ (September 23, 2014).
Defenders of Wildlife v. Lujan, 792 F. Supp. 834 (D.D.C. 1992).
Defenders of Wildlife v. Norton, 239 F. Supp.2d (D.D.C. 2002).
Defenders of Wildlife v. Norton, 258 F.3d 1136 (9th Cir. 2001).
Defenders of Wildlife v. Salazar, Case 9:09-cv-00077-DWM (September 8, 2009).
Defenders of Wildlife v. Salazar, 729 F. Supp. 1207 (D. Mt. 2010).
Defenders of Wildlife v. Secretary of Interior, 354 F. Supp. 2d 1156 (D. Or. 2005).
DOW v. Salazar, CV 09-77-M-DWM, CV 09-82-M-DWM (April 9, 2011)
Duke Power v. Carolina Study Group, 438 U.S. 59 (1978).
Environmental Protection Information Center (EPIC) v. NMFS, Case No. C-02-5401 EDL (D.D.C. 2004).
Federation of Fly Fishers v. Daley, 131 F. Supp.2d 1158 (N.D. Cal. 2000).
Friends of Swan v. U.S. FWS, 12 F. Supp. 2d 1121 (D. Or. 1997).

Fullilove v. Klutznick, 448 U.S. 448 (1980).
Fund for Animals v. Babbitt, 903 F. Supp. 96 (D.D.C. 1995).
Glidden v. Zdanok, 370 U.S. 530 (1962).
Gojack v. U.S., 384 U.S. 302 (1966).
Greater Boston Television Corp. v. FCC, 444 F.2d 841 (D.C. Cir. 1970).
Grove City College v. Bell, 465 U.S. 555 (1984).
Hampton v. Mow Sun Wong, 426 U.S. 88 (1976).
Hunt v. U.S., 278 U.S. 96 (1928).
In re ESA Deadline Litigation, 277 F.R.D. 1 (D.D.C. 2011), aff'd 704 F.3d 972 (D.C. Cir. 2013).
In re ESA Section 4 Deadline Litigation, 270 F.R.D. 1 (D.D.C. 2010).
In re Steuart Transp. Co., 495 F. Supp. 38 (E.D. Va. 1980).
INS v. Cardozo-Fonseca, 480 U.S. 421 (1987).
INS v. Chadha, 462 U.S. 919 (1983).
Kimel v. Florida Board of Regents, 528 U.S. 62 (2000)
Kleppe v. Sierra Club, 427 U.S. 390, (1976).
Kline v. Burke Construction Co., 460 U.S. 226, 234 (1922).
Light v. U.S., 220 U.S. 523 (1911).
Lockerty v. Phillips, 319 U.S. 182 (1943).
Marbury v. Madison, 5 U.S. (Cranch) 137 (1803).
Martin v. Hunters Lessee, 14 U.S. (1Wheat.) 304 (1816).
Martin v. Waddell, 41 U.S. (16 Pet.) 367 (1842).
Matthews v. Eldridge, 424 U.S. 319 (1976).
Merrill Lynch, Pierce, Fenner & Smith v. Curran, 456 U.S. 353 (1982).
Misretta v. U.S., 488 U.S. 361 (1989).
Motor Vehicle Manufacturers' Assoc. v. State Farm Mutual, 463 U.S. 29 (1983).
National Assoc. of Home Builders v. FWS, CV No. 12-2013 (March 31, 2014).
National Ass'n of Home Builders v. Norton, 340 F.3d 835, 841(9th Cir. 2003).
NLRB v. Robbins Tire & Rubber Co., 437 U.S. 214 (1978).
NWF v. NMFS, 481 F.3d 1224 (9th Cir. 2007).
National Wildlife Federation v. Secretary of Interior, 386 F. Supp. 2d 553 (D. Vt. 2005).
Nevada v. U.S., 512 F. Supp. 166 (1981).
Oregon NRC v. Daley, 6 F. Supp.2d 1139 (D. Or. 1998).
Palmore v. U.S., 411 U.S. 389 (1973).
Panama Refining Co. v. Ryan, 293 U.S. 388 (1935).
Pennsylvania v. Wheeling & Belmont Bridge, 59 U.S. 421 (1855).
Plyler v. Doe, 457 U.S. 202 (1982).
Robertson v. Methow Valley Citizens Council, 490 U.S. 332 (1989).
Robertson v. Seattle Audubon Society, 503 U.S. 429 (1992), 914 F.2d 1311 (9th Cir. 1990).
Romer v. Evans, 517 U.S. 629 (1996).
Ruddy v. Rossi, 248 U.S. 104 (1918).
Schecter Poultry Corp. v. U.S., 295 U.S. 495 (1935).
Seminole Tribe v. Florida, 517 U.S. 44 (1996).
Sewing Machine Co. Case, 85 U.S. 553 (1873).
Sheldon v. Sill, 49 U.S. (8 How.) 441 (1850).
Sierra Club v. Morton, 405 U.S. 727 (1972).
Southwest Center for Biological Diversity v. Norton, Civil Act No. 98-934 (RMU/JMF) (D.D.C. 2002).
Springer v. Philippine Islands, 277 U.S. 189 (1927).
Stop H-3 v. Dole, 870 F. 2d 1417 (9th Cir. 1989).
Stryker's Bay Neighborhood Council v. Karlen, 444 U.S. 233 (1980).
Trout Unlimited v. Lohn, 559 F.3d 946 (9th Cir. 2009).
TVA v. Hill, 437 U.S. 151 (1973).
U.S. v. Ballin, 144 U.S. 1 (1892).
U.S. v. Carolene Products, 304 U.S. 144 (1938).
U.S. v. City & County of San Francisco, 310 U.S. 36 (1940).

U.S. v. Dickerson, 310 U.S. 554 (1940).
U.S. v. Hudson, 11 U.S. (7 Cranch) 32 (1812).
U.S. v. Klein, 80 U.S. 128 (1871).
U.S. v. Lopez, 514 U.S. 549 (1995).
U.S. v. McKittrick, 142 F.3d 1170 (9th Cir. 1998).
U.S. v. Missouri Pacific Railroad, 278 U.S. 269 (1929).
U.S. v. Padelford, 76 U.S. (9 Wall.) 531 (1870).
U.S. v. Students Challenging Regulatory Agency Procedures, 412 U.S. 699 (1973).
U.S. v. Union Pac. R.R., 98 U.S. 569 (1878).
Vermont Yankee Nuclear Power Corp. v. NRDC, 435 U.S. 519 (1978).
Winter v. NRDC, 129 S. Ct. 365, 374 (2008).
Wyoming Farm Bureau Association v. Babbitt, 987 F. Supp. 1349 (D. Wyo. 1997); 199 F. 3d 1224 (10th Cir. 2000).
Yakus v. U.S., 321 U.S. 414 (1944).
Yellin v. U.S., 374 U.S. 109 (1963).

Index

About the Author

Edward A. Fitzgerald is professor of political science at Wright State University. He has taught at Northeastern University, Saint John's University, the University of Massachusetts Fitchburg, and the University of Dayton Law School. Dr. Fitzgerald received his B.A. from Holy Cross College in 1971, J.D. from Boston College Law School in 1974, M.A. from Northeastern University in 1976, and Ph.D. from Boston University in 1983.

CPSIA information can be obtained at www.ICGtesting.com
Printed in the USA
BVOW03*1945010215

385636BV00005B/6/P

9 781498 502672